Nutshell Series

of

WEST PUBLISHING COMPANY

P.O. Box 64526

St. Paul, Minnesota 55164–0526

Accounting—Law and, 1984, 377 pages, by E. McGruder Faris, Late Professor of Law, Stetson University.

Administrative Law and Process, 2nd Ed., 1981, 445 pages, by Ernest Gellhorn, Dean and Professor of Law, Case Western Reserve University and Barry B. Boyer, Professor of Law, SUNY, Buffalo.

Admiralty, 1983, 390 pages, by Frank L. Maraist, Professor of Law, Louisiana State University.

Agency-Partnership, 1977, 364 pages, by Roscoe T. Steffen, Late Professor of Law, University of Chicago.

American Indian Law, 1981, 288 pages, by William C. Canby, Jr., Adjunct Professor of Law, Arizona State University.

Antitrust Law and Economics, 2nd Ed., 1981, 425 pages, by Ernest Gellhorn, Dean and Professor of Law, Case Western Reserve University.

Appellate Advocacy, 1984, 325 pages, by Alan D. Hornstein, Professor of Law, University of Maryland.

Art Law, 1984, 335 pages, by Leonard D. DuBoff, Professor of Law, Lewis and Clark College, Northwestern School of Law.

Banking and Financial Institutions, 1984, 409 pages, by William A. Lovett, Professor of Law, Tulane University.

Church-State Relations—Law of, 1981, 305 pages, by Leonard F. Manning, Late Professor of Law, Fordham University.

Civil Procedure, 2nd Ed., 1986, 306 pages, by Mary Kay Kane, Professor of Law, University of California, Hastings College of the Law.

Civil Rights, 1978, 279 pages, by Norman Vieira, Professor of Law, Southern Illinois University.

Commercial Paper, 3rd Ed., 1982, 404 pages, by Charles M. Weber, Professor of Business Law, University of Arizona and Richard E. Speidel, Professor of Law, Northwestern University.

Community Property, 1982, 447 pages, by Robert L. Mennell, Former Professor of Law, Hamline University.

Comparative Legal Traditions, 1982, 402 pages, by Mary Ann Glendon, Professor of Law, Boston College, Michael Wallace Gordon, Professor of Law, University of Florida and Christopher Osakwe, Professor of Law, Tulane University.

Conflicts, 1982, 470 pages, by David D. Siegel, Professor of Law, St. John's University.

Constitutional Analysis, 1979, 388 pages, by Jerre S. Williams, Professor of Law Emeritus, University of Texas.

Constitutional Power—Federal and State, 1974, 411 pages, by David E. Engdahl, Professor of Law, University of Puget Sound.

Consumer Law, 2nd Ed., 1981, 418 pages, by David G. Epstein, Dean and Professor of Law, Emory University and Steve H. Nickles, Professor of Law, University of Minnesota.

Contract Remedies, 1981, 323 pages, by Jane M. Friedman, Professor of Law, Wayne State University.

Contracts, 2nd Ed., 1984, 425 pages, by Gordon D. Schaber, Dean and Professor of Law, McGeorge School of Law and Claude D. Rohwer, Professor of Law, McGeorge School of Law.

Corporations—Law of, 1980, 379 pages, by Robert W. Hamilton, Professor of Law, University of Texas.

Corrections and Prisoners' Rights—Law of, 2nd Ed., 1983, 386 pages, by Sheldon Krantz, Dean and Professor of Law, University of San Diego.

Criminal Law, 1975, 302 pages, by Arnold H. Loewy, Professor of Law, University of North Carolina.

Criminal Procedure—Constitutional Limitations, 3rd Ed., 1980, 438 pages, by Jerold H. Israel, Professor of Law, University of Michigan and Wayne R. LaFave, Professor of Law, University of Illinois.

Debtor-Creditor Law, 3rd Ed., 1986, 383 pages, by David G. Epstein, Dean and Professor of Law, Emory University.

Employment Discrimination—Federal Law of, 2nd Ed., 1981, 402 pages, by Mack A. Player, Professor of Law, University of Georgia.

Energy Law, 1981, 338 pages, by Joseph P. Tomain, Professor of Law, University of Cincinnatti.

Environmental Law, 1983, 343 pages by Roger W. Findley, Professor of Law, University of Illinois and Daniel A. Farber, Professor of Law, University of Minnesota.

Estate and Gift Taxation, Federal, 3rd Ed., 1983, 509 pages, by John K. McNulty, Professor of Law, University of California, Berkeley.

Estate Planning—Introduction to, 3rd Ed., 1983, 370 pages, by Robert J. Lynn, Professor of Law, Ohio State University.

Evidence, Federal Rules of, 1981, 429 pages, by Michael H. Graham, Professor of Law, University of Miami.

Evidence, State and Federal Rules, 2nd Ed., 1981, 514 pages, by Paul F. Rothstein, Professor of Law, Georgetown University.

Family Law, 2nd Ed., 1986, about 418 pages, by Harry D. Krause, Professor of Law, University of Illinois.

Federal Jurisdiction, 2nd Ed., 1981, 258 pages, by David P. Currie, Professor of Law, University of Chicago.

Future Interests, 1981, 361 pages, by Lawrence W. Waggoner, Professor of Law, University of Michigan.

Government Contracts, 1979, 423 pages, by W. Noel Keyes, Professor of Law, Pepperdine University.

Historical Introduction to Anglo-American Law, 2nd Ed., 1973, 280 pages, by Frederick G. Kempin, Jr., Professor of Business Law, Wharton School of Finance and Commerce, University of Pennsylvania.

Immigration Law and Procedure, 1984, 345 pages, by David Weissbrodt, Professor of Law, University of Minnesota.

Injunctions, 1974, 264 pages, by John F. Dobbyn, Professor of Law, Villanova University.

Insurance Law, 1981, 281 pages, by John F. Dobbyn, Professor of Law, Villanova University.

Intellectual Property—Patents, Trademarks and Copyright, 1983, 428 pages, by Arthur R. Miller, Professor of Law, Harvard University, and Michael H. Davis, Professor of Law, Cleveland State University, Cleveland-Marshall College of Law.

International Business Transactions, 2nd Ed., 1984, 476 pages, by Donald T. Wilson, Professor of Law, Loyola University, Los Angeles.

International Law, 1985, 262 pages, by Thomas Buergenthal, Professor of Law, Emory University and Harold G. Maier, Professor of Law, Vanderbilt University.

Introduction to the Study and Practice of Law, 1983, 418 pages, by Kenney F. Hegland, Professor of Law, University of Arizona.

Judicial Process, 1980, 292 pages, by William L. Reynolds, Professor of Law, University of Maryland.

Jurisdiction, 4th Ed., 1980, 232 pages, by Albert A. Ehrenzweig, Late Professor of Law, University of California, Berkeley, David W. Louisell, Late Professor of Law, University of California, Berkeley and Geoffrey C. Hazard, Jr., Professor of Law, Yale Law School.

Juvenile Courts, 3rd Ed., 1984, 291 pages, by Sanford J. Fox, Professor of Law, Boston College.

Labor Arbitration Law and Practice, 1979, 358 pages, by Dennis R. Nolan, Professor of Law, University of South Carolina.

Labor Law, 1986, 397 pages, by Douglas L. Leslie, Professor of Law, University of Virginia.

NUTSHELL SERIES

Land Use, 2nd Ed., 1985, 356 pages, by Robert R. Wright, Professor of Law, University of Arkansas, Little Rock and Susan Webber Wright, Professor of Law, University of Arkansas, Little Rock.

Landlord and Tenant Law, 2nd Ed., 1986, about 320 pages, by David S. Hill, Professor of Law, University of Colorado.

Law Study and Law Examinations—Introduction to, 1971, 389 pages, by Stanley V. Kinyon, Late Professor of Law, University of Minnesota.

Legal Interviewing and Counseling, 1976, 353 pages, by Thomas L. Shaffer, Professor of Law, Washington and Lee University.

Legal Research, 4th Ed., 1985, 452 pages, by Morris L. Cohen, Professor of Law and Law Librarian, Yale University.

Legal Writing, 1982, 294 pages, by Lynn B. Squires and Marjorie Dick Rombauer, Professor of Law, University of Washington.

Legislative Law and Process, 2nd Ed., 1986, about 300 pages, by Jack Davies, Professor of Law, William Mitchell College of Law.

Local Government Law, 2nd Ed., 1983, 404 pages, by David J. McCarthy, Jr., Professor of Law, Georgetown University.

Mass Communications Law, 2nd Ed., 1983, 473 pages, by Harvey L. Zuckman, Professor of Law, Catholic University and Martin J. Gaynes, Lecturer in Law, Temple University.

Medical Malpractice—The Law of, 2nd Ed., 1986, about 337 pages, by Joseph H. King, Professor of Law, University of Tennessee.

Military Law, 1980, 378 pages, by Charles A. Shanor, Professor of Law, Emory University and Timothy P. Terrell, Professor of Law, Emory University.

Oil and Gas, 1983, 443 pages, by John S. Lowe, Professor of Law, University of Tulsa.

Personal Property, 1983, 322 pages, by Barlow Burke, Jr., Professor of Law, American University.

Post-Conviction Remedies, 1978, 360 pages, by Robert Popper, Dean and Professor of Law, University of Missouri, Kansas City.

Presidential Power, 1977, 328 pages, by Arthur Selwyn Miller, Professor of Law Emeritus, George Washington University.

Products Liability, 2nd Ed., 1981, 341 pages, by Dix W. Noel, Late Professor of Law, University of Tennessee and Jerry J. Phillips, Professor of Law, University of Tennessee.

Professional Responsibility, 1980, 399 pages, by Robert H. Aronson, Professor of Law, University of Washington, and Donald T. Weckstein, Professor of Law, University of San Diego.

Real Estate Finance, 2nd Ed., 1985, 262 pages, by Jon W. Bruce, Professor of Law, Vanderbilt University.

Real Property, 2nd Ed., 1981, 448 pages, by Roger H. Bernhardt, Professor of Law, Golden Gate University.

Regulated Industries, 1982, 394 pages, by Ernest Gellhorn, Dean and Professor of Law, Case Western Reserve University, and Richard J. Pierce, Dean and Professor of Law, University of Pittsburgh.

Remedies, 2nd Ed., 1985, 320 pages, by John F. O'Connell, Professor of Law, Western State University College of Law, Fullerton.

Res Judicata, 1976, 310 pages, by Robert C. Casad, Professor of Law, University of Kansas.

Sales, 2nd Ed., 1981, 370 pages, by John M. Stockton, Professor of Business Law, Wharton School of Finance and Commerce, University of Pennsylvania.

Schools, Students and Teachers—Law of, 1984, 409 pages, by Kern Alexander, Professor of Education, University of Florida and M. David Alexander, Professor, Virginia Tech University.

Sea—Law of, 1984, 264 pages, by Louis B. Sohn, Professor of Law, University of Georgia and Kristen Gustafson.

Secured Transactions, 2nd Ed., 1981, 391 pages, by Henry J. Bailey, Professor of Law Emeritus, Willamette University.

Securities Regulation, 2nd Ed., 1982, 322 pages, by David L. Ratner, Dean and Professor of Law, University of San Francisco.

Sex Discrimination, 1982, 399 pages, by Claire Sherman Thomas, Lecturer, University of Washington, Women's Studies Department.

Taxation and Finance, State and Local, 1986, 309 pages, by M. David Gelfand, Professor of Law, Tulane University and Peter W. Salsich, Professor of Law, St. Louis University.

Taxation of Corporations and Stockholders, Federal Income, 2nd Ed., 1981, 362 pages, by Jonathan Sobeloff, Late Professor of Law, Georgetown University and Peter P. Weidenbruch, Jr., Professor of Law, Georgetown University.

Taxation of Individuals, Federal Income, 3rd Ed., 1983, 487 pages, by John K. McNulty, Professor of Law, University of California, Berkeley.

Torts—Injuries to Persons and Property, 1977, 434 pages, by Edward J. Kionka, Professor of Law, Southern Illinois University.

Torts—Injuries to Family, Social and Trade Relations, 1979, 358 pages, by Wex S. Malone, Professor of Law Emeritus, Louisiana State University.

Trial Advocacy, 1979, 402 pages, by Paul B. Bergman, Adjunct Professor of Law, University of California, Los Angeles.

Trial and Practice Skills, 1978, 346 pages, by Kenney F. Hegland, Professor of Law, University of Arizona.

Trial, The First—Where Do I Sit? What Do I Say?, 1982, 396 pages, by Steven H. Goldberg, Professor of Law, University of Minnesota.

Unfair Trade Practices, 1982, 444 pages, by Charles R. McManis, Professor of Law, Washington University.

Uniform Commercial Code, 2nd Ed., 1984, 516 pages, by Bradford Stone, Professor of Law, Detroit College of Law.

Uniform Probate Code, 1978, 425 pages, by Lawrence H. Averill, Jr., Dean and Professor of Law, University of Arkansas, Little Rock.

Hornbook Series

and

Basic Legal Texts

of

WEST PUBLISHING COMPANY

P.O. Box 64526

St. Paul, Minnesota 55164–0526

Administrative Law, Davis' Text on, 3rd Ed., 1972, 617 pages, by Kenneth Culp Davis, Professor of Law, University of San Diego.

Agency and Partnership, Reuschlein & Gregory's Hornbook on the Law of, 1979 with 1981 Pocket Part, 625 pages, by Harold Gill Reuschlein, Professor of Law Emeritus, Villanova University and William A. Gregory, Professor of Law, Georgia State University.

Antitrust, Sullivan's Hornbook on the Law of, 1977, 886 pages, by Lawrence A. Sullivan, Professor of Law, University of California, Berkeley.

Civil Procedure, Friedenthal, Kane and Miller's Hornbook on, 1985, 876 pages, by Jack H. Friedental, Professor of Law, Stanford University, Mary K. Kane, Professor of Law, University of California, Hastings College of the Law and Arthur R. Miller, Professor of Law, Harvard University.

Common Law Pleading, Koffler and Reppy's Hornbook on, 1969, 663 pages, by Joseph H. Koffler, Professor of Law, New York Law School and Alison Reppy, Late Dean and Professor of Law, New York Law School.

Conflict of Laws, Scoles and Hay's Hornbook on, 1982, 1085 pages, by Eugene F. Scoles, Professor of Law, University of Illinois and Peter Hay, Dean and Professor of Law, University of Illinois.

HORNBOOKS & BASIC TEXTS

Constitutional Law, Nowak, Rotunda and Young's Hornbook on, 2nd Ed., 1983, 1172 pages, by John E. Nowak, Professor of Law, University of Illinois, Ronald D. Rotunda, Professor of Law, University of Illinois, and J. Nelson Young, Late Professor of Law, University of North Carolina.

Contracts, Calamari and Perillo's Hornbook on, 2nd Ed., 1977, 878 pages, by John D. Calamari, Professor of Law, Fordham University and Joseph M. Perillo, Professor of Law, Fordham University.

Contracts, Corbin's One Volume Student Ed., 1952, 1224 pages, by Arthur L. Corbin, Late Professor of Law, Yale University.

Corporations, Henn and Alexander's Hornbook on, 3rd Ed., 1983, 1371 pages, by Harry G. Henn, Professor of Law, Cornell University and John R. Alexander.

Criminal Law, LaFave and Scott's Hornbook on, 1972, 763 pages, by Wayne R. LaFave, Professor of Law, University of Illinois, and Austin Scott, Jr., Late Professor of Law, University of Colorado.

Criminal Procedure, LaFave and Israel's Hornbook on, 1985 with 1985 pocket part, 1142 pages, by Wayne R. LaFave, Professor of Law, University of Illinois and Jerold H. Israel, Professor of Law University of Michigan.

Damages, McCormick's Hornbook on, 1935, 811 pages, by Charles T. McCormick, Late Dean and Professor of Law, University of Texas.

Domestic Relations, Clark's Hornbook on, 1968, 754 pages, by Homer H. Clark, Jr., Professor of Law, University of Colorado.

Economics and Federal Antitrust Law, Hovenkamp's Hornbook on, 1985, 414 pages, by Herbert Hovenkamp, Professor of Law, University of California, Hastings College of the Law.

Environmental Law, Rodgers' Hornbook on, 1977 with 1984 Pocket Part, 956 pages, by William H. Rodgers, Jr., Professor of Law, University of Washington.

Evidence, Lilly's Introduction to, 1978, 490 pages, by Graham C. Lilly, Professor of Law, University of Virginia.

HORNBOOKS & BASIC TEXTS

Evidence, McCormick's Hornbook on, 3rd Ed., 1984, 1156 pages, General Editor, Edward W. Cleary, Professor of Law Emeritus, Arizona State University.

Federal Courts, Wright's Hornbook on, 4th Ed., 1983, 870 pages, by Charles Alan Wright, Professor of Law, University of Texas.

Federal Income Taxation of Individuals, Posin's Hornbook on, 1983 with 1985 Pocket Part, 491 pages, by Daniel Q. Posin, Jr., Professor of Law, Southern Methodist University.

Future Interest, Simes' Hornbook on, 2nd Ed., 1966, 355 pages, by Lewis M. Simes, Late Professor of Law, University of Michigan.

Insurance, Keeton's Basic Text on, 1971, 712 pages, by Robert E. Keeton, Professor of Law Emeritus, Harvard University.

Labor Law, Gorman's Basic Text on, 1976, 914 pages, by Robert A. Gorman, Professor of Law, University of Pennsylvania.

Law Problems, Ballentine's, 5th Ed., 1975, 767 pages, General Editor, William E. Burby, Late Professor of Law, University of Southern California.

Legal Ethics, Wolfram's Hornbook on, 1986, about 1050 pages, by Charles W. Wolfram, Professor of Law, Cornell University.

Legal Writing Style, Weihofen's, 2nd Ed., 1980, 332 pages, by Henry Weihofen, Professor of Law Emeritus, University of New Mexico.

Local Government Law, Reynolds' Hornbook on, 1982, 860 pages, by Osborne M. Reynolds, Professor of Law, University of Oklahoma.

New York Estate Administration, Turano and Radigan's Hornbook on, 1986, about 575 pages, by Margaret V. Turano, Professor of Law, St. John's University and Raymond Radigan.

New York Practice, Siegel's Hornbook on, 1978 with 1985 Pocket Part, 1011 pages, by David D. Siegel, Professor of Law, St. John's University.

Oil and Gas, Hemingway's Hornbook on, 2nd Ed., 1983, 543 pages, by Richard W. Hemingway, Professor of Law, University of Oklahoma.

Poor, Law of the, LaFrance, Schroeder, Bennett and Boyd's Hornbook on, 1973, 558 pages, by Arthur B. LaFrance, Dean and Professor of Law, Lewis and Clark College, Northwestern School of Law, Milton R. Schroeder, Professor of Law, Arizona State University, Robert W. Bennett, Dean and Professor of Law, Northwestern University and William E. Boyd, Professor of Law, University of Arizona.

Property, Boyer's Survey of, 3rd Ed., 1981, 766 pages, by Ralph E. Boyer, Professor of Law, University of Miami.

Property, Law of, Cunningham, Whitman and Stoebuck's Hornbook on, 1984, 916 pages, by Roger A. Cunningham, Professor of Law, University of Michigan, Dale A. Whitman, Dean and Professor of Law, University of Missouri, Columbia and William B. Stoebuck, Professor of Law, University of Washington.

Real Estate Finance Law, Nelson and Whitman's Hornbook on, 1985, 941 pages, by Grant S. Nelson, Professor of Law, University of Missouri, Columbia and Dale A. Whitman, Dean and Professor of Law, University of Missouri, Columbia.

Real Property, Moynihan's Introduction to, 1962, 254 pages, by Cornelius J. Moynihan, Professor of Law, Suffolk University.

Remedies, Dobb's Hornbook on, 1973, 1067 pages, by Dan B. Dobbs, Professor of Law, University of Arizona.

Secured Transactions under the U.C.C., Henson's Hornbook on, 2nd Ed., 1979 with 1979 Pocket Part, 504 pages, by Ray D. Henson, Professor of Law, University of California, Hastings College of the Law.

Securities Regulation, Hazen's Hornbook on the Law of, 1985, 739 pages, by Thomas Lee Hazen, Professor of Law, University of North Carolina.

Torts, Prosser and Keeton's Hornbook on, 5th Ed., 1984, 1286 pages, by William L. Prosser, Late Dean and Professor of Law, University of California, Berkeley, Page Keeton, Professor of Law Emeritus, University of Texas, Dan B. Dobbs,

Professor of Law, University of Arizona, Robert E. Keeton, Professor of Law Emeritus, Harvard University and David G. Owen, Professor of Law, University of South Carolina.

Trial Advocacy, Jeans' Handbook on, Soft cover, 1975, 473 pages, by James W. Jeans, Professor of Law, University of Missouri, Kansas City.

Trusts, Bogert's Hornbook on, 5th Ed., 1973, 726 pages, by George G. Bogert, Late Professor of Law, University of Chicago and George T. Bogert.

Uniform Commercial Code, White and Summers' Hornbook on, 2nd Ed., 1980, 1250 pages, by James J. White, Professor of Law, University of Michigan and Robert S. Summers, Professor of Law, Cornell University.

Urban Planning and Land Development Control Law, Hagman and Juergensmeyer's Hornbook on, 2nd Ed., 1986, about 600 pages, by Donald G. Hagman, Late Professor of Law, University of California, Los Angeles and Julian C. Juergensmeyer, Professor of Law, University of Florida.

Wills, Atkinson's Hornbook on, 2nd Ed., 1953, 975 pages, by Thomas E. Atkinson, Late Professor of Law, New York University.

Advisory Board

LEGISLATIVE
LAW AND PROCESS
IN A NUTSHELL

By

JACK DAVIES
Professor, William Mitchell College of Law
State Senator, Minnesota 1959–82

SECOND EDITION

St. Paul, Minn.
WEST PUBLISHING CO.
1986

COPYRIGHT © 1975 By WEST PUBLISHING CO.
COPYRIGHT © 1986 By WEST PUBLISHING CO.
                        50 West Kellogg Boulevard
                        P.O. Box 64526
                        St. Paul, Minnesota 55164–0526

Library of Congress Cataloging in Publication Data

Davies, Jack, 1932–
  Legislative law and process in a nutshell.

  (Nutshell series)
  Includes index.
  1. Legislation—United States. I. Title. II. Series.
KF4933.Z9D38 1986   328.73'077   86–7768
ISBN 0–314–21437–2

Davies, Leg.Law & Process, 2d Ed., NS

This book is dedicated to the Minneapolis voters who from 1958 through 1982 made the legislature a subject of more than academic interest to me.

Jack Davies

PREFACE

During 24 years as a state senator, I had the opportunity to view the legislative institution from a surprising variety of perspectives. I started as the youngest senator, a liberal law student in an institution of mature, conservative patriarchs. I was, at first, a member of the minority caucus in a partisan body, and I entered in a bitterly partisan year. Later, actually quite soon, the rulers of the institution accepted me as a useful member deserving a place on the best committees. Though a minority member, I felt I was almost "in the club." But, during fourteen years as a minority member, I learned to press my objectives by amendment, to blur partisan lines, and always to recruit majority caucus allies. I learned to wait, to educate, to let others take the credit. And I learned to love the legislature.

Then, political fortunes changed; for the next ten years I served as a leader in the majority caucus. As a majority member, I authored and passed dozens of major bills. Partly because I was a law professor, the procedures of the body became my responsibility. I served on the organizing committee that wrote the rules, that designed the committee structure, that named the chairmen and committee members, that hired the senate staff. For ten years I chaired the judiciary committee. I headed the subcommittee responsibile for higher education appropriations. For six years I was the senior member of the senate, its historian, its memory. In my last term I presided as senate president.

I wrote the first edition of this book while serving as the senior member of the majority caucus in the Minnesota Senate. My hope was to describe the nature of the legislative process, to give readers a realistic understanding of how legislatures work. I think I succeeded, for it has become common to spot my Nutshell in the hands of new lobbyists starting their careers in the Minnesota Capitol and having them tell me that some old pro had recommended it as "The best guide you'll find."

The most satisfying review of the first edition came from a friend who is also a college teacher, a lobbyist, and a former senate colleague. He said that as he read the book he kept saying to himself: "Yes, that's the way it is."

Why then a second edition? A few things had to be added: a fuller discussion of ethics, the review of campaign "reform" in the past decade, comment on the new idea of a common law function for courts in an age of statutes. I have expanded the treatment of statutory interpretation, particularly the material on legislative history. Also, a few sections have been brought up to date, like the material on the legislative veto.

The style throughout has been sharpened. And I have mixed in the pronoun "she" in equal measure with the old pronoun "he."

The book presents legislation as one long and intellectual journey. Legislation starts before the legislature is involved, when there exists only hope or anger or disappointment or concern in someone's mind. The book describes what is needed to turn these emotions into ideas and then into effective legislative bills. It describes the process used by legislative institutions to test and refine ideas. It examines the tactics of advocates which speed, impede, or redirect legislative action. The dynamic life of legislative law after enactment is described, including how agencies, local governments and businesses use statutes and how citizens, lawyers and courts adjust them to fit life's realities.

The basic emphasis is on the power of ideas in the legislative process. This tale is seldom told, yet it provides the most accurate and practical look into legislative law and process. After all is said and done, ideas dominate legislative life.

PROFESSOR JACK DAVIES

St. Paul, Minnesota
January, 1986

*

OUTLINE

PART II: MAKING A BILL

PART III: PERSPECTIVES ON LEGISLATIVE POWER

PART V. STATUTORY INTERPRETATION

Chapter 13. Fundamentals of Statutory Interpretation

*

LEGISLATIVE
LAW AND PROCESS
IN A NUTSHELL

SECOND EDITION

*

PART I

THE LEGISLATIVE PROCESS

CHAPTER 1

FOUR FUNDAMENTAL IDEAS

A. LEGISLATION IS IMPORTANT

§ 1-1. Legislation has an impact. A state legislature passes an act and creates a university— or a state park, or a utilities rate board, or an unemployment compensation system, or an environmental protection agency, or a department of insurance, or a state board of fine arts, or a state board of cosmetology, or . . . .

The legislature passes an appropriation act and gives that university money to operate for a biennium; and the state park is maintained; and utility rates are regulated; and the unemployed are compensated through payroll taxes; and the environment is studied and protected; and financial records are examined to assure that insurance companies follow accepted accounting practices; and artists are subsidized; and beauticians are told to clean their combs; and . . . .

The legislature passes an act and a convicted burglar is sentenced to an indeterminate term of one to ten years, with the actual stay in prison decided by prison officials whose advice is relied on by the legislatively-created parole board. Then the legislature passes an act changing the rules on sentencing. Now a judge, exercising a new sentencing power, orders another burglar to serve a determinate sentence of exactly twenty-two months. Then the legislature passes yet another sentencing act, again allowing prison officials to influence, though not control, time served by authorizing the daily award of "good behavior" credits against the prisoner's sentence. Then the legislature passes another act and . . . .

The legislature passes an act and the cost of probate is decreased by twenty percent. The legislature passes an act and divorce is allowed upon a showing of "irretrievable breakdown," rather than exclusively on the ground of adultery. The legislature passes an act and motorcyclists wear helmets. Another act, and motorists are commanded to use seat belts (and thousands more use them than did before). Another act, and . . . .

Legislatures are important. It is useful, from time to time, to think about the reach of legislative power.

§ 1–2. The tasks that make legislatures important.

Operating government. Under the American political system, the executive administers the government. But the legislature creates the machinery of government—establishes its departments, its boards, its commissions, its bureaus. The legislature defines the missions of these agencies—their service responsibilities, their research and educational undertakings, their regulatory roles, their obligation to manage public resources. The legislature allocates the resources; it taxes and it makes appropriations of money that set the level of activity in the various government programs. And the legislature establishes the fundamental rules of government operations—its administrative procedure acts, its civil service rules, its appointing processes, and its election procedures.

Making private law. Historically, in Anglo-American jurisprudence, the law matured through the common law process of accumulating judicial precedent—by Shelly's case, Hadley v. Baxendale, Raffles v. Wickelhaus, and Palsgraf. Occasionally the legislative institution engrafted on the common law a new rule of private law, for example, the Statute 13 Elizabeth Chapter 5 (1570) (the statute on fraudulent conveyances), and the Statute 29 Charles II, Chapter 3 (1677) (the statute of frauds). Later came copyright law, patent law, real estate recording acts, bankruptcy code, corporation codes, Uniform Partnership Act, workers compensation, Uniform Commercial Code, no fault auto insurance laws, and more and more.

Now, because the greater part of private law has become legislative law, the law's growth and refinement must come through legislative action amending various statutory codes. For the first time in our system of Anglo-American jurisprudence, legislatures have assumed the dominant responsibility for the quality and character of the private law of contract, tort, property, and business associations.

Making public law. The law of crimes, taxes, commercial regulation, land use, and environmental protection is also legislative law. Even when the rules of public law are hemmed in by constitutional law principles, the detailed lawmaking falls to legislatures. In addition, a current majority on the Supreme Court claims devotion to the principles of a greater legislative and smaller judicial (constitutional) role and a greater state and smaller federal role in making public policy.

It is a fundamental truth that legislation and legislatures are important. A lawyer must understand not only how these institutions work, but also how they can be used to serve the lawyer's clients.

B. OBLIGATION TO PETITION

§ 2–1. Board of review. Contrary to the conventional wisdom of editorial writers and good government groups, legislatures respond; they seldom lead. Those who want something from a legislature must ask for it. The single most important duty of legislators is to vote *yes* or *no* on proposed legislation, thereby passing judgment on petitions from individuals and groups who ask for legislative action. When petitions for legislation are imaginative and sensible, legislators produce good legislation. When proposals are weak and ill-conceived, legislative performance reflects those qualities. Legislatures work almost exclusively as boards of review to judge proposals brought forward by various groups.

§ 2–2. **The silver platter.** Legislators are aware in a general way of most problems and are ready to make reasonable responses. But they need detailed advice on how to respond; they need a request for specific legislation. The effective petition is served on a silver platter as a soundly conceived and well-drafted bill. It is accompanied by supporting advocacy which convinces legislators that the bill is sensible and that they will not incur serious political vulnerabilities if they support it.

Legislators themselves seldom invent an idea, draft that idea into a bill, educate the press and public to a bill's merits, or lead a lobbying effort in both houses of the legislature and with the executive branch. It is unrealistic to expect them to do so. What actually happens is that new ideas in the form of bill drafts are brought to legislators by citizens, scholars, lawyers, bureaucrats, and lobbyists. These non-legislators then help pass the bill by explaining its merits to legislators and to the public. A bill coming from outside the legislature has political legitimacy, a credential that the rare bill a legislator personally dreams up does not enjoy.

§ 2–3. **Malapportioned lobbying.** Lobbyists—persons employed as legislative advocates—do not represent the myriad groups affected by legislative action. The fact that many interests have no lobbyists distorts public policy. The legislative process uses an adversary system in which silence is treated as acquiescence. If those affected do not object to a bill, legislators tend to accept assertions about its merit from its supporters. Of course, good legislators try to fill the lobbying void with their own examination of each bill presented, but the sheer number of bills undermines this effort. Legislators are generalists who lack specialized knowledge that would aid their review of bills. The pace of most legislative sessions allows them to do little more than judge the cases presented by advocates. In the same way that lawyers are essential to judges in appellate and trial courts and to officials in administrative proceedings, the informed advocacy of lobbyists is essential to legislators.

It is unrealistic to expect that a few dozen elected legislators, acting alone, can provide informed public policy leadership for a state. The unreasonableness of that expectation is obvious when one considers that most legislators are in legislative session only part of each year, are modestly compensated, and are usually attempting to pursue some other vocation along with their legislative work. Besides, most legislators avoid speaking bold words and taking controversial actions that could cost them reelection and the opportunity for political advancement.

C. THE FORCES AT WORK

§ 3–1. **Acquiescence.** Legislatures are organized to divide and share work loads and to build consensus from which decisions emerge. Division of labor cannot occur without acquiescence in the decisions made by other members and by the committees or subcommittees to which primary responsibility for policy making on various subjects is assigned. Consensus cannot develop unless individual viewpoints are submerged or adjusted so as not to interfere with finding a common ground upon which group agreement can be built.

The most frequent decision by legislators is to go along—to acquiesce—in decisions made by others. Acquiescence includes supporting subcommittees and committees, not offering amendments, not speaking, not raising alternatives or questions; it means accepting compromises already made. Going along is easy, for the legislator generally lacks information to support a dissent. But sometimes going along requires great restraint; on occasion, the legislator has information and reason to object. A legislator's decision then must take into account the continued effectiveness of the division of labor provided by the committee structure. If a legislature habitually overturns committee work, each legislator faces more and more decisions in floor session. When acting on the chamber floor the legislator has no help from specialization, from hearings, from extensive discussion, from thinking time, or from between-meeting compromises. This makes persuasive the leadership plea to uphold the system of divided labor and responsibility. The leader's argument in favor of "going along" is usually made, not for the particular decision, but rather for the system.

Each legislator has two other reasons to support committee decisions. First, she does committee work which she wants respected and accepted. If she successfully undercuts other committees, her own committees become less sovereign. Second, acceptance by other legislators always depends on playing by the rules. Among the human relations rules of legislative institutions is that one must show respect for the opinions of others and defer to those who bear primary responsibility for specific decisions.

§ 3–2. **Inertia.** Inertia is a law of physics defined as "the tendency of matter to remain at rest, if at rest, or, if moving, to keep moving in the same direction unless affected by some outside force." Inertia is a universal characteristic of legislative institutions, just as it is universal in our physical world. Its two aspects, inertness and momentum, serve to describe and explain legislatures better than any other analogy.

Legislatures are organized to keep unnecessary or deleterious bills bottled up in committee where they will not consume legislative energy. Committees are expected to hold a bill until its sponsors meet a difficult burden of persuasion. A bill stays pigeonholed and "at rest" in a committee unless outside forces provide the push to get it moving.

When public demand, skilled lobbying, or an effective sponsor (and the merits of the proposal) start a bill moving, legislators usually allow the bill to continue forward. They accept early decisions of drafters, sponsors, subcommittee, and committee. Unless someone steps forward with an amendment and with persuasive information supporting that amendment, a proposal will move to passage *as is,* propelled primarily by legislative momentum. It will be adopted in a form consistent with the initial bill unless outside forces cause modification.

Legislative procedure is premised on the idea that a bill escapes its initial resting place in committee when its supporters have demonstrated a need for the bill. The presumption then follows that the bill deserves to be taken up and acted upon favorably at the next step and each step thereafter. The bill will become law unless along the way some force prompts the unusual decision to re-evaluate prior affirmative action.

As a bill gets closer to passage, it is harder to kill, or even to amend; the burden of persuasion for making any change becomes heavier. Therefore, energy expended early in the process is more effective than energy applied late in the process. Early lobbying has another advantage. Since fewer members are involved in decisions at the start of the process, the task of persuading is less time consuming. The lobbyists can accomplish their purpose by contacting a handful of decision makers.

D. LEGISLATION IS WORDS

§ 4–1. **A bill for an act.** The formal procedural work of a legislature begins with a set of words called "A bill for an act." Under all parliamentary procedure, debate is out of order until a motion is made. The purpose of requiring a motion is to give focus to the discussion. In a legislative institution this practical principle is carried forward by the requirement that a written bill be the object of consideration. Because deliberations are centered on bill drafts, those interested in an issue know who is affected and how. The words in the bill tell what is involved. Throughout the process the focus is on words—words which communicate the underlying values, judgments, and purposes of the bill.

A legislature decides whether the words should be enacted and thus be accorded the legal force of official legislative action. Public policies adopted by a legislature must be expressed in the words of an act. Once an act is passed, the legislature's job is done. It is then up to other forces in society—governmental, commercial, cultural—to implement the policy, to put the legislative words to work in real life. The legislature cannot change policy without enacting new words, passing new legislation.

§ 4–2. Legislative initiative through bill drafting. Those who propose actual words contribute the vital initiative for legislative policy. Words come into the process in two ways, in draft bills as introduced and as amendments to bills. An idea becomes an item of legislative business only when someone turns it into a bill or offers it as an amendment to a bill.

Bills provide the basis for the legislative work of deciding public policy. The process of making a bill—moving an idea into a first draft and then into a draft suitable for introduction—is difficult intellectual labor. In fact, the process appears so challenging that it scares off most of those who desire to petition the legislature.

But potential petitioners must realize they are not expected to complete the bill draft by themselves. The petitioner can share the burdens with many others, including full time legislative bill drafters. The petitioner's responsibility consists of reducing the idea to some kind of written form and then bringing it to a supportive legislator. The legislative machinery completes the process, taking the petitioner's idea and creating a polished draft. Rather than being deterred by the enormous task, potential petitioners should be encouraged by the fact that the burden—intellectual and otherwise—can be shared.

§ 4–3. Legislative initiative through amendment drafting. Changing the words of a bill by amendment is the means to accomplish two important legislative tasks—the accommodation of concerned groups and the elimination of technical defects. Amending out its effective provisions is also one method to defeat the purpose of a bill. Legislators give a greater part of their attention to decisions on amendments than to the question of whether a bill will be passed or defeated. The nimble legislator or lobbyist probes to find word changes that will silence the opponent or even turn an objector into a supporter. The legislative machinery uses amendments to reconcile conflicting viewpoints and to make the words of an act reflect the collective judgment of all those concerned with the issue.

The advocate who wants to be more effective should work with the words of legislation. The dominant legislators and lobbyists ask for specific amendments, argue the merits of specific amendments, write amendments, and, most significantly of all, think up amendments.

CHAPTER 2

LEGISLATIVE INSTITUTIONS

A. HOW LEGISLATURES VARY— AND DON'T

§ 5–1. **Common threads.** To a considerable extent all legislatures are alike. Each is surrounded by staff which influences the decisions of the members. Each is followed and worked by lobbyists who bring to it the messages from the various interest groups of the community—the many publics of "public opinion." Each creates an internal structure of committees and subcommittees to divide the work into manageable pieces. Each has a cadre of leaders who, with or without formal title, handle institutional housekeeping, scheduling, and peacekeeping. Each has other leaders for matters of substance who, with or without formal titles, design the large compromises and who, more than other members, set policy agendas and priorities. Each legislature is controlled by formal rules and by pervasive custom. Each is an arena where the tides of political philosophy ebb and flow. Each is a stage where members of varying temperment and character play out their roles as public policy decision makers.

How alike are legislatures? A lobbyist at the New Hampshire House of Representatives (a 400-

member, ill-paid, understaffed, high-turnover institution) was asked how lobbyists handle that as-
toundingly large legislative body. The answer was
simple: "The same as you work the New York
State Senate. You talk to the four or five members who will make the decision on the issue you're
interested in."

§ 5–2. **Federal Congress and state legislatures.** The great majority of members of the United States Congress give legislative work (and re-
election) their full professional attention. In
contrast, a majority of state legislators are paid
part-time salaries and combine legislative service
with another vocation. Holding office is usually a
financial burden to the best state legislators.

The 535 members of Congress—in session nearly
year around—are now served (or plagued) by nearly 20,000 employees, thirty seven per member.
The fifty state legislatures average 320 full time
employees, a number low enough to assure that the
members themselves remain the effective center-
pieces of their five to seven month sessions.

Legislators in a few of the largest states—California and New York especially—are more similar
to their congressional colleagues than to other
state legislators with respect to pay, duration of
sessions, and the potential for domination by staff.

§ 5–3. **Year to year.** With the legislative devotion to custom, to know a legislature once is to
know it forever. But change is also a constant.
Each watershed year in political life brings to state

legislatures a flood of new members with different agendas. Imagine the Republican faces that departed from state legislatures in the election of 1974 with the Grand Old Party demoralized by Watergate. The figures from Iowa tell the story. In 1972 the GOP held sixty three of 100 seats in the Iowa House. The average member had 6.3 years of service. In 1975 the GOP held thirty nine seats and the average tenure was only 4.3 years. By 1983 the GOP had rebuilt its strength to 58 seats and the average tenure of members had grown back to 6.1 years.

Technology also changes legislatures. Try to imagine the changes in legislative institutions caused by the development of the Xerox copier. The legislatures of 1961 were institutions of carbon paper, mimeographs, and oral amendments. Bills and amendments were often explained only in speeches because there were few ready copies. The institutions worked effectively because of pervasive trust among their members.

By 1971 legislatures were institutions of photocopying, with written amendments thoroughly reviewed by bureaucrats, lobbyists, staff, and members. Ten years later, in 1981, legislatures had become institutions of computer bill-drafting, word processor constituent letters, and paper shredders.

§ 5–4. **Senate and assembly.** A bicameral legislature consists of two separate and different institutions. Senates, the smaller of the two legislative houses, have less specialization of members, smaller committees and subcommittees, more staff per member, and larger constituencies to serve. Because of realities not so obvious from simple arithmetic, the smaller body also has shorter debates, less need for centralized leadership and thus more widely dispersed leadership responsibilities, and many other distinct qualities.

The amount of experience in a legislative body changes the allegiance to custom, attitudes toward decorum, and in a variety of other ways significantly affects how a legislative body works. Senate members are favored with longer terms and slightly greater prestige than are representatives. One consequence is that assembly members regularly abandon assembly seats to move to the senate. These moves, along with the fact that senators face the hazards and burdens of election half as often as assembly members, cause senators to have much longer average legislative tenure than do their assembly counterparts.

Senators who have assembly experience retain respect and affection for the other house after they switch to the senate. But representatives who aspire to, but fail to attain, senate membership tend to carry small resentments against the "upper house" and against their former colleagues who moved "over." Having served in two legislative bodies is likely to give a legislator a somewhat richer base of experience and greater understanding of the essentials of parliamentary law and practice. A member switching from assembly to

senate carries to the senate memories of a variety
of tactical devices and inventive housekeeping
ideas used in the assembly.

On the first day of a term, a representative looks
forward to another election in just twenty-two
months, an election day that may end the legislative career. During half of each senator's term,
that worrisome reality is two years further off than
it is for each representative. Senators, as a consequence, are more courageous, but less politically
responsive. Senators are more emotionally committed to the legislative life and institution, but
are less committed to political party and other
machinery of election. The size of districts also
makes the houses different. Assembly districts are
only one-half, one-third, or one-fourth as large as
senate districts. Large districts mean less homoge-
neous constituencies.

Because of these physical, temporal, and personnel variations, there are always in every legislature substantial differences in the decision-making
processes of the two houses.

§ 5–5. **Committee to committee.** Legislative
committees are not peas in a pod. Each takes on
an individuality through the interplay of its members and its work. In the weeks before a new
legislative session, the majority caucus organizing
committee faces the task of putting together the
roster of committee members and chairmen for the
session. The work is done thoughtfully, for the
success of the session depends on the quality of

committee work. Predictably, the weak, lazy, or unreliable member who is eligible by seniority for a chairmanship is assigned to chair a minor committee where there is less opportunity to do damage. In contrast, the strong, aggressive, wise, and reliable members are chosen to head the important and sensitive committees.

As the rest of the committee is chosen, the risk of damage caused by the weak chairman may be hedged by giving the committee a strong vice chairman or a core of more competent members. At other times the same criteria that caused assignment of a weak chairman is applied as members are named. Then one discovers the weak chairman surrounded by lazy members and the thoughtful chairmen strengthened by a committee roster of reliable craftsmen. The performance of the two committees differs as day differs from night. One committee must be constantly rescued by leadership intervention or by floor amendment; the other committee works with near autonomy as the institution defers to its consistent good sense. One is manipulated by outside forces; the other offers a tough-minded panel to judge the merits of contending arguments.

Most committees screen a multitude of bills in order to select a few dozen for submission to the floor of the body. Each committee is responsible for a given subject area. The subject jurisdiction of a committee influences its membership and its characteristics. For example, one committee, with jurisdiction over government structure, will draw legislators with a political science turn of mind. A committee dealing with banking and insurance, on the other hand, will interest members whose focus is commerce. These two committees will behave differently.

When committees have different functions, their processes become distinct. In contrast to the bill screening function, appropriation committees construct a few omnibus appropriation bills. To do this different task, appropriations committees have special procedures. They hold months of hearings on spending requests and devote a few intense weeks to allocation meetings.

A tax committee usually oversees the technical aspects of state tax laws, but, more significantly, it shapes one bill each session to balance the state budget by assuring that the state tax code will produce revenue equal to state expenditures. While other committees set the legislative agenda, the tax committee controls a subject that is inevitably on the agenda.

Because of function, subject jurisdiction, and quality of members, each committee—welfare, government operations, local government, commerce, appropriations, or tax—displays significantly different characteristics.

§ **5–6. Issue to issue.** Legislative performance changes from issue to issue. Compare the legislative approach to these two kinds of problems: first, the stark alternatives raised by abortion; second, the subtle decisions required to construct a workable system to protect private information in an age when computers can store millions of records on individuals and retrieve in seconds any single record.

On abortion questions, emotional tides in the electorate have locked most legislators into unbreakable alliances with one side or the other. Therefore, there is little inclination to deliberate thoughtfully on any abortion-related proposal. For a legislator even to appear to have a second thought will offend both sides in a milieu of single-issue voters.

On the problem of keeping some government records private, public attention is minimal. The Herculean struggles of the three or five-person subcommittees evaluating proposed bills go nearly unnoticed, even by legislative colleagues. The whole process is a desperate search to find sense, justice, and accommodation. This effort occurs in seminar-like subcommittee meetings attended only by a handful of bureaucrats and a few media lobbyists, most offering narrow-minded, self-serving advice.

§ 5–7. **Good days and bad days.** Bismarck's comment that "No man who loves laws or sausages should see how either are made" is not universally applicable. Sometimes legislatures are a joy to behold. Like other human institutions, legislatures and legislative committees often rise to the occasion. At other times, they muddle. Political

pressures, fatigue, incomplete information, interpersonal tensions, conflicting ideology, and other
destructive forces impact the legislative processes
in different ways in various circumstances. Legislators will perform like statesmen one day and
cave in to pressure or misjudge reality the next.

Ironically, when a legislature performs the best,
it may look the worst. When an issue is vital and
differing opinions are strongly held, the public sees
bitter debate and stalemate. The media report
stubbornness and posturing. Press, radio, and television find it too complex to convey the reality that
(between public outbursts) each side in a protract-
ed legislative struggle is looking for merit in the
arguments made by the competing side, pressing
the merit of its own position, and engaging in
subtle bargaining. Though the fight looks bad, it
is worthwhile on an important issue. For one side
to have quietly acceded to prevailing opinion without vigorously pressing its cause would have looked
efficient and fair; but it would have been bad
legislating. Sometimes only a good fight will reveal truth and yield the best public policy.

§ 5–8. At the deadline.   All legislatures
change their procedures between the start and the
end of each yearly session. As the work changes,
so does the process. In early weeks the focus is on
hearings and subcommittee study. As the session
progresses, the focus shifts to committee action,
followed by floor consideration of the bills reported
by committee.

In many states, constitutional deadlines for adjournment turn the last days and hours of a session into a frantic drive to dispose of accumulated business. In other states and in Congress, the deadline—and the scramble to meet it—is imposed by political and practical realities. Media reports generally suggest that all the work of the session is concentrated in the few weeks during which the legislature is acting under the compulsion of its deadlines. In reality, deadlines merely end study and reflection and force the institution and its members to turn tentative decisions into final ones. A lobbyist who has not made a client's case earlier is often denied the opportunity to make it during the closing days. Legislators are so busy casting votes based on previously acquired information that they cannot take time to listen to additional evidence or argument. The institution is not acting without thoughts or facts; it is acting without *new* thoughts or facts.

B. THE UNIVERSAL INSTITUTION

§ **6–1. Bicameral-unicameral.** The United States Congress and forty-nine state legislatures are organized as bicameral bodies. The Nebraska legislature and most county and municipal legislative institutions are organized on a unicameral basis. A bicameral legislature is really two institutions. The two houses of a legislature have separate procedures and leadership. Joint committees and joint hearings are the exception. Some members of one house may be complete strangers to some members of the other house. This amazes those citizens who reasonably expect legislative work to throw together the few score of individuals in their state who enjoy the status of legislator. But a legislative bill-passing effort must occur in two really separate arenas. It involves a journey through the upper house (senate) and a journey through the lower house (assembly).

§ 6–2.　**The extended institution.** One reason for the separateness of house and senate is that members represent but a part of the legislative institution. Legislative staff, reporters, lobbyists from private and public entities, and other interested citizens swell the ranks of the real legislature to hundreds of persons. To participate effectively in deliberations on an issue in either house requires familiarity with the extended institution— all the players who contribute to consideration of the issue in that house. Those players become more important than almost any member of the other house, for each house gives a proposal consideration independent of the other body. For a legislator who is effectively involved in legislative work in his own house, time constraints require him to ration the amount of energy he can spend on acquaintance-making in the other house. A senator may not cross paths with new or inactive members of the assembly for weeks or months. He will know lobbyists, news reporters, and obscure staff members of his own house much more quickly.

Davies, Leg.Law & Process, 2d Ed., NS—3

§ 6–3. **Lobbyists.** A legislative institution is a huge fact-finding and educating machine. The elected members have a special role in that machine, but ample opportunity exists for other citizens to participate in its work and to influence the legislative product. Foremost among citizen participants in the legislative institution are the lobbyists. The hired lobbyists have no credential as they arrive at the legislature, other than that somebody pays them to show up to represent a particular point of view. The citizen who comes as a volunteer lacks even that credential. While the volunteer may assert conviction and integrity of motive as a substitute credential, experienced legislators expect more honest and reliable information from hired lobbyists. The professional lobbyists— and their clients—have a stake in maintaining long term credibility. That keeps the professionals honest. On the other hand, the unknown volunteer has no past legislative record and may have no legislative concerns beyond the current issue. The volunteer may be a narrow ideologue or may be concealing a significant personal economic interest. To be effective, the volunteer must build trust by being around the legislature over a period of time and by demonstrating respect for the institution and its members.

Hired or volunteer, lobbyists play a major role in the legislative institution. They prepare its bills, write amendments to those bills, advocate bills, and argue for amendments. They develop compromises and facilitate communication between the two houses. When a legislator shares decision making with staff, the lobbyists extend advocacy to the staff. When public opinion is critical, they provide information to reporters and editorial writers. Lobbyists show up on the field of battle armed with information and backed by politically potent constituencies, making them an essential part of the legislative institution.

§ **6–4. Committees.** Woodrow Wilson, as a political science scholar, wrote, "The Congress in committee is Congress at work." The work of all legislative bodies is done through committees in order to divide the labor. Nearly every legislative action follows a committee recommendation that is reported to the floor of the house, confirmed by floor action, and becomes the official action of that house. However, not all bills are reported to the floor. Committees pigeonhole bills which the committee decision makers decide to leave off the committee agenda or which are laid over by the committee after hearing.

The autonomy of committees in their decision making varies from institution to institution and from time to time. The degree of committee autonomy is probably the most significant variable among legislative bodies. It determines the amount of control that leadership cliques hold over the work of the institution. Institution-wide leadership competes with a more decentralized control by the committee chairmen, who often exercise pre-eminent power in the area of their jurisdiction.

The degree of committee autonomy also affects the opportunity for legislators to attack problems beyond their own assignments. In some legislative bodies, notably the United States House of Representatives, a legislator can work with real effectiveness only on issues handled in committees on which the legislator serves. When the issue produces an intense floor fight, members of the committee that processed the bill will lead the battle on the two sides of the issue. Even the most powerful legislators, if not members of the relevant committee, exercise their leadership on an issue in backstage roles. Where committee autonomy is not so dominant, legislators are free to sponsor bills before any committee and to participate actively in the floor advocacy on any bill and any amendment.

The role of the committee in the legislative process can hardly be exaggerated. Still, the committee is subject to the consensus of the body. A committee seriously out of step with majority opinion within a house will be attacked and reversed. The leadership of the committee will respond by modifying its future actions to avoid provoking floor rejection of its decisions.

Generally, the committee structure of a legislative body is determined by the steering committee of the majority group, although in some jurisdictions and in the United States Congress a statute establishes the structure. Where the pattern of organization is left to each newly elected legislature, the number and jurisdiction of committees varies from session to session. The number often depends on how many members are eligible for committee chairmanships on the basis of seniority; for example, a committee may be established for each majority caucus member with at least two prior terms.

The jurisdiction of committees may be adjusted to fit the talent and ambition of the various chairmen. Strong chairmen expand the variety and significance of bills referred to their committees at the expense of less assertive chairmen. When jurisdictional disputes arise, legislative leaders direct bills to preferred committees, usually to a committee chaired with a steady hand by an established member of the body's hierarchy.

§ 6–5. **Subcommittees.** The labor of the institution is further divided through the use of subcommittees. There may be standing subcommittees to deal with particular subject areas or *ad hoc* subcommittees to deal with a specific bill. Sometimes a subcommittee is used as a repository for a bill that the committee or committee chairman does not wish to be bothered with again. More commonly, subcommittees are used to do the hard work of taking testimony, redrafting language, and developing the consensus necessary before a bill is submitted to the full committee and to the floor.

One indication of the need for division of labor in legislatures is the reverse relationship between the number of standing committees and the number of subcommittees. Inevitably, the fewer the standing committees, the greater the number of policy-making subcommittees that are required to conduct legislative business. An often suggested "reform" in legislative structure is to reduce the number of standing committees so each legislator will have fewer assignments. This recommendation fails to take into account the phenomenon of multiplying subcommittees. It also ignores the fact that, as the number of committees is reduced, each surviving committee must carry a heavier work load because it covers a wider subject area. Therefore, each committee must give consideration to more bills and members will have as much work as before.

A more efficient division of legislative resources occurs, instead, with smaller, but more numerous, standing committees. Having fewer members on each committee reduces the number of assignments for each legislator. And these reduced assignments are to committees without expanded subject areas.

Often policy-making subcommittees are duplicative and time wasting, but this criticism is not applicable to small subcommittees which polish a bill prior to full committee consideration. Such work-horse subcommittees save legislative energy by putting a minimum number of minds to the initial task of sharpening the issues, screening out avoidable conflicts, and inserting perfecting amendments.

§ 6–6. **Leadership.** Leadership in a legislative body is profoundly affected by the committee structure of the body. To understand a legislative institution, one must know the interrelationships of its formal leaders—speaker, majority leader, minority leader, president, steering committees and committee chairmen. It is essential to know who makes what decisions in order to influence the legislative product most efficiently. In some legislatures, a small clique of majority caucus leaders dominate. In other institutions, decisions are made by committee chairmen and their supporters; the formal legislative leadership then plays a housekeeping and coordinating role rather than a substantive role. Even where the legislative committee is quite autonomous, there are decisions on which leaders gauge the consensus of the house and of the public and communicate it to the committee. On these issues the committee structure serves largely to rubber-stamp leadership decisions and, within the parameters of those decisions, to polish and flesh out the bill.

The size of the body also plays a determinative role in legislative leadership. Generally, the larger a legislative body, the more centralized the leadership. This makes the speaker of the assembly the most powerful single legislator in most jurisdictions. The assembly speaker and majority leader often serve as a team, overseeing the committee work of the assembly and stepping in with directions on the substance of legislation on key issues. Senates, because of their smaller size, are more likely to be dominated by an oligarchy of committee chairmen. Longer service gives senators more automatic prerogatives and reduces the leverage available to the formally elected leaders.

The formal apportionment of power within an institution is reflected in the committee structure, the elected leadership of the body as a whole, and the leaders of its separate political caucuses. This power apportionment is adjusted in a variety of ways, especially to account for the extra, informal influence of members with extraordinary ability and personality. The legislator who holds a particular title may exercise the power that should go with the title. But the possessor of the title may be so deferential to the opinions of other members that lobbying efforts intended to influence the title-holder's actions are most effectively channeled through more dominant members. A common mistake in dealing with legislative institutions is to assume that the power of the institution coincides with the formal titles, rather than to examine the real relationships and lines of power within the institution.

§ 6–7. **Legislative norms.** Superimposed on the formal legislative structure and official rules of procedure and organization are legislative norms—established patterns of behavior. Some unwritten rules conflict directly with the written rules of the

institution. For example, written rules always authorize a motion to close off debate, but unwritten
norms of many state legislatures dictate that the
motion is never made. The rules of a legislature
may authorize unlimited co-sponsorship on bills,
but custom may dictate that sponsors are held to a
low number.

Unwritten rules vary from institution to institution and from time to time, but the following are
universally present to some degree. This list of
norms is drawn from the Jewell and Patterson
study, *The Legislative Process in the United States.*

Legislative work. Legislators are rewarded
with expanded influence in the institution as they
work at the task of being a legislator. Legislators
who demonstrate interest in personal advancement
or publicity, rather than in the quality of the
legislative product, lose some legislative influence,
even if their non-legislative political power grows.

Specialization. Legislators are expected to concentrate their energies in a limited number of
fields, demonstrating an understanding of the necessity for division of labor and of the prerogatives
of other members who carry responsibility for decision-making in different fields. The legislator who
flits from issue to issue is usually a dilettante and,
when recognized as such, is denied the deference
given those "who mind the store."

Institutional patriotism. A legislator is expected to respect the institution, demonstrating
that respect by working at the job and by behaving

in other ways that contribute to the esteem in which it is held by the public. Occasionally, the issue of institutional loyalty arises in power clashes between the executive and the legislative branch. When the issue is perceived as a matter of legislative prerogatives, the legislator who sides with the executive rather than with the legislative institution loses influence.

Party loyalty. Loyalty is a political commodity of high value and legislatures are political institutions. Therefore, the pressure of party caucus loyalty is significant. The degree to which party discipline is asserted in legislative bodies varies, but when an issue arises in which the majority of a caucus asserts a party position and requests all members of that caucus to stay in line, acceptance of the request is expected. To stray is excused, however, when the legislator's constituency is antagonistic to the caucus position or when the member is already on record on the other side of the issue.

Reciprocity. Legislators are expected to help one another. This involves geographic and ideologic tolerance. A legislator finds himself out of step with the spirit of the institution if he approaches each issue with the narrow viewpoint of what it will do for him and for his constituency, ignoring broader interests and ignoring the political imperatives facing his colleagues. He also finds himself short of accumulated goodwill when he faces a legislative situation in which the broad-minded understanding of colleagues is needed.

Interpersonal courtesy. Goodwill among members of the legislature increases the capacity of the institution to do its work effectively. Facing a multitude of conflicts—some bitter—a legislative institution can be torn apart by personal animosities. To protect against this development, the norm in legislatures is to separate personalities from issues. Motives of members are not questioned. Debate is carried on in the most impersonal and respectful of terms. When debate on an issue is concluded, that conflict is forgotten and the body turns to its next task with a minimum of retained rancor. The norm is to "disagree without being disagreeable."

§ 6–8. Seniority. One legislative norm universally applied is the rule of seniority. In any legislative institution, newcomers serve an apprenticeship during which they learn the rules of the institution—written and unwritten—and develop some specialization through their committee assignments. Members who return for second, third, and subsequent terms are favored with assignment to more preferred committees, or at least are allowed to retain their assignments from prior sessions. The strictness with which seniority is applied varies from legislature to legislature, but is followed in all to a significant extent.

The seniority system as utilized by most legislatures is justified. Justification lies partly in recognizing the value of experience and the sounder judgments of maturity. An even more valid justification is that seniority avoids fratricide within the legislative body. Any method of assigning committee memberships and chairmanships less cut-and-dried than seniority opens the door to factionalism, political maneuver, vote-trading, resentment, and periodic disintegration of discipline and order. Seniority is retained in the process of legislative organization because it is the only way to avoid problems much greater than the problems of seniority itself. It is hard to imagine a way to bind up the wounds that would follow a biennial struggle for committee assignments and chairmanships conducted without the restraint of seniority guidelines.

The seniority system earned a bad name through slavish adherence to it in the United States Congress. However, the evils in the pre-1975 congressional system should not be imputed to state legislatures. Turnover of membership causes a less rigid adherence to the seniority system in state legislatures where weaker members, even after long service, are often side-tracked into chairmanships of minor committees. Furthermore, the incidence of senility in state legislative committee chairmen is lower than it was in congressional committees. State legislators are closer to home and exposed to their constituencies on a more regular basis, the perquisites of office are fewer, and staff pressure to hold on to the office is less.

Whatever problems arise from seniority generally are reduced by modifications in the rigidity with which the system is applied. Reducing the opportunities for autocratic behavior by individual committee chairmen—old or young—can also help. The legislative process, a consensus procedure, usually operates in a way that counteracts the evils of weak, senile, or dictatorial committee chairmen. Even the United States House of Representatives has abandoned its unquestioning adherence to seniority; in 1975, three senior chairmen were replaced and in 1985 one sitting chairman was ousted.

C. THE MEMBERS

§ 7–1. **Impact of politics.** Legislators come to their position through politics. Every legislator has some quality attractive to voters. That quality may be good sense; or it may be captivating friendliness and good humor. Or it may be impressive intelligence, irresistible ambition, utter decency, or some combination of these traits. By and large legislators are attractive, pleasant, and reasonably capable citizens selected by peers to hold positions of responsibility. To demean their individual and collective quality is cynical and destructive.

Still, legislators seldom stand apart from the constituencies that send them to the legislature. Voter trust of a political candidate seems to grow as the degree of identification with the candidate increases. This produces legislators who reflect the community in both its strengths and its weaknesses, its common sense and its ignorance, its dedication and its fickleness, its caution and its caprice.

§ 7–2. **Legislative roles.** In 1965, when legislators were almost all part-time office holders, James Barber in *The Lawmakers* categorized them according to the various roles they assume in the legislative process. The increasing professionalization of state legislatures has eroded the universality of Barber's work, but not the validity of his underlying premises. The main lesson to be learned from his classification system is that legislative advocates must view legislators as individuals and adjust their advocacy to address each legislator in a way consistent with the role each plays. The roles Barber describes provide useful insights into the legislative process.

The lawmaker. The lawmaker is Barber's legislative hero. Each lawmaker comes to the legislature with a purpose. Personal satisfaction comes not from public reputation, or from high political position, but from results. The formulation and production of legislation are foremost, and the lawmaker spends more energy and attention on this than any other legislative type. The lawmaker is often a career legislator, and becomes and expert at using the structure and processes of the institution as effective means to further public policy goals.

The advertiser. The advertiser, bursting with ambition, comes to the legislature, not with an agenda of lawmaking, but rather with an agenda of personal advancement. Legislative office was sought and won, not because it was dreamed of, but rather because it was there, like Mount Everest, and climbing it would bring honor and profit. Since the advertiser's personal advancement depends so heavily upon reputation, the advertiser selects a few high visibility issues and pursues them aggressively. Legislative service is only a temporary interest for the advertiser. After one or two terms the advertiser is ready to use the public recognition earned in the legislature for personal advancement elsewhere.

The reluctant. The reluctant does not come to the legislature to pursue a personal agenda of issues, or to achieve personal notoriety and success. She desires merely to be competent in her role as a cog in the legislative machine. Emphasizing rules of legislative process over the substance of particular bills, she believes that proper procedures will ensure proper legislation. The reluctant provides the legislative balance wheel, protecting the institution from those who would pursue their lawmaking or advertising at all cost.

The spectator. A born follower, the spectator lacks the ability or self confidence to promote his own legislation. Having a low standard of success, he is content to bask in the prestige of office, and act as a supporter of the party leaders. Since his participation in legislation is strictly vicarious, an advocate in the legislature need not worry about the spectator. If the support of the party leaders is gained, the support of the spectators will soon follow.

§ 7–3. **Other legislative types.** Other commentators have used descriptive categories as a way to give insight into Congress. Although aimed at the national legislature, these descriptions reveal attributes of all legislative institutions. Roger Davidson identified several legislator types in his 1969 book, *The Role of Congressmen.*

The tribune. Historically, the tribune's function was to fight the people's battles against the Crown. The tribune in the legislature today is concerned mainly with taking care of problems at home; doing case work for constituents that does not necessarily have anything to do with legislation. If the tribune is involved with the formulation of legislation, it is a bill to aid the home district.

The ritualist. The ritualist is an expert at the intricate procedures, rules, etiquettes and formal understandings of the legislative process. The ritualist emphasizes the formal aspects of capitol hill duties and routines; legislative work, overseeing, investigation and committee specialization serve as the means to gain influence.

The inventor. An inventor emphasizes problem solving or policy innovation, and takes a broad view of the role as a legislator.

The broker. This is congressman as politician in a pluralistic society, balancing and blending diverse interests, including home district interests versus national interests.

The opportunist. This legislator stresses the job of campaigning and re-election. Although all members of Congress have a primary interest in re-election, some have no other interest.

J. McIver Weatherford has categorized three roles of legislators in *Tribes on the Hill.*

The shaman. This little known legislator is most visible after a crisis (such as Three Mile Island) dispensing shame for greater self glory. The shaman's power does not derive from the authority of position, or from any practical results produced, but from the confidence displayed, and the emotion extracted from followers. The shaman is an expert at making real the threats of unseen demons: world communism, the Mafia, monopoly cabals, the moral majority, or the immoral minority.

The warlord. This legislator carefully chooses one piece of legislative terrain, slowly dominates it, strengthens it, and gradually extends it outwards, increasing its scope. The warlord concentrates on intensive, rather than extensive politics. As a group, warlords hold the real power. Although each controls only a part of the whole organization, they have strategically selected every spot to maximize a particular brand of power.

The godfather.   Ignoring the committee structure, this tactician concentrates on the political
party structure, seeking elected posts within Congress as party whip and party leader, putting together ad-hoc coalitions and deals, and playing a
fast·game.   Like warlords, the godfathers have a
career commitment to Congress, but unlike them,
they are too impatient to accrue power slowly in a
single area.   Godfathers act as brokers, keeping
warlords in balance by treating them as any politician treats a constituency.   They are backroom
negotiators and group facilitators.

Two other types of legislators must be added to
the cast of characters.

The dependable friend.   Soon after a person is
seated as a member of a legislative body, observers
spot patterns in the votes cast.   The legislator may
demonstrate consistent allegiance to party, to farm
bloc, to management, to labor, to the chief executive, or to the local courthouse crowd, editor, or
industry.   Sophisticated legislative advocates learn
upon whom they can depend for support and who
will likely be in opposition.   They start each lobbying effort with a quick visit to sure friends, then
work through the likely supporters, and finally
contact those whose position cannot be predicted.
The advocate's presentation becomes more refined
and effective with practice.   This is a reason to
start with easy votes first.   Another reason is to
gauge better what compromises may be necessary.
If the advocate has difficulty with dependable

friends, the votes of those legislators of more questioning attitudes will not be available. With this knowledge, the advocate can trim the proposal to acceptable size early in the process, before lines of opposition have hardened.

For the legislator, being thought of as a dependable friend creates problems. When a vote is cast against political allies, they feel double-crossed and resentful, or at least let down. A respected political slogan is, "You dance with them what brung you." A legislator votes against traditional allies with reluctance because the price for doing so is high.

The problem of being *no one's* dependable friend is daunting. If the performance of a legislator is so unpredictable that it earns the loyal support of no constituency, the legislator seeks re-election lacking a strong base of support. It is difficult to be a maverick in an institution and in a profession where loyalty is a highly valued quality.

The ideologue. The ideological legislator takes a totalitarian stand on the few issues which are near and dear to his heart, while all but ignoring the other issues before the legislature. The ideologue will settle only for the perfect solution to pet projects, not for a workable solution. This hard line approach and an interest in only a few issues makes the ideologue an ineffective and short lived legislator. Only an advocate who shares his ideological position will find this legislator to be useful.

D. QUESTIONS OF ETHICS

§ 8–1. **On the merits.** The bottom line of legislative ethics ought to be that public policy is made on the merits, with no extraneous considerations twisting judgment.   Ideally, no influence should deter legislators from fulfilling their obligation to promote the great purposes of government: to seek for all citizens the right to life, liberty and property and the pursuit of happiness; to seek the greatest good for the greatest number; to attain order and justice.   The ideal is to have every decision made honestly toward these ends, free of distorting influences.

Reality, of course, falls short of the ideal.   But reality, even in the worst legislature, more closely reflects the ideal than does the cynic's morose view.   A cynical attitude paralyzes its holder from hoping for, asking for, and working for reasonable legislation.   It deters one from bringing petitions based on merit.   It cuts short research to assemble facts for truth-based advocacy.   It leads the petitioner to appeal to legislator self interest, rather than to his honesty and intellect and judgment.

But if cynicism is so bad, why does it flourish? The reasons are complex.

§ 8–2. **Negative publicity.** The negative publicity about legislatures is so pervasive that it seems inevitable that conventional wisdom should hold legislators to be ignorant, bungling, bumbling, and self-serving.   That view is constantly re-enforced because legislatures are easy targets. Human frailties—intellectual and ethical—exist wherever people gather. But the open deliberations of the legislature expose those frailities as does no other milieu. Personal decisions and most business decisions are made behind the scenes, in private. It is accepted as normal that they are concealed from review by the community. But legislatures conduct public business in public; they are always in the news and always the object of critical examination.

Legislators themselves broadcast much of the criticism of their institution. Legislatures are partisan places and the combat of political campaigns commonly includes negative comment. Candidates barrage the voters with criticisms of how the other side handles the public business. These charges cause the public to generalize legislator fault.

Most people are always looking for a laugh. Editorial cartoonists exploit our love of humor, and they thrive on the vulnerability of politicians. The portrayal of legislatures as comic places extends beyond the cartoons, it pervades the press. Actually, legislative humor, like the humor of a wartime army, makes each legislative session bearable to participants. Legislators laugh along with the public, but the institution pays a price, even when the ridicule is gentle.

Another seemingly universal human quality, much less attractive than love of humor, is the blaming of scapegoats. Legislators play the scapegoat role. It is both inevitable and healthy in a representative democracy for legislators to be the community scapegoats. That means both legitimate and scapegoat blame fall on a powerful institution of government. No solution to society's problems is ever perfect. But when an institution of power falls short of what is expected, there is a tendency to mistrust its motive, rather than assuming its failures came from honest mistake.

These are the publicity reasons, but there are also substantive reasons for the public disillusionment with legislatures.

§ 8–3. The causes of cynicism. The following catalogue of reasons for distrust of legislatures and legislators is too credible. These are the reasons for public cynicism, but they do not justify it. Like a list of jargon to be avoided, the enumeration itself may reinforce negative thoughts instead of improving perspective.

The ambiguity of truth. Even legislators deeply committed to decision on the merits find it difficult to live up to that commitment 100 percent of the time. The merits are sometimes hard to pin down. Uncertainty arises because new facts challenge the conventional wisdom of the community and of the legislative institution. More uncertainty arises when the view of a trusted advisor disagrees with the opinion of the expert specialist. With some of these persuaders aligned with the legislator's self interest and some aligned against it, even the finest legislator from time to time loses the ability to follow the winding road of truth.

Compromising the merits. Many people view the legislative propensity to compromise as proof of an inherent contradiction between legislative mores and decision-making on the merits. They ask: How can I respect a process that requires its participants to bargain away what they know is correct policy? How can I accept the compromises of the legislative process that preclude adherence to honest conviction?

Legislative compromise often is judged to be unconscionable wheeling and dealing; and unprincipled accommodation is assumed to be inevitable. This belief leads to the conclusion that legislatures are so prone to unscrupulous behavior that they are too evil to bother with, or, if not evil, at least so lacking in reasoned decision-making that it is undignified to bring petitions to that arena.

Parochial obligations. Sometimes a legislator confronts an issue of parochial interest to his district. What test of merit is then to be applied? Is the test what is best for the state or, rather, what is best for the home district? Either choice fuels the mistrust of the cynic.

The ambiguity of responsiveness. Many voters suffer ambivalent feelings as to whether they really want elected representatives to be courageous and independent, deciding each issue on the merits without worry about reelection. Even voters who usually want courageous conviction sometimes hope for the kind of "flexibility" from their own representative that at least allows her to respond to their own demands. Ironically, to the extent voters demand responsiveness, they deny legislators freedom to cast pure votes based on known facts and compelling logic.

Of course, many voters think a legislator can be both responsive and courageously wise. The representative simply needs to vote as the constituent directs. The average voter associates and talks politics with others who have similar backgrounds, who live in similar circumstances, and who hold similar political views. The voter concludes, therefore, that his own opinions are majority opinions and that a legislator who disagrees is, not only wrong, but also unresponsive. The legislator's every disagreeable vote—if discovered—thus is double fuel for the fires of cynicism.

The ambiguity of team loyalty. A legislature is a complicated institution with large and conflicting responsibilities. Legislative leaders give the advice: "To get along, go along." Sometimes members are asked to yield their individual judgments to make a majority concensus on the one road to be taken of several that are available. When individual members refuse to bend, the institution will stall. Commentators today generally lament the inability of congressional leaders to "whip the members into line" in response to national needs. The commentators are, in effect, arguing for a system under which legislators have less control over their individual votes, where the orders of leaders can be enforced.

But both leading and following contribute to a cynical view of legislative decision making. Decision-making on the merits, in a simple view of things, does not contemplate the yielding to entreaty or the acceptance of orders.

The problem of prior obligation. Sometimes an interest to whom the legislator has been a dependable friend demands a bad vote. The legislator's choice, then, is to cast a vote encumbered by prior obligation or, instead, to take a position that creates the appearance of ingratitude and disloyalty. Either choice—the encumbered or the disloyal vote—supports a cynical judgment.

The temptation of favors. The misuse of power for personal gain is a major theme of movie and novel. The occasional bribery indictment proves the theme is not without its real life antecedents. The power of a legislative vote carries the opportunity to prosper. Some individuals offer the bribe or the business favor. Some individuals chosen to serve as legislators are vulnerable to corrupt influences.

All these cynic-making factors arise naturally out of the inherent complexity of legislative choices. But, as the following sections show, it is possible to avoid destructive impulses by keeping the ambiguities of legislative behavior in perspective.

§ 8–4. Perspective on honesty. Although temptation is inherent to the legislative function, corruption is not. In the big picture bribery affects such a miniscule percentage of legislative decisions that it hardly counts as having a meaningful impact on public policy.

All states make bribery a felony. The payment of money for a legislative vote is everywhere thought of as an ultimate corruption of the law-making process. Bribery is intolerable, but it is generally under effective control in American jurisdictions. Wherever and whenever it occurs, the response must be vigorous insistence on exposure and prosecution. In any venue where it is more than an occasional and random perversion, that political habit must be challenged by press, business, labor, and "good" people so the practitioners of corruption can be routed out—both givers and takers. Cynicism hinders, instead of helps, this effort.

§ 8–5. Perspectives on legislative compromise. It takes just a little tolerance to reconcile legislative compromise and decision-making on the merits.

Resolution comes by viewing compromise as a legitimate process of accommodation, as a necessary and proper method to balance—on the merits—the competing interests of claimants to a limited supply of benefits. For example, when the legislature proposes to give one city a community college, the legislators from another region may demand approval for a new highway bridge "in trade" for their support for the college. The rule of decision-making on the merits is not inevitably violated by the demand. Rather, the demand may propose a bargaining compromise to assure an appropriate dispersal of the largess of public spending.

Of course, compromise can be illegitimate. When either side of a bargain views its own or the other side's demand as not founded on honest belief, it is participating in a legislative decision not grounded on the merits. An honest bargain requires an honest demand and a legitimate objective; otherwise it proposes an "ill-gotten" gain. It buys a benefit with a corrupted vote.

Even an accommodation made where one side views the demand of the other as unsupportable is not necessarily an expedient and corrupt vote exchange. It can be a decision on the merits if the other side is thought to be making its demand in good faith; if its position is honestly believed, even though mistaken. The accommodation to differences of *opinion* is wholly legitimate. Each legislator must give the benefit of the doubt in exchange for others giving the benefit of the doubt in return. Resolution of legislative dispute frequently comes to splitting the difference to reach a workable consensus. It comes down to averaging the right and the wrong judgments of the two sides and arriving, quite precisely, at a collective wisdom that is, at bottom, decision-making on the merits.

Two half wrongs, in the world of the legislature, often make a right.

§ 8–6. **Perspectives on responsiveness and independence.** The way legislators respond to the competing claims for responsiveness and adherence to the merits does not cool cynical fires. Whether one wants responsiveness or independence, legislators act in ways that disillusion. Assume for the moment that the ideal is Edmund Burke's delegate, who acts always on the basis of what her own judgment tells her is in the best interest of her constituency. Legislators campaigning for election deny this ideal; they seldom declare their intention to vote their personal convictions regardless of popular opinion. During election campaigns—winning campaigns—legislators play the theme of responsiveness. They renounce the delegate's role, feeding the cynicism of those who dream of being served by bold delegates.

These candidates will later also disappoint those voters who believe the candidate claim of responsiveness. Those voters will be distressed when the legislator in office takes a position that is not responsive, but is, instead, based on all the evidence, including that disclosed in legislative hearings. The legislator who casts a vote on merit, rather than on the weight of political mail, often breaks a campaign promise about how she intends to make policy decisions.

§ 8–7. **How legislators represent.** The perception of politicians mollycoddling the voters is much exaggerated. Despite campaign rhetoric, legislators live up to the ideal of the delegate much of the time. They have good reasons to vote on most issues in accord with their own best judgment. They spend hours studying questions that most voters, even those with strong opinions, hardly consider. They attend to issues with the helpful advocacy of lobbyists for the affected interests, while voters evaluate the questions with fact and thought filtered through print and broadcast journalists or, worse yet, through cheerleaders for the voter's narrow and biased self interest.

Often legislators have little choice but to make up their own minds, for they mistrust opinion polls and letter writing campaigns as gauges of public opinion. But even when constituent attitudes are quite clear, legislators rise above ill-founded demands from the public. The office holder learns that most voters tolerate a legislator who thoughtfully defends a position, even when it conflicts with the voter's expectation. Furthermore, a legislative vote of the past is seldom a political issue in a later campaign. The electorate looks ahead to future issues. Finally, voters pass judgment more on the candidate than on the issues. Voting for the "best candidate" and for the "party" are still the most common—and the most intelligent—election day practices.

Even granting an intellectual preference for Burke's delegate over the pressured representative, it is possible to construct a respectable case for the legislator who responds. First of all, can one fault so democratic a behavior? Is it not elitist and absurdly idealistic to suggest that legislators, to serve the greater good, ought to rise above the unsound demands of their constituencies? That the old question of how independent a legislator should be is still given so much thought—and that public attitudes are so mixed—suggests that responsive political behavior ought not invariably be viewed cynically.

The best case to be made for responsiveness is a pragmatic argument for limited responsiveness. Yielding or not yielding to political pressure is just one element in the calculus by which legislators allocate their time and energy to family, to job, to recreation, to health, to re-election, and to the duties of public office. Legislators have a limited measure of time to meet all the responsibilities. Taking a stand that offends the "folks at home" requires explanation. Constituents who discover the bold vote will have to be educated, or at least mollified. The burden of explanation intrudes into the time the legislator has for serving family, health, and the other responsibilities of office.

All legislators play it safe sometimes; a legislator who never did so would be a martinet and unbearably self-righteous. But all legislators have a bit of Edmund Burke in them; most have courage in large measure when the power and responsibility of choice clearly rests with them.

§ 8–8. A balancing test on political courage.

The law uses balancing tests to reflect the necessity of trade offs. The considerations a legislator must balance to take appropriate account of political benefit and loss are subtle and difficult. Issues range in significance from nuclear death for the planet to designating the state mushroom. Perceptions of political hazard range from near-certainty that the vote or speech is a career-ender to vague notions that one position is somewhat safer than another. The certainty of the merits varies from "I'd bet my life on it" to "I wish I could flip a coin." The impact of the legislator's decision runs from voting after being told, "It's now or never, and you are the deciding vote," to a choice to cast one ineffectual *no* against four affirmative votes in a subcommittee. The negative implications of casting an uncompromised vote can be serious. It can be as hurtful as breaking the spirit and confidence of a promising young politician or as dangerous as enraging a vindictive power broker. Or the negative implications can be as insignificant as giving momentary offense to an ineffectual ignoramus.

The ethical significance of every decision depends on where it fits on each of these continua. For those who know a legislature well, watching members struggle with the interplay of all these factors is high drama. Balancing the considerations well takes intelligence, energy, and character. Whether the members in any legislature have those qualities in adequate measure ultimately depends on the electorate.

CHAPTER 3

PROCESSING BILLS

A. DUE PROCESS OF LEGISLATION

§ 9–1. **Limited constitutional mandates.**
Constitutional law does not require of legislatures
the same procedural due process as is demanded of
administrative agencies and courts. Nonetheless,
looking at legislative procedure from a due process
perspective gives insight into how legislatures
work. The next three sections explore how legislatures provide, and do not provide, the three essentials of due process of law—notice, opportunity to
be heard, and fair tribunal.

§ 9–2. **Notice.** No legislature provides to interested persons anything like the notice required
in judicial and administrative agency proceedings.
But the legislative process, when soundly constructed, does abound with efforts to make effective notice *available* to those interested persons
who go a little out of their way to "notice the
notice."

Bill introductions. The first step in the official
legislative process is the formal introduction of a
bill for an act. This document tells everyone what
action the institution has been asked to take. To
improve the effectiveness of this notice function,
each bill must be given a constitutionally-mandat-

ed title expressing the subject of the bill. Lists of these titles are available throughout the community. Alert individuals and organized interests skim the lists to find out which bills it might be well for them to study. After examining the bills relevant to their interests, they will know if it is worth their while to show up; they will know there is something to lose or to gain while the bill is being considered. The purpose of bills and titles is to insure that an interested citizen or group can find out that the legislature has been asked to address a certain subject in a certain way.

Who receives lists of bills introduced? Those who ask. The interested citizen or lawyer must subscribe to a proprietary news service that publishes these lists or must get on the mailing list for the daily legislative journal. The journal, an official history of legislative action, includes a report of bill introductions together with the record of all other official legislative actions. Subscribers to private and official legislative information services are a select group. Consequently, most of the community, including many persons directly and significantly affected, know nothing of day-to-day legislative business. Nowhere does the general press provide adequate notice of impending legislative activity.

Committee hearing. When a bill is placed on a committee agenda for hearing and action, the time and place of the meeting is posted and published. However, it may be posted only a day or even just a few hours before the committee meeting. If interested persons have asked committee staff to give them telephone notice of hearings on a bill, they usually will be accommodated—but not always. Therefore, knowledgeable lobbyists constantly watch legislative bulletin boards to keep track of meetings relevant to their clients. Committee agendas may be reported in the daily journal.

Amendments. While a bill awaits action in committee (and while it awaits floor action as well), its friends and foes plan amendments. One amendment may sweep dozens (or thousands) more persons into or out of the ambit of the bill, or the amendment may change the impact from beneficial to troubling for one interest or another. All who might want to advise the institution on the merit or demerit of an amendment would like to know that the amendment is to be proposed and when; without notice it is impossible to engage in timely lobbying. But advance notice of amendments need not be given. In fact, surprise is often a part of the amending strategy. The due process right to notice is not constitutionally required and legislative institutions have not constructed procedures to provide certain notice, even for the most alert, on-the-scene lobbyist.

Subsequent notice that an amendment has been adopted is also deficient, if judged by litigation or administrative law standards. When a bill is amended, who is notified of the change? Floor amendments are promptly reported in the journal, but committee amendments usually are recorded in the journal only when the committee concludes work on a bill and submits its favorable report to the house floor. That may be days after the committee first approves the amendment. A private legislative news service may attempt to report amendments to major bills. News of a few amendments finds its way into the general press. At bottom, though, in many legislatures the only way to keep track of committee amendments is to personally monitor committee meetings.

Floor schedules. Each house maintains printed calendars of pending business, essentially committee-reported bills awaiting floor action. Occasionally, a measure is scheduled at a time-certain to accommodate the media, but usually the bill is taken up when the bills ahead of it are disposed of or temporarily passed over; that is a highly unpredictable timetable. Therefore, the day and hour any particular bill will be taken up is not noted on the calendars and interested parties find it necessary to monitor floor sessions, just as it is necessary to monitor committees. This will be true throughout the remaining steps of the process, including meetings of conference committees to resolve differences between the two houses.

The essence of legislative notice is to make notice available only to those who reach out to help themselves. Self-help notice does not meet the ordinary standard for due process. Usually, those

who seek action through a legal process must give
specific notice to those they know will be directly
affected by the proposed action. Notice in all cases
must be given in a way reasonably calculated to be
effective, usually by personal service or by first
class mail directed to the last known address. Of
course, the cost of mailed notice to all those affected by legislative action would be frightful. Even
published notice is unrealistic. So the reality is
that legislative work will be done in public, with
some general notice provided to those who come
looking for the notice, and with the expectation
that those few who show up will represent adequately all others with similar interests.

§ 9–3. **Opportunity to be heard.** Not everyone who wants to be heard by a legislative panel is
given that opportunity. Not even members have
the privilege to say as much as they might want;
time pressure is too severe. Legislators have developed a variety of ways to ration their limited
capacity to listen so that greater attention is directed to the most helpful petitioners. Inevitably,
the screening blocks out or discourages some persons with valuable information.

Those who know how to get through the screen
and to be heard—really heard—are said to have
"access." Not having access means, basically, that
one does not have an assured opportunity to be
heard in the due process sense. But even in the
judicial and administrative law worlds, one must
follow correct procedures and demonstrate a cer-

tain status to assure a right to be heard. The judicial and adminstrative law idea of having the petitioner show standing—direct interest in the matter—parallels the notion of legislative access. Advocates are more readily heard by a legislature after they make a threshold showing that the issue is legitimately their business.

The hired spokespersons for large interests have access on any issue identifiable as affecting their clients. The lobbyists for the independent and holding company banks, the electric utility, the telephone company, the auto dealers, the doctors, the employers' association, the AFL–CIO, the organized teachers, the lawyers, and the other major economic interests have legislative standing because hearing them satisfies the procedural necessity of not wasting legislative energy listening to busybodies. These lobbyists know better than to waste legislative energy with talk of matters that do not concern their clients; when they speak up, they contribute to legislative understanding.

Even among the lobbyist for major interests, access varies. Some have demonstrated a capacity for quick, clear explanation. They deliver information efficiently—whether it is offered by them or sought from them. Legislators—always fighting clock, calendar, and fatigue—open their doors and minds to these lobbying stars while closing off the same degree of access to most others. A lobbyist whose client is viewed as friend or valued political supporter also wins legislator attention. This has to do with standing—and with trust and human nature.

Does one, then, have to represent large economic interests to have access? The answer is "no" as demonstrated by an occasional lone petitioner who earns attention with a sensible public policy idea. But few persons without an economic interest even try to gain access.

§ 9–4. Fair tribunal. The third principle of due process is a fair tribunal. Generally in judicial and administrative law terms this means having a judge who is without prior commitment on the question to be decided. But a legislator in committee or on the floor is unlikely to be without some degree of commitment on any controversial issue.

Even more certainly, a fair tribunal means having judges who have not been approached privately on the question to be decided. In judicial and administrative law it means that there has been no *ex parte* contact between the judge and any party to the proceeding. Not so in the legislative arena; advance contact is anticipated and recommended. This legislative reality, to a considerable extent, can be reconciled with our due process concepts.

If a legislative decision-maker takes a position not consistent with known proclivities, most advocates politely confront the legislator to ask the basis for the unexpected stance. The answer reveals any private contact and permits the lobbyist to counter the unilateral advocacy. A ping-pong game of *ex parte* exchanges soon becomes the equivalent of an acceptable hearing. The fairness of this process is strengthened by the fact that both decision-maker and advocate have time to reflect, to gather additional evidence, to confront informally, and to hone arguments.

An additional factor affecting the fairness of legislative tribunals is that legislative decision making occurs as a series of decisions over a period of time. The decisions made in each house include: to sponsor, to schedule in subcommittee and committee, to amend, to recommend out of committee, to approve in committee of the whole, to approve formally and to concur in the actions of the second house. Thus, the interest group that finds itself frustrated by a close-minded tribunal anywhere in the legislative process usually has a shot at another panel on another day. Further, rehearing is common practice and clearly within the customs of most legislatures. Reconsideration is usually based on a claim of inadequate attention on first consideration. The motion to reconsider is adopted much more frequently in legislatures than is the grant of a rehearing in courts and administrative agencies.

§ 9–5. Dealing with failures of due process.
A legislative advocate, whether insider or outsider, must be prepared to deal from time to time with being denied due process. When the insider has a decision made behind his back, he can respond by asserting his previously earned standing and demanding the procedural rights that go with it.

The regular lobbyist can insist that the procedurally illegitimate decision should be reversed and redone in accordance with legitimate procedures. The demand prevails when those who used the procedural shortcut did not have the votes to reach their objective by normal processes.

But what can the beginning lobbyist and outsider do about being denied legislative due process? Not much, except to complain, for in truth, when one is an outsider, little can be done immediately about being treated as an outsider. One without standing does not have to be heard. The newcomer can deal with the situation only by earning legislative standing—winning access. Access is attained by showing up regularly, by explaining to legislators the stake the client has in the legislative decision, and by explaining the stake the community has in the wellbeing of the client. It also helps gain access if one pays the dues of political contributions (a user tax imposed on those who seek to influence governmental policy).

§ 9–6. The responsibilities of other institutions. When the legislature in any jurisdiction slips away from providing an acceptable level of "legislative" due process, the groups who are procedurally shortchanged must speak out. Leaders of the legislative institution then will likely change their ways, for responsive politicians cannot bear to have their institution accused—with cause—of failing to provide anyone notice, an opportunity to be heard, or a fair opportunity to win on the merits.

Unfortunately, groups shy away from making complaints about procedure for fear of offending the legislature. This is short-sighted because many legislators—probably most—welcome the pressure to do things correctly. No group has a bigger stake in legitimate process than legislators themselves. Therefore, they are not likely to retaliate. Furthermore, good procedure is more important to every group over the long run than is any sanction that might be imposed against it in the short run.

B. BILL PASSING MANDATES AND RULES

§ 10–1. **Variability.** The procedure used to enact legislation varies from jurisdiction to jurisdiction, from house to house within a jurisdiction, and even within a house. The following materials, therefore, must be treated as a general survey and as a foundation for a study of the details of procedure in a specific legislative institution.

§ 10–2. **Constitutional mandates.** Constitutions, the basic governmental charters, typically lay down various procedural mandates for legislatures. However, these mandates vary so widely that legislative practitioners in each state must check the constitution of that state. One typical mandate requires three separate readings of a bill. In some jurisdictions, constitutions provide for

reading "at length," a requirement which is of
necessity circumvented in practice. Constitutions
often require for final passage in each house the
affirmative vote of a majority of those elected (not
just those present). Another requirement may be
that the names of those voting *aye* and *nay* be
recorded in the journal. A common mandate is
that a particular kind of legislation, for example a
capital expenditure, requires an extraordinary
vote. Constitutions may prescribe the period during which a legislature's work must be completed.

Authority for an executive to veto legislation is
constitutionally established and the procedure for
vetoing and for overriding may be spelled out in
detail. Constitutions may prescribe that certain
officers, such as speaker and president *pro tem,* be
elected by the respective houses and may assign
them tasks. One common requirement, not applicable to the United States Congress, is that a bill
contain a single subject which must be expressed
in its title. This requirement limits the packaging
of legislative work and thus significantly affects
procedures.

The procedural restrictions imposed by constitutions may or may not be subject to judicial enforcement depending on whether the state follows the
journal entry or the enrolled bill rule. (See §§ 13–
1 to 13–5).

§ 10–3. **Legislative rules.** Every senate and
assembly adopts rules to spell out the organization
and the procedure of the body. These rules gener-

ally incorporate *Mason's Manual of Legislative Procedures* as the controlling authority for any situation not covered by a specific rule. For the serious student of legislative procedure, *Mason's Manual* is the authoritative source. Legislative bodies usually adopt a supplemental rule after an incident occurs in which the general rules of parliamentary practice led to some difficulty. Afterward, locking the barn door, the body adopts a special rule to prevent repetition of the difficulty. Some rules modify the general rules of parliamentary practice; other rules simply reaffirm the ordinary parliamentary practices and place them in the rules of the body where they are not so likely to be overlooked.

Legislatures frequently need to depart from regular order to do essential work. Therefore, suspension of the rules is used so often that it, along with unanimous consent to shortcuts, is an integral part of normal procedure. A rules suspension requires a two-thirds vote, so minorities are protected from unfair or unexpected departures from regular procedures.

Procedures involving both houses of a bicameral legislature may be included in joint rules adopted by both or may be adopted in the separate rules of each house.

§ 10–4. **Resolutions.** Some legislative work is done through joint, concurrent, assembly, or senate resolutions, rather than through bills. The use of resolutions is largely a matter of custom. Typically, a joint resolution originates in one house and, with the concurrence of the other house, has the force of official legislative action. It is used to propose state constitutional amendments and to ratify federal constitutional amendments, actions which do not require the signature of the governor. In some jurisdictions a joint resolution may substitute for a bill if submitted to the executive and signed.

A concurrent resolution, like the joint resolution, originates in one house and is concurred in by the other. It does not have the legal impact of a joint resolution. It is commonly used to express opinion on some issue. Petitions from state legislatures to the federal Congress or President are drawn as concurrent resolutions. Commendations to statesmen and winning basketball teams are further examples of concurrent resolutions. Internal housekeeping involving both houses, like the rules and dates of joint conventions and of *sine die* adjournment, is also handled by concurrent resolution.

A senate or assembly resolution is used to accomplish internal housekeeping. For example, resolutions are used to adopt the rules of the house, to establish committees, to initiate investigations, to authorize and hire employees. Most things accomplished through a one-house resolution could be accomplished by motion, but a resolution is used for greater formality. However the day-to-day work of the body is conducted through simple floor motions.

C. TYPICAL HURDLES IN ONE HOUSE

§ 11–1. **A bill for an act.** With the warning—repeated—that legislative procedure varies from institution to institution and from time to time, the following sections describe typical steps a bill must take in a legislative body. Technical and tactical considerations are discussed for each of these steps.

The official legislative process starts and ends with a bill for an act. From the moment of introduction to final approval, all procedures of the institution focus on a bill. The significance of this concentration cannot be overstated. Having a specific bill under consideration forces a legislature to tackle issues directly rather than to engage in philosophical debates. The decision-making process of legislative bodies has a crispness superior to that of most other group-led institutions. The focus on a written proposal in the form of a bill for an act produces this characteristic.

§ 11–2. **Obtaining sponsors.** A bill is introduced into the legislature through the sponsorship of an elected member. Depending on the rules, a limited or unlimited number of co-sponsors is allowed. It is advantageous to obtain co-sponsors who provide political, geographic, and ideological balance, since balanced sponsorship reduces the suspicion with which a bill is examined.

Knowledgeable lobbyists choose chief sponsors with utmost care, for the wrong sponsor can seriously handicap a bill's progress. The chief author or sponsor is the legislator who manages the bill as it passes through the institution, making tactical decisions and carrying a heavy responsibility of explanation and advocacy in committee and on the floor. Consequently, legislators in the majority caucus with special talent for managing legislation are besieged with requests to handle bills.

It is efficient and effective to seek as chief sponsor a member of the committee with jurisdiction over the bill. Obtaining co-sponsors from the same committee is also advantageous because a co-sponsor is somewhat committed, although not duty-bound, to cast an affirmative vote in committee. Starting with three, four, or five semi-secure affirmative committee votes is extremely helpful. Even when a committee member turns down a request to sponsor or co-sponsor a bill, the time spent explaining the bill may pay off later when the committee considers the measure. The request to sponsor a bill provides an early opportunity to present the bill's merits to key decision makers.

§ 11–3. **Introduction of bill.** After the chief sponsor's and co-sponsors' names are signed on a bill, it is ready for introduction. Introduction may be a routine matter or may involve a number of tactical decisions. Some bills are introduced on slow news days and are accompanied by press releases with the hope of attracting news coverage.

Other bills are saved for times when the bill will receive a minimum of attention. The decision depends on whether the sponsors feel public attention is more likely to work for or against the bill.

At the time of introduction the bill is referred to a standing committee. When there is room for judgment on the reference, sponsors attempt to arrange a favorable reference. This is accomplished by contacting the speaker, the president of the senate, the parliamentarian, or a ministerial officer or staff member who can arrange reference to the desired committee. In most legislatures, committee jurisdiction is so flexible that the proper reference is often not cut and dried. In the case of major legislation, sequential reference to two or more committees may be required; which committee gets the bill first may then be of critical importance.

§ 11–4. **Committee action.** When a bill has been introduced and referred to a committee, the tasks of its advocates are to win a place on the committee agenda and then to obtain a favorable committee recommendation. Committee agendas are largely controlled by the committee chairman, so the conventional view is of autocratic committee chairmen deciding which bills will be passed and which will be pigeonholed. This view is not without validity, but group consensus plays a significant role in committee agenda making, as it does throughout the legislative process. A committee chairman does not maintain the allegiance of com-

mittee members and the highest degree of effectiveness by disregarding committee attitudes on
what ought to be scheduled. Therefore, the most
dictatorial-appearing decisions of committee chairmen often are consensus decisions from the committee itself or from the majority members and
caucus leaders. Other legislators hide behind the
chairman.

The competition for committee time is intense.
Bills heard are essential, or popular, or generally
beneficial, or non-controversial, or particularly appealing to the committee chairman. Sometimes,
though, a bill is scheduled mainly to head off a
more obnoxious proposal. Proponents of a bill
may request subcommittee consideration if a spot
cannot be won on the committee agenda. In subcommittee, a partially developed proposal can be
polished into a solid draft which then deserves and
gets full committee time.

The most effective lobbying occurs while the bill
rests in committee. Due to the legislative system
of division of labor, the committee decision usually
becomes the decision of the whole body. If that
decision is for inaction (laying over or pigeonhol-
ing), the bill is effectively stopped for that session
of the legislature. If the committee recommends
that the bill be formally killed (indefinitely postponed), that recommendation is reported to the
floor as a committee report to be confirmed by
house vote. Adoption of the committee report officially kills the bill. Committees keep from the

floor, and from passage, the great mass of proposals.

If the committee recommends passage of the bill, it is sent to the floor with a favorable committee report. This recommendation carries the bill past the major obstacle in the legislative process. An affirmative committee recommendation is the most significant single forward step in the process.

Some bills include provisions within the jurisdiction of more than one committee. The first committee then must refer the bill to another committee for further consideration. Although the second committee may want to kill the bill, momentum provided by the first committee's affirmative recommendation puts pressure on the second to act favorably. When the second committee is hostile to the bill, it may water down the bill by amendment, even when it does not challenge directly the first committee's recommendation that the bill be passed.

§ 11–5. **Re-referral.** After a legislative body adopts a committee recommendation that a bill pass, the bill is placed on the calendar for floor action. That agenda may be long. During its wait for floor action, and at any time until final passage, a bill is subject to a motion to re-refer it to the committee which recommended it or to some other committee. The tactic of re-referral is a favorite for opponents of a bill. It avoids a direct decision on the bill and, if successful, forces the bill to confront again the obstacle of committee approval.

From the proponents' perspective, the motion to re-refer is dangerous for three reasons. First, opponents control the timing of the motion so it will be made when it is most likely to prevail, when absences, events, or concentrated lobbying make the bill's opponents strongest. Second, because of the time pressures under which legislatures work, a *prima facie* case of inadequate committee consideration can be made in support of a re-referral motion against virtually any bill. Third, a basic principle of legislative tactics is to seek the softest method of accomplishing an objective. The motion to re-refer is the classic example of the gentle but deadly motion. It is much easier for legislators to vote to re-refer a bill than to cast a hard negative vote on final passage. The re-referral vote is cloaked in procedural or right-to-be-heard camouflage; there is comforting and protective ambiguity in a motion to send a bill back to a committee for interminable further consideration.

§ 11–6. Committee of the whole. The first floor consideration of a bill in most state legislatures occurs in committee of the whole. This means an entire house sits as a committee to consider the bill. The historical foundation for the committee of the whole procedure was the desire of early parliaments to act on legislation in semi-secrecy, without recorded votes, and thus to be independent of the king's sanctions. The commit-

tee of the whole has survived partly to allow legislators to act on bills free of the political consequences of recorded votes. More basically it
provides an opportunity for less formal debate
without limitations on the duration or number of
times a member may speak. Consideration of a
bill in committee of the whole also provides an
interval between that preliminary floor consideration and final passage. This day or two interval
allows members and lobbyists to reflect on the
debate, on any amendments, and on the press
reports. It provides an opportunity for a few more
hours of thought and lobbying.

§ 11–7. **Alternatives to committee of the
whole.** For better or worse, use of committee of
the whole procedure is declining. A body may
omit that step of the process for selected types of
bills, in special circumstances, or totally. For example, in almost every legislature there exists a
"consent calendar" procedure for bills identified by
committee reports as noncontroversial. The consent calendar is taken up at a designated time,
each bill is briefly explained, and the final-passage
vote is taken. Then the next bill is taken up for a
similarly brief explanation and quick vote. If just
two or three members of the body object to a bill
on a consent calendar, their objections bump the
bill back to a regular calendar for more careful
examination. The consent calendar device permits
a legislative body to dispose of minor bills with a
minimum of energy.

Another set of bills likely to bypass the committee of the whole procedure are the major bills that legislative leadership wishes to process with a tighter rein than is possible in committee of the whole where votes may be unrecorded and attendance is somewhat unpredictable. The device used for processing these major bills is a special order or special rule to schedule the bill for debate, amendment, and passage at a single sitting. The body may designate a bill for special order in a variety of ways. Sometimes an extraordinary majority (two-thirds) of the body designates the bills. More commonly, authority to select bills for special orders is delegated to a majority caucus policy committee, to the bipartisan leadership of the body, or to a priority setting committee. Bills from appropriations and tax committees may get automatic special order privileges.

It is increasingly common for legislative bodies to take up bills for debate and amendment, then put them immediately to final vote. The advantages are that the vote is taken while the subject is fresh in members' minds and that time is saved because the bill is addressed only once on the floor. The disadvantage is loss of the more deliberative process of consideration on two separate days.

§ 11–8. Priority setting committees. In some legislative bodies, standing committees regularly report to the floor more bills than the body has time to consider. In this situation, machinery must be established to pick out some bills for floor consideration and to leave other bills to die with adjournment. The machinery usually established is a priority setting committee. The most famous example is the rules committee of the United States House of Representatives. This committee may designate for priority consideration any bill reported to the floor of the House by another committee. Bills adopted by the House of Representatives reach final passage either through a consent calendar procedure, through a two-thirds vote suspending the rules, or by rules committee action. Since mustering a two-thirds suspension-of-the-rules vote is an impossibility for any measure with substantial opposition, the major pieces of national legislation must pass through the House rules committee. This is the key to its great power.

In the United States Senate, priority setting is the task of the majority party policy committee. In practice, floor agendas are usually agreed to by the majority and minority leaders and reflect a consensus of the entire Senate.

The devices used in state legislatures are some variety of special order procedure, a variation on the Congressional rules committee procedure, or an informal consensus device similar to that of the United States Senate.

§ 11–9. **Final passage.** Under a few constitutions, including that of the United States, a vote on final passage may be oral and unrecorded unless the *ayes* and *nays* are called for by a member of the body. A call for the *ayes* and *nays* is a right on final passage. In many states, the constitution requires that a bill must receive an affirmative vote from a majority of all members to pass and that the votes must be recorded in the journal. Since previous steps of the process usually require only a simple majority of those voting on the question, the final vote is the highest formal hurdle. By the time a bill has reached this point in the process, however, accommodations have been made with some of those in opposition, and on most bills there is such momentum that defeat on final passage is rare.

The vote on final passage may be reconsidered for a limited period of time. When the vote is close, those on the losing side look for converts among those on the prevailing side. If vote switches are found, a motion to reconsider may succeed. In a situation where reconsideration is likely, the winners also look for members with whom some additional advocacy may be effective in order to hedge against reconsideration; occasionally the makers of a motion to reconsider are surprised by the loss of some of their own supporters.

Parliamentary rules permit reconsideration of any vote only once. Therefore, when those on the losing side seem likely to undertake a campaign for reconsideration, those on the prevailing side may ask that the vote be reconsidered immediately and urge that the motion be defeated. If the motion is defeated, the losing side is precluded from moving to reconsider at a later time (after a campaign to change votes). In Congress the motion to reconsider is routinely made and laid on the table to give finality to votes. The number of successful reconsiderations is not substantial, but it is a device which occasionally proves useful to open the door for additional compromise.

D. THE OTHER HOUSE AND THE EXECUTIVE

§ 12–1. **Agreement.** In a bicameral legislature, passage of a bill by one house carries the bill a significant way toward passage. Passage by the first house usually makes affirmative action by the second easier to achieve. Reasons for this include: the bill requires less work in the second house since rough edges have been removed by the first; opponents have had input in the first house and, if accommodated there, may hold their fire as the bill is processed in the second; inter-house relationships may be improved by passage of the bill and harmed by its rejection; and concern about wasting time on a bill that will not pass is reduced since the bill has already cleared the other house. There also exists a momentum from previous affirmative action. Members of the second house assume the affirmative vote in the first had a logical basis. Thus some of the burden of persuasion shifts to the negative side.

After the final affirmative vote for passage by the first house, the bill is officially engrossed and transmitted to the other house for consideration. Each house must act on the same document. Therefore, if the senate acts on a bill first, the senate bill becomes the subject of consideration in the assembly. If the assembly acts first, its bill is the document taken up in the senate. Some procedural device will advance on the agenda any bill from the other house if its companion bill has had any formal action. For example, an assembly bill will be substituted for the companion senate bill on the senate committee of the whole calendar.

If the house giving second consideration to the bill accepts verbatim the version adopted by the first house, it returns the bill with a message so indicating. The first house then enrolls the bill, obtains the signatures of the officers of the two houses, and transmits the bill to the executive for signature.

However, if the second house has amended the bill, the message returning the bill requests concurrence in those amendments. Sponsors of the bill in the first house, consulting with interested lobbyists and other legislators, determine whether the other body's amendments are acceptable. If so, a motion is made to concur in the amendments and to place the bill on repassage. If the motion passes, the formalities of a final vote are repeated for the bill in its amended form. This means again recording the *ayes* and *nays* if required by the constitution. If repassed, the bill is enrolled in its amended form, signed by the legislative officers, and transmitted to the executive for signature.

If the house of origin refuses to concur in the amendments of the second house, the complex conference committee procedure described in the next section is used to resolve the differences between the two houses.

§ 12–2. Disagreement; conference committees.

The mechanism for compromising differences between senate and assembly is a conference committee. It usually consists of three to five members from each house who are appointed after each body adopts a motion calling for the conference. The speaker generally names assembly conferees, after consultation with chairmen of relevant committees and minority leadership. In senates the appointment is likely to be made by a policy committee or a committee on committees drawn from senate leadership. Bill authors and leaders on the committee which processed the bill are given priority in conference committee selections.

After their selection, the two delegations sit down together, choose a chairman from their membership, note the differences between the two versions of the bill, and dispose of secondary issues involving minor differences. Then, through give and take, they resolve the significant policy differences.

In state legislatures, the members representing each body are expected to uphold the position of their house against the contrary position of the other house. In Congress, minority party members must be included as conferees from both houses. This statutory requirement occasionally leads to the incongruous situation of the minority membership from both houses uniting with the majority membership of one house to dictate terms of the conference report. In all bodies, conference committee members regularly suffer the discomfort of conflicting obligations. It is not unusual for a senate conferee to prefer an assembly position, for his party caucus to prefer the assembly position, or for his constituency to be better served by the other version. In these circumstances he will be a soft conferee, eager to compromise and less than vigorous in his support of his body's position.

In a conference, as is true throughout the legislative process, there is more effort to discover and willingness to accept the merits of opposing positions than is realized by those who have not had close contact with legislative institutions. Differences are generally resolved after discussion of the merits. Even if the compromise amounts to averaging the values of the assembly and senate by splitting the difference, this reflects the collective judgment of the whole institution.

Once the differences are resolved, a conference committee report is submitted to the two houses. The committee report goes first to the house that initially passed the bill. If the report is adopted, the bill is placed on repassage in its compromise form. After the final vote, the conference committee report and the bill are sent to the other house where again the report of the conference committee is submitted for approval and, when the report is approved, the bill placed on repassage. After repassage, the bill is returned to the house of origin, enrolled, signed by the officers of the legislature, and submitted to the executive for signature.

A conference committee may deal generally with the subject matter before it or it may be limited to resolving the precise differences between the two houses. Even where the conference committee is not by rule limited in its jurisdiction, legislative custom severely limits the freedom with which new subject matter can be inserted into the conference bill. But occasionally a conference committee produces unexpected results, results beyond its mandate. These excursions occur even where the rules impose strict limitations on conference committee jurisdiction. This is symptomatic of the authoritarian power of conference committees. Conference reports are returned to assembly and senate on a take-it or leave-it basis, and the bodies are generally placed in the position that to leave-it is a practical impossibility.

Conference committee action is the most undemocratic procedure in the legislative process; it is an appropriate target for legislative critics. But conference committees are essential in a bicameral system; the only way to eliminate them is to substitute the unicameral for the bicameral sys-

tem. Short of this far-reaching change, the conference committee is an evil which must be endured.

§ 12–3. **Same bill document.** A single document must be passed by both houses and signed by
the governor. Passage by each house is verified by
the signature of its presiding officer and its chief
clerical official. These signatures must go on the
enrolled act before that document is ready for the
executive's signature. If the houses pass identical
but separate bills, the action is without effect.
One of the houses must approve the official bill
document from the other house.

§ 12–4. **Veto or signature.** The final steps in
the legislative process are the signature on an
enrolled bill by the executive and filing of the
signed bill (now an act) with the secretary of state.
When an executive declines to sign a bill while the
legislature is still in session, the bill is returned to
the legislature, usually with a veto message explaining the reasons for the governor's disapproval.
With the house of origin acting first, the legislature may override the veto by an extraordinary
vote of each house (usually two-thirds). Some state
constitutions provide that the governor may select
particular items from appropriation bills for item
veto. In these cases the veto message identifies
particular disapproved items, and the opportunity
to override exists on each item.

If the governor does not return a bill to the
legislature with formal disapproval, it becomes law
without the governor's signature after a specified

number of days. The executive deposits the bill in the secretary of state's office and the fact that it became law without the executive's signature is duly noted. However, when the legislature adjourns before the time for signature runs out, the adjournment prevents the executive from returning the bill with a veto message. Since the adjournment of the legislature cut short the executive's time for consideration of the bill, the governor is permitted to kill the bill by inaction, a "pocket" veto.

The veto power gives the executive a central role in the legislative process, especially if the governor chooses to assert it. For example, threatening to use the veto can force amendments that would otherwise be unacceptable to the legislature. The extent to which this power is used varies greatly, depending on the personality of the executive, the political allegiances of the houses, the custom in the jurisdiction, the political independence of the legislators, and the quality of legislative performance. If a legislative body is doing quality work, reflective of popular opinion, and the legislators hold significant political independence in their home constituencies, a governor runs political risks with each veto cast. Furthermore, the legislature has retaliatory power through appropriations, appropriation riders, and a variety of other devices. Therefore, the great power of the veto is used cautiously by all executives.

E. JUDICIAL SUPERVISION OF LEGISLATIVE PROCEDURE

§ 13–1. **Enrolled bill rule.** The legislative process ends when an official bill document is filed with the secretary of state. This document is the enrolled act. It bears the signatures of the officers of each house certifying action on the measure by their respective bodies. It also carries the signature of the executive, indicating approval, or appropriate documentation of the legislature's override of a veto.

For acts of Congress, and in somewhat less than half the states, the enrolled bill is conclusively presumed to have been validly adopted. This presumption bars judicial inquiry into legislative procedure, treating such inquiry as an intrusion into the internal affairs of the legislature. The enrolled bill rule is based in part on the fact that courts cannot claim greater ability to judge procedural legitimacy, since constitutional rules on legislative procedure are easily mastered. Procedural disputes are over facts—whether or not the bill had enough votes, or three readings, or whatever—not over the meaning of the constitution. Legislators, as eyewitnesses, are in a better position than a court to rule on the facts. The argument is also made that legislatures would be offended if courts examined legislative procedure.

An additional rationale for the enrolled bill rule is that it gives stability to the law. Citizens reasonably assume that filed acts are valid. To avoid an act on procedural grounds traps those who in good faith relied on the legislation. Many courts hold that legislation must "carry its death warrant in its hand" (that is, on its face) before a court can invalidate it. Defects of due process, equal protection, free speech, double subject, title, special legislation, delegation, and other defects of legislative content and style appear on the face of legislation and therefore are discernible by a reader.

§ 13–2.　Journal entry rule.

Under the journal entry rule, followed by those jurisdictions that do not adhere to the enrolled bill rule, a court may examine the official journals of the legislature to determine if constitutional mandates on procedure were met. The journal entry rule bars any inquiry into the legitimacy of procedure beyond looking at journal entries. The rule also protects stability of law by a presumption that every procedural requirement was met unless the journal affirmatively shows otherwise. In one appellate case, the *aye* and *nay* votes recorded in the journal showed the absence of a two-thirds vote on a motion for which that margin was constitutionally required, yet a court asserted that the journal entries did not establish that the same motion was not put at another time, carried with sufficient votes, and omitted from the journal by oversight. The court excused the journal defect because the bill received better than a two-thirds vote on final passage.

The rationale for the journal entry rule is necessity. If a court cannot enforce a constitution's procedural orders, the legislature can ignore those mandates with impunity. It is also claimed on behalf of the journal entry rule that a procedural check offends legislatures no more than a check on the substance of legislation. In reality, to have a court overturn an act because of a procedural defect bothers legislators less than to have legislation overturned on substantive grounds. The procedural check protects the institution itself—and particularly legislative minorities—from abuse of its rules. The court reinforces legislative self-discipline by providing an outside procedural check. Most significantly, by repassage of the bill, a legislature can always correct a procedural error which invalidated an act.

§ 13–3. Limited effect of journal entry rule. The judiciary imposes strict restraints on its review of legislative procedure even where the journal entry rule prevails. The powerful presumptions favoring validity of an act in actual cases dim the practical difference between the enrolled bill rule and the journal entry rule. The difference is so slight that it barely justifies the intellectual energy that has been devoted to examining the distinction. To stop the examination of legislative procedure at the official record maintained by the legislature means there is no judicial review of any violation willfully concealed by false entries in the journal.

A case can be made for review of procedure which looks at the facts, rather than stopping at journal entries. For example, legislatures with fixed adjournment dates have sometimes continued the journal of the last legal day for a number of days thereafter. Everyone who reads news reports, including the judges of the state, are aware the constitution is being evaded. However, the journal entry rule proscribes subsequent attack upon acts passed after the deadline because the journal shows action on an earlier, legal date.

The journal entry rule is a convenient and effective compromise between unlimited oversight of procedure and no oversight at all. A legislature is reluctant to falsify its official record, so review of the journal does reveal most procedural defects. When the journal is written to misrepresent the facts, it is usually done with unanimous consent because the constitutional provision violated is unrealistic. Constitutions are living documents and a legislature must sometimes adjust procedural provisions to get its job done, just as courts do.

§ 13–4. **Defects subject to journal entry review.** State constitutions impose a variety of procedural requirements and prohibitions. In a jurisdiction that follows the journal entry rule, the following legislative procedures are typically subject to judicial review:

Non-identical bills. Assembly and senate must pass a bill and the executive must sign it to make it a valid act. Each house and the executive must put its official imprimatur on a single document. A court will declare the legislation invalid if a review of the journal discloses any variation in the text acted on by any one of the three. Under the enrolled bill rule, on the other hand, the document the governor signs and delivers to the secretary of state is conclusively presumed to be the version passed by assembly and senate.

Ayes and *nays* recorded. Many state constitutions (but not the federal constitution) require that the *ayes* and *nays* be recorded on final passage votes. If sufficient names are not recorded in the yes column in the journal, the act is subject to successful challenge.

Sufficient affirmative votes. Recording names on final passage or recording the number of votes for or against are ways to meet the common constitutional requirement that some minimum number of affirmative votes be cast for a measure. Usually a majority of all members elected is required. Some bills—usually those to authorize capital expenditures, borrowing, or special taxes, or to propose constitutional amendments—require more votes. The journal entry may be examined to confirm that the bill received sufficient votes. A South Dakota case held that where a bill contained some appropriation items requiring a two-thirds vote and other items requiring a simple majority, the latter were valid and the former were severed as invalid because the recorded vote fell between a majority and two thirds.

PROCESSING BILLS

Three readings. A common requirement is that a bill receive three readings, each on a separate day. The journal may be examined to see if the mandate was met or if some emergency loophole was properly utilized. When the requirement is that any of the readings be at length, journals falsely imply that at-length readings occur. Since courts do not inquire into the reality behind the journal, this pretense works in most jurisdictions. But in a few states, courts locked themselves into a literal interpretation and the legislature was forced to hire a chorus of readers to chant the words of pending legislation when the chamber was not being used for the real work of the legislature. The practical need for oral reading ended, of course, long ago when most legislators became literate.

Revenue bills from assembly. Following the pattern of the federal constitution, state constitutions usually require tax-raising bills to originate in the lower house. This means simply that an act for taxation must pass the assembly first. It is of no consequence what amendments the senate adds. Occasionally this mandate, usually insignificant, snares a piece of legislation by accident. This occurs when the tax aspect is overlooked because it is incidental to the larger purpose. Then a senate bill, rather than an assembly bill, may be processed and turn up in the office of the secretary of state. If challenged, the bill is subject to invalidation in its entirety or in its tax aspects.

§ **13–5. No review of rules violations.** Each legislative body adopts rules to make its procedures regular and fair. These rules protect minorities from arbitrary action. A two-thirds vote may suspend a rule and fewer than that cannot excuse the body from its self-imposed procedural requirements. But even if a body's journal shows breach of its rules, courts cannot invalidate an act on that ground. The violation, by custom, is treated as a suspension of the rule. The only rules judicially enforced are those mandated by the constitution; a court may interfere with the internal procedures of its coordinate branch only to uphold the constitution.

CHAPTER 4

LEGISLATIVE ADVOCACY

A. TO MOVE THE LEGISLATURE

§ 14–1. **Education and persuasion.** Legislators are generalists forced to make policy decisions on thousands of specific questions during each legislative session. They are guided by their general education, their common sense, their instincts, their biases, and the information and advice brought to them by advocates for various segments of the community. Legislators spend most of their time gathering information upon which to base decisions.

Legislative advocacy is an educational process. It means providing the information desperately desired by legislators—and some information they might prefer to ignore. The education of legislators and legislative staff occurs at many times and locations: at campaign meetings, at endorsement screening committees, at trade association conventions, at interest group dinners, in governors' offices, in attorney generals' offices, in party platform committees, and in the lobbies of capitol buildings. Legislative advocates seek to inform wherever a legislator or legislative staff member can be addressed directly or indirectly with facts,

91

with logic, with opinion, with suggestions, with entreaties.

While there may be a best time and place for most things, the only general rule about lobbying is to adjust to the circumstances. With some legislators on some issues, the best move is to step forward just before a vote and ask a relaxed question like: "You don't need any more information supporting our bill, do you? We haven't run across serious problems yet." On some occasions even that approach is too much; it is best to let legislative momentum carry the bill along. With other legislators and other issues, lobbying may require contacts long before the legislature convenes. The outcome may depend on the time consuming process of dislodging old biases and conventional wisdom.

Most legislatures work under constitutional limits on meeting periods. Since these limits create severe time pressures during sessions, lobbyists use non-session periods for basic educational efforts. They sow ideas in the off season and reap legislation in due time. But legislators have other careers which demand their attention. They often want to be left alone when they are away from the capitol, so only compelling and complex issues should be forced upon them then. Requests for attention at any time, but especially during non-session time, must be carefully presented to insure a willing and open-minded listener.

Lobbying in the off season, more than lobbying during a session, seeks to educate rather than to win a commitment on how a vote will be cast. Circumstances, including the words of a bill, change; the responsible legislator usually wants to be free to adjust to new situations and to new words. She is unlikely to commit herself early if there is any doubt about how she will vote. She is also likely to resent being pushed for a commitment. Demanding a firm promise is rarely the best method to win a legislator's vote. But in the heat of a session it occasionally is essential to get a vote count in order to choose tactically between a bold push for passage and a drastic amendment to salvage part of an otherwise lost cause.

Lobbying technique depends in other important ways upon the character and personality of the legislator. Some legislators relish all the attention they can get. Because they do not resent impositions on their time, the lobbyist should press the cause to them early and often. Other legislators place high value on their time and resent a second explanation. Some want explanations in writing to allow for homework and staff analysis. Some legislators want the merits presented; some want a tally of groups supporting and opposing the action; some want to squeeze in their own amendments; some only want to know that the issue is coming up so they can at their leisure recall memories of the pros and cons from past debates and reflect on them. Some listen politely, but burn slowly as the

explanation drags; others appear impatient and
unresponsive, even when they are appreciative of a
full explanation.

Clearly, the lobbyist who knows the members
well can adjust lobbying style to the circumstances
much better than the drop-in lobbyist. This is one
reason lobbying is one of the most specialized fields
among practicing lawyers. (The failure of most
lawyers to recognize that their clients have problems that could be relieved by legislation is a more
distressing reason for the specialization. See § 2–
3.)

§ 14–2. Significance of committee hearing.
Legislators spend a great percentage of their time
at committee hearings. Cynics sometimes suggest
that decisions are cut-and-dried and that hearings
are just window dressing. But legislators are too
busy to spend so much time in any activity that is
mere show. Committee hearings, in fact, provide a
decision-making forum of utmost importance. Legislators spend more time in hearings and less time
reading than is efficient, but politician-legislators
commonly are extroverts. Most of them enjoy the
group situation of a committee meeting more than
lonely closed-door study at office or home. Also no
one watches homework being done, so more political points are scored in the public arena of the
committee hearing. A politician who is at work
(learning) likes to have someone watching.

Formal legislative advocacy is concentrated at
committee hearings. Hearings give the legislative

advocate an official opportunity to confront the decision makers with arguments for or against a bill or amendments. The give and take of questioning provides the opportunity to test information in a confrontational procedure. The advocate may, however, fill out the story and respond to questions from committee members in less formal circumstances between meetings.

Legislative committee meetings vary greatly in purpose and style. On major legislation, committee action usually starts with a hearing at which statements are presented to inform the committee members and to educate the public through press coverage of the meeting. The committee carefully accords proponents and opponents equal time. After these formal hearings, the committee meets at mark-up sessions where members discuss the issues and adopt amendments to prepare the bill for floor consideration.

On routine bills and in legislatures with more informal practices, the committee meeting procedure is less structured. Public testimony, committee discussion, action on amendments, and final committee approval or disapproval of the proposal are mixed together and piled one atop the other. Fast-moving committees require lobbyists to think and act quickly. The lobbyists must prepare so well that they can cope with unexpected developments.

State legislatures commonly report only the approved committee amendments and the recommendation that the bill pass. But some committee hearings are designed to build a written record. The record may seek to justify a policy judgment already made, or it may be designed to provide background materials to scholars and others interested in the problem so that legislative solutions to the problem can be constructed. This is especially true in Congress.

§ 14–3. Societal pressure. A part of legislative advocacy is communicating the pressures for legislative action present in the community. In the evolution of public knowledge and opinion, a time comes when the pressure for specific legislation is irresistible. Thus, in the decade beginning in 1910, almost all state legislatures adopted workers compensation laws. For a half-century before 1910, the idea of workers compensation was gathering academic, business, and public support. Yet the political force to produce legislative action did not mature until New York and Wisconsin acted within a few months of each other. Then the tide of compensation legislation swept through most of the country. Writings by scholars, journalists, and judges had convinced public, workers, and employers that the programs made sense. Once two states had broken the ice, without disastrous consequences, the pressures from society to reform compensation for victims of industrial accidents made action a legislative certainty.

The opinion molder who builds a perception of the need for legislation is a legislative advocate, even if he does not carry the message personally. However, the legislative response is more prompt if identifying a problem is followed quickly by drafting proposed legislation and by presenting the idea in the form of a bill. The improvement of our society lags tragically because creative individuals fail to convert their good (and brilliant) theories into concrete legislative proposals and thus effectively to present their ideas to legislatures. There is a serious break in the communication line from the people who work in the ivory towers to those who work in the marble chambers of capitols.

§ 14–4. **Persuasion by members.** Popular folklore about legislatures includes a dominant leader calling in other legislators and with smile, frown, heavy handshake, backslap, or bearhug passing the word as to how a vote is to be cast. This scene is not drawn entirely from fiction. Legislative leaders with dominating personalities do exist. The impact of the aggressive, self-confident personality upon the legislative institution is no different from the effect of that personality on other institutions. Such a person produces decision, movement, action. Another personality type with strong impact on legislative performance is the charming leader who whistles through legislative tasks like the Pied Piper of Hamelin, picking up a coterie of friends who follow on many occasions. Legislatures are very human institutions. They respond affirmatively to dominant and to charming personalities.

But appearances are deceiving. Individuals who earn reputations for legislative virtuosity are less likely to redirect the institution than to reflect its consensus. In ideology they usually represent the middle ground. They often hold formal leadership positions which give them access to the channels of communication so they can learn where compromise is likely to occur. Their leadership role may make them messengers to the rest of the body from interest groups such as organized labor, organized agriculture, or the business community. In this situation they represent less their personal power than their power as agents of the organized voting blocs of the electorate. Power and political muscle do influence legislative decision making, but it is more the muscle of external pressure groups than the muscle of individual, dominant legislative personalities. Much more significant in the legislative process than "This is the way it's going to be," is "We've worked out this compromise which we hope is acceptable to you." The latter statement often follows by an hour, a day, a week or a month the standard question, "What can we do to the bill so you can go along?"

There are other legislators who change the character or direction of decisions in a legislature. Measured by historical perspectives, their impact may be enormous though they have fewer victories day by day than the consensus-finding leaders. These legislators may be ahead of the consensus, clearing the way for others to follow. They lead with intellect and courage. There is significant incompatability between playing the out-front role and being the consensus-finding leader. The latter uses a reputation for winning as a basic tool. Occasionally, the roles are combined by an exceptional personality who can communicate to colleagues which of these conflicting roles—captain or pathfinder—is being played at different times.

B. CHOOSING AUTHORS

§ 15–1. **Picking the right quarterback.** At least one member must sign on as the formal sponsor in order to have a bill introduced into a house of a legislature. The sponsoring member, usually euphemistically called its author, delivers the signed bill to the proper office or to the chamber desk. During the next daily session of the house, the bill will be given its first reading and referred to the appropriate standing committee. Thereafter, public notice of the bill's introduction and its listing among pending legislative proposals will more often then not include the name of its legislator-author.

The selection of a chief author seals the fate of many bills. The legislator-author of a bill acts as its manager in committee, on the floor, and in negotiation sessions. The chief author is spokesperson for the bill in the house and often in public. An author who possesses sound judgment and a competitive nature can steer to passage a bill that in less talented hands would not pass. Consequently, proponents give great care to selecting and recruiting the best possible legislative authors for their bills. The selection is like picking a jockey, drafting a quarterback, or choosing a lawyer. Quality makes a difference.

Other legislators sign onto a bill as co-authors. Generally they are endorsers of the bill, rather than co-managers. Co-authors affect the fate of a bill much less than the chief author, but they can make a difference. The general tactical rule on selecting co-authors is to use them to create the impression of broad-based support. To the extent possible, a lobbyist for a bill recruits co-authors who politically, ideologically, and geographically counter-balance the qualities of the chief sponsor.

§ 15–2. **Other criteria for authors.** A lobbyist looking for a legislative author seeks a number of other characteristics besides talent.

The right committee. In selecting an author the lobbyist will first review the roster of members of the committee to which the bill will be referred. A committee member can handle a bill more efficiently than a nonmember. Attending meetings when the bill is scheduled is no extra work; the member is supposed to be in attendance anyway. Soliciting support, discussing amendments, discovering doubts, and all the other tasks of managing a bill during its pendency in a committee are easier for an author whose daily routine is to spend hours working with other members of the relevant committee during deliberations on its other bills. The committee member also knows the personality quirks of its members and can more skillfully gauge tactics of timing and argument selection.

Having an author from the committee also gives the lobbyist one firmly committed vote in the struggle for a committee majority. For the same reasons, co-authors are recruited from the committee that will process the bill. Finally, soliciting authors requires a sales talk; it gives the lobbyist an invaluable excuse to corner a legislator to explain the proposal. For best effect, the explanation should be made to members of the committee that will decide its fate. This is a lobbying opportunity too valuable to squander on legislators whose votes do not count at the critical committee stage.

The right party. Generally, a lobbyist chooses an author from the majority party in the house. Partisanship varies among legislatures, but many bodies treat authorship of successful bills as a kind of patronage to be reserved for majority members. Congressional practice is extreme on this point. Major legislation is often taken over, not just by a majority member, but by the chairman of the committee processing the bill. Even a trailblazing author is relegated to co-authorship.

The right enthusiasm. The most talented author is sometimes not the right author. A legislator whose commitments have outrun available time cannot do justice to the job of managing yet another bill. Or the first choice legislator-author may be unwilling to give the lobbyist's bill as high a priority as required. Then the calculation must be: Do we go with the best or with the most enthusiastic?

§ 15–3. Someone to make the motion; moving an amendment. A lobbyist must find a member-sponsor for whatever other action, besides bill introduction, he seeks from the legislature. When the lobbyist wants to block passage, an agent must be found. Some legislator must make the killing motion, or urge a negative vote, or ask for a rollcall, or move to refer to the graveyard committee, or move to postpone action, or object to suspension of the rules, or execute whatever other tactic will stop the bill.

In getting a motion made—just as with choosing a chief author—the lobbyist may find the right person or may end up with a loser. Particularly in floor deliberations, who is making a point counts for a great deal. Some legislators are always listened to, some are listened to rarely. Some are viewed as invariably partisan; some as irrelevant; some as reliable.

Often a lobbyist desires to have an amendment placed on a bill. If so, a legislator must formally move the amendment. The best procedure is to have the legislator-author agree to and offer the amendment because an author's amendment is often routinely accepted. (An author's amendment early in the committee process is usually adopted without examination; it is treated as if it were pre-introduction drafting, which is entirely within the control of the author.) Other times the author resists the amendment and the lobbyist must find another member who will formally move the amendment and wage the battle necessary to overcome the resistance to it.

C. MAKING A CONSENSUS

§ 16–1. **Battle of the bills.** Legislative rules require that proponents build a consensus of more than half the members. Often a legislative majority wants to respond to a problem, but there is no consensus on the means by which to attack the problem. Until proponents put together an agreement on one scheme and on the words to implement it, the majority necessary to approve legislation is not achieved. The legislative tactician opposing action works in this situation to reinforce fears that each option (each separate, competing bill) carries destructive secondary consequences. The advocate of action, on the other hand, works out compromises among those supporting action so that one bill ultimately receives majority support. Pride of authorship is one cause of difficulty when several competing bills address a single problem. Each sponsor believes hers is the one true solution. Other times the battle of the bills arises from legislators or political parties vying for political credit.

Bicameralism also contributes to this battle. When the two houses give separate consideration to a complicated issue, conflicting approaches to it are nearly inevitable. To minimize the problem, legislative advocates must promptly relay messages between sponsors in the separate houses as each modification occurs, asking for quick amendments to conform to the action of the other house. Conforming amendments are more easily placed on a bill early in its consideration, before attitudes in the second house become firm. Also, if most differences between the houses are resolved as the process moves along, it is less likely that an accumulation of minor differences will push the bill into a conference committee. And even if a conference committee is necessary; the fewer the differences remaining, the easier they are to resolve.

§ 16–2. **Irresistible title.** The battle of the bills may slow agreement on precisely what to do, but the pressure to pass a particular bill may be overwhelming. Occasionally, there develops a powerful consensus for legislative action because someone attaches an irresistible title to a proposal. For example, effective public relations efforts have made a crackdown on drunk driving, probate reform, and environmental rights irresistible titles in recent years.

Strategically, an irresistible title situation is volatile, even dangerous; a bill so blessed can carry extra baggage without faltering. Therefore, legislative opportunists try to hitch onto the bill secondary propositions which could not be enacted by themselves. Sponsors lose the check they normal-

ly have on friends of the bill, since there is little
hazard of overreaching and thus killing the whole
package. The normal restraint on those who want
to make it the perfect bill (that is, the most extreme bill) is absent. The sponsors themselves
may exploit to the fullest the unusual situation in
which compromise and moderation are not legislative necessities. A legislature, in other words,
occasionally finds itself on a runaway horse, with a
bill it must pass.

§ 16-3. **Hostage bills.** Legislatures look worst
when assembly and senate are locked in bitter
power struggles. Since the work of the two houses
is so separate, some of the moderating influences of
shared conviviality and apportioned responsibility
are missing when feelings run high between the
houses. Also, the tool of compromise is not used
daily between houses as it is within each. Finally,
dispute often arises as to whether a bill will be
passed, rather than what will be in it when it does.
If the dispute is over content, the conference committee is available to work out compromise. But
no formally established mechanism of compromise
is present when the assembly enthusiastically passes a measure and watches its bill disappear into a
pigeonhole of some senate committee.

The assembly response to this situation is often
to take hostage a bill that senate leaders want
enacted. The word is passed to the senate that it
will get its bill passed when the bill desired by the
assembly is approved by the senate. Suddenly

issues are mixed and the game is brinkmanship and bluff. Even in this most undisciplined of legislative situations, the principals—without any offical or structural machinery for compromise—usually turn, in the end, to the merits and to accommodation. Each house lets go of its hostage bill or bills, the session work is wrapped up, and everyone returns home with a forgiving heart—most of the time.

§ 16–4. **Prepackaged compromise.** One way a legislative institution deals with difficult issues is through prepackaged compromise. Prepackaged compromises occur in issues so complex that negotiation of the final product is best left to the interests directly involved. An example is the role of organized employers and organized labor in helping legislative bodies work out acceptable unemployment and workers compensation benefits. These interests are so powerful politically that the final bill should strike a balance. If it is not balanced, but instead fully exploits recent election day successes of one side, the bill puts too high a value on political victory. Labor and employers have a continuing relationship that outlasts temporary legislative advantages. Therefore, these interests must remember that today's political strength is too fickle a determinant of the law. By the prepackaged accommodation, labor and management can smooth out the peaks and valleys of their relative political fortunes—and protect their legislative friends.

Legislatures process prepackaged compromises with the understanding that members will not untie the package by supporting disruptive amendments, no matter how attractive the amendment appears at the moment. The legislature and its members obviously benefit by having a difficult, emotional issue delivered to the institution as a compromise ready to be ratified.

§ 16–5. Splitting the difference and rolling the log.

In the legislative world of compromise—and pursuit of the merits—there comes a time when the different value judgments of the various decision-makers must be accommodated to one another. The classic accommodation is to split the difference. For example, if the two houses have equal authority to make a spending decision, and the senate comes up with the judgment that $800,000 for the activity is appropriate, whereas the assembly fixes on $700,000, the logic of settling on $750,000 to represent consensus is overwhelming. Knowing this, the senate is tempted to write in an appropriation of $900,000 to provide an extra $100,000 as trading stock. This complicates the task of finding what fairly reflects consensus, because a splitting-of-the-difference compromise then requires that the trading stock be discounted.

Splitting the difference is also practiced on issues where positions are not measured in dollars. Sometimes a legislature allows the assembly to have its way in issues A and B and lets the senate prevail on issues C and D. This gives each house its share of the decisions.

On some subjects, particularly appropriations, consensus comes by assembling a multitude of allocations to balance and accommodate the requests of the various geographic and economic interests in the state. Even in this situation, the allocations must satisfy enough members on the merits so the log will keep rolling; and the allocations must be sufficiently balanced so as not to offend to the point of rebellion those members whose constituents are left out.

§ 16–6. Passionate minorities. One type of petitioning group, a passionate minority, has less trouble forging a majority than their bare numbers would justify. A passionate minority often has more political impact than a passive majority. Political and legislative strengths reflect the depth as well as the breadth of support for a position. In elections, the passionate minority is represented most dramatically by one-issue constituencies that measure candidates by a single legislative vote out of hundreds cast. The general character of an incumbent's service or a challenger's potential is ignored, and the candidates are evaluated on whether they say the right thing about one proposition. An unfortunate by-product is the impact on other issues. Conscientious and skilled legislative work earns little political appreciation in normal circumstances, but when the electorate includes significant numbers of one-issue voters, the reward for good legislating over the whole spectrum of issues is even less.

D. TACTIC OF SOFTENING ISSUES

§ 17–1. **The softening amendment.** The legislative advocate always attempts to make it as easy as possible to agree with and as difficult as possible to oppose the advocate's position. Each motion is framed to accomplish the objective with the least ruffling of feathers. Soft motions increase the temptation to acquiesce, to go along.

A classic legislative dilemma occurs when either a friend or foe offers an amendment to water down (soften) an objectionable bill. The motion to amend presents the possibility of no loaf, half a loaf, or a full loaf. The opponent of the bill intellectually favors whatever will weaken the proposal, but at the same time fears the amendment may moderate the bill just enough to win sufficient votes for passage. She may decide to join supporters of the pure bill to defeat the amendment in the expectation that the pure bill will die. Conversely, she may vote for the amendment so that if the bill does pass, it will be more acceptable. "Vote for the amendment and against the bill" is a standard instruction from opposition leaders.

Either supporters or opponents of the bill may initiate the softening amendment, which complicates the decision on how to vote. The decision might be easy if legislative votes could be counted in advance. But almost invariably there are a handful of legislators keeping private counsel on how they intend to vote. This forces sponsors of the bill and leaders of the opposition to make tactical guesses on critical amendments.

A variation on this dilemma regularly confronts the legislator cursed with a compulsive drafter's pride in the legislative product. When confronted with a bill that seems foolish or obnoxious, this legislator, by an intensely critical reading of it, may discover a defect in the bill that makes it unworkable or even constitutionally invalid. When the bill seems destined to pass, the legislator's dilemma is whether to alert its sponsors to the defect, so the bill may be turned into a technically sound legislative product, or, instead, to leave the defect in the bill where it may prove fatal to the sponsors' objective. Working conscientiously on an objectionable proposal is referred to as "building a bridge over the River Kwai."

The dilemma has yet another aspect. A legislator (or interest group) may find a proposal objectionable in general, but abhorrent in some detail. If the sponsors agree to amend the bill to eliminate the most objectionable provision, the legislator (or interest group) faces a problem of sportsmanship. There is a general attitude that if a legislator is given a requested amendment, she should give the bill her vote. When she has been accommodated, sponsors of the bill resent her vote against passage and will be less likely to accept her amendment suggestions on subsequent bills. If a legislator is not going to support the bill after winning an amendment, it is important that sponsors be told in advance that the legislator intends to stay negative even though the amendment is added. Of course, proponents of a bill may agree to put an opponent's amendment on the bill even if doing so does not win that opponent's vote. The amendment may win her silence; she may refrain from expressing what might be effective opposition. The amendment may win over other legislators; and it may improve the bill.

§ 17–2. **Foot-in-the-door.** Another soft legislative maneuver, the foot-in-the-door strategy, is to introduce and pass a bill in a limited form to open the way for subsequent stronger legislation. Faced by a small bill with large potential, a legislator is hard put to determine the appropriate course of action. Are the cries that the floodgate are being opened honest or alarmist? Should the bill be evaluated by what appears on its face today or by what it portends for the future? An opponent of the bill, to demonstrate its long range implications, may propose to amend it to a form consistent with its sponsors' ultimate objectives.

A variation of this problem occurs when a bill has precedent-setting potential. One of the great legislative battles of the 1970's concerned a federal guarantee of loans to Lockheed Corporation. By Congressional standards the money involved was modest, yet the implications of the bill as a precedent in the area of business-government relations gave it a significance far beyond its own dimensions. The dilemma faced by members of Congress on the Lockheed loan legislation is not uncommon. Legislators often first measure short-term pros and cons and then find the debate, and their decision, turning almost entirely on the long-range precedent the bill will set if passed.

§ 17–3. **Raising the stakes.** Because there is a general tactic of softening issues, there are responsive tactics. When one side attempts to make as little of something as possible, the other side will attempt to raise the stakes, that is, to show that the question is more significant than is being made to appear. The classic stake-raising device is to decry the precedent being set. Legislators instinctively understand that what is done once is likely to be done again; they know that resistance weakens with each yielding. "We don't want to start down *that* road," is an effective legislative appeal.

Another effective line is: "They took your friends out of the bill this time, but they'll be after you next session." And: "They're just trying to get their foot in the door." And: "If it's a good idea to take this inch, then next time there will be no way to keep them from taking the mile." Sometimes opponents of a bill, knowing they have the votes to kill a bill, resist all softening amendments, even those they would normally favor. They resist the amendments in order to keep the bill from being softened enough to pass. They try to keep the stakes high enough to defeat the whole proposal.

The ultimate stake-raising tactic is to put a bill in jeopardy by "friendly" amendments. Opponents may seek to topple a proposal by making the bill top-heavy with amendments that extend its reach beyond politically acceptable limits. Its foes add provisions to the bill consistent with its main purpose, hoping to shoot it down on the basis of the added provisions. For example, if a bill proposed to impose a sales tax on architects' services, opponents might offer an amendment to extend the tax to lawyers, accountants, barbers, and beauticians as well. If the amendment is adopted, the bill will die; what the architects could not kill alone will quickly expire under the assault of all five interest groups. Another example would be a proposed public subsidy for "the arts". Opponents might move to add more dollars to the bill, claiming that if a modest subsidy makes sense, a greater subsidy should make more sense. The additional appropriation is designed, not to win support, but to create enough new expense to kill the whole idea.

§ 17–4. **Compromise to acquiescence.** Legislative compromise is more than a legislative tactic (some observers view the whole process as compromise), but it does soften an issue. Legislators respect minority viewpoints and understand the need to accommodate those who have somewhat different goals. As the majority on one issue wins its way and finishes its work, it is replaced by a different majority and a new line-up of votes on another issue. Each time this occurs, tolerance becomes more deeply ingrained in a legislator's character. Allies and opponents change in kaleidoscopic fashion during a legislative session. Therefore, legislatures give dissent a respect it enjoys in few other arenas.

There are several classic divisions within a legislature—Democratic versus Republican, liberal versus conservative, labor versus management, rural versus urban, establishment versus young Turk. Each of these divisions splits the body along varying lines on different subjects and puts a member first into alliance and then into disagreement with every colleague on one or another issue.

Legislative compromise does not enjoy, and does not deserve, an entirely spotless reputation. But compromise goes with legislative work. Those who do not like this reality would do better to challenge specific compromises that benefit undeserving interests rather than to damn the habit of accommodation; accommodation is essential to legislative work and to the political health of our society.

E. OTHER TACTICS AND SOME REALITIES

§ 18–1. **Delayed impact debate.** During a legislative session, the pace limits thoughtful reflection. Committee discussions and presentations by lobbyists compete for attention with other issues, with political concerns, and with personal responsibilities. The legislator takes office with the comfortable biases that carried him successfully through the election campaign. Neither a legislator's mind nor position is easily changed. However, debate and lobbying have an impact. Often the case made during consideration of a bill takes root in the mind of the legislator and emerges as a new attitude and a new position months later when the issue arises again.

Legislative advocacy is education. In legislative learning, as elsewhere, ideas often must be presented several times before they are grasped. Good legislative advocates need a combination of patience and impatience. Patience keeps them at the task of persuading the slow-learning institution and its slow-learning members. Impatience prevents them from allowing time to run without fighting to speed along the change desired. Advocates, when convinced they are correct, maintain their morale by presuming eventual victory while battling and hoping for quick success.

§ 18–2. Leaning on the door. Some legislative advocates make an opponent feel like a guard at a door against which the relentless advocate continually leans. The opponent knows that if she ever stops pushing back, the door-leaner will move through. Few legislative experiences are more disheartening than to be caught in an unending pushing match. A quick test on the merits leaves the participant free to move on to other issues, but a test of endurance does not.

Within legislative institutions a reputation as a door-leaner is invaluable. If the advocate seldom abandons a cause, opponents are tempted to give in with the attitude of "Eventually, why not now?" For example, the leaner may want a public institution constructed. He has a constituency behind him and is rewarded for his continual effort by praise and reelection whether he prevails or not. The guardian of the public treasury—the no-sayer—may not receive similar appreciation from a constituency; she may actually lose popularity. Victory finally goes to the person or group with the greater endurance and a more impressive reputation for persistence.

§ 18–3. **Using up political points.** Public cynicism about the legislature often develops from news reports of special interest victories in legislative battles. Unfortunately, press reports of legislative activities tend to focus on the few pitched-battles in the institution, the very situations in which power dominates and merit yields. Much public disillusionment with legislative institutions is traceable to the media's preference for reporting legislative controversy rather than legislative work.

Power does play a role in legislative institutions, but taking a slightly longer perspective will erase much cynicism. Power only buys time. Even the weakest legislators free themselves from political and other commitments in a year or two. They can then vote the merits when the issue next arises. The lobbyist cannot complain convincingly about a current vote when the legislator says: "I voted your way last time when you asked me, but this time I see the merits of the issue the other way."

When a power-broker sees support eroding, his best tactic is to give up on killing the bill and to cut the loss by designing a moderating amendment. After the amendment is incorporated into the bill, the retreating lobbyist abandons the battle completely so that the bill passes overwhelmingly. He thereby avoids the appearance of having lost power and suffering defeat; and the public never recognizes the bill as a victory over a vested interest.

The legislative advocate with a meritorious case should press the cause even in the face of certain defeat; this forces the opposition to use its political IOU's immediately. Once those IOU's have been expended, the institution is freed to act later on the merits. Then the advocate, previously blocked by entrenched interests, can pursue the strategy of leaning against the door, secure in the knowledge his cause will prevail.

§ 18–4. **Skin the cat.** The legislative process is essentially simple. Nonetheless, the legislative tactician enjoys a variety of choices throughout the process. Many participants fail to realize how many alternative routes exist; they therefore fail to select the winning strategy and lose battles that should be won. The point is that there are many ways to skin a cat.

The preferred strategy is to follow the ordinary legislative process and to make as few waves with a proposal as possible. But superior advocates maintain an attitude of flexibility that allows them to make end runs around obstacles that cannot be overcome directly. They come up from losses smiling, with a new request for at least a half or a third of what they want. They turn defeat into partial victory. Or, when the legislature is unwilling to approve their bill, they try to delerate the decision to an agency or they call for a study. They ask opponents how to solve the problem. They try to ride on another bill, or to find a friendlier committee.

Flexibility should also be applied to the substance of what clients want. The advocate must compromise, invent, adjust, and borrow ideas. A valuable legislative motto is: If at first you don't succeed, try another way.

§ 18–5. **To oppose or ignore.** Proponents of legislation must attract attention for the proposal. If legislators know of the proposal, they become sensitive to the problem it addresses. By communicating opposition, opponents do some of the proponents' work. They unavoidably alert legislators to the fact that the bill will have an impact, that in real life some things will be affected by its passage. If opponents ask that attention be paid to the bill, they are likely to be accommodated. Since attention is exactly what proponents of the bill need, vocal opposition aids significantly in starting the bill down the path toward passage.

Should, then, the legislative tactician faced with an objectionable bill ignore it, hoping it will die quietly? That may be a dangerous course. Proponents might quickly and privately present the case for the bill. The case may sound sensible in the absence of opposition; and proponents will urge prompt action. Once a bill begins to move in a legislative institution, arguments against it may be too late. The dilemma is obvious. Should the opponent step forward and pay the price of drawing attention to the proposal; or should she treat the bill as unworthy of legislative attention and run the risk of quick action based on a one-sided story?

The legislative advocate may be able to cope with this dilemma by dealing directly with the agenda setters of the legislature. The advocate can discuss the basis for opposition with the committee chairman or staff and declare a readiness to marshal opposition if the bill begins to move. This may eliminate the hazard of quick, affirmative action. The opponent may also contact the sponsor of the bill, explain the reason for opposition, request accommodation, and communicate that there will be a fight ahead. Since the sponsor already knows of the bill, this tactic does not draw additional attention to the proposal.

§ 18–6. Hairy arm. A bill is sometimes introduced with some obnoxious feature. Critics pounce on that frightening "hairy arm" as the point of vulnerability in the proposal. Sponsors may defend the provision for a time, but before the critical vote they delete it. Opponents are left fighting the rest of the bill, which they may not have previously criticized or even studied. Inclusion of the provision may have been tactical from the beginning; deleting the hairy arm gives the appearance of compromising with the bill's critics.

Passage of Minnesota's criminal code provides an example of this technique at work. The code as introduced made significant changes in both procedural and substantive criminal law, including the repeal of a number of provisions relating to sexual behavior. The proposed repeal of laws against sodomy, adultery, and fornication brought vigorous attacks on the code. But when sponsors deleted those provisions late in the session, opponents were literally left speechless. The remainder of the code passed easily.

§ 18–7. Timing. Timing is the most pervasive tactical decision. When should the lobbyist approach the legislator or staff member? When should information be released to the media? When should the bill be introduced? When should the hearing be scheduled? When should the amendment be offered? When should the new argument be made? When should strategic retreat occur? When should the agency be approached? When should the secret ally surface? Finally, when should the vote be called for?

The most unruly spot in the legislative process is committee of the whole. This is when bills are taken up in a floor meeting of the entire body, usually without a procedure for rounding up absent members. On tough bills proponents and opponents jockey to control the timing of action to take advantage of absences. When an issue turns on one or two votes, the absent members decide the outcome. And timing fixes who is absent. Of course, the tactic of timing votes is a staple of committee action as well.

§ 18–8. **When you have the votes, vote.** The ultimate tactic in the legislative process is to press for action when you will win; vote when you will gain your objective. Imagine a legislator or lobbyist standing before a committee with nearly all the members ready to cast favorable votes. Now imagine the advocate giving a prepared speech, running through all ideas in notes prepared the night before. And imagine the committee members deciding, one by one, that there must be more to this bill than they first thought. They each start a careful reading of the bill to discover what defect in the bill makes its sponsor so nervous and defensive.

When this scene starts to pay out, a delightful legislative practice is for a senior member to interrupt with the questions: "Is this a good bill? Do you have the votes to get it passed?" On receiving affirmative answers, the experienced member makes the gentle suggestion: "Why don't you let us vote?" At other times no one gives the hint and the proponent talks her own bill to death. The filibuster, engaging in unnecessary discussion to prevent a matter from coming to vote, is a classic tactic. It is regularly used by shrewd opponents of a bill. But the filibuster is sometimes implemented mindlessly by supporters of a bill who should want the vote to occur at once because they already have the votes to win.

One way to avoid damaging one's cause with excessive discussion is prompt use of this useful statement: "If there are no questions, I move that the bill pass." This puts to the opposition the burden of speaking up and raising doubts. The tactic of pressing for a quick vote accords with a fundamental principle of parliamentary practice. The principle is that a majority in a legislative body can have its way; the majority rules. All other rules, in essence, exist to provide minorities with the opportunity to persuade. Most rules that control legislative deliberation simply give to those who do not, at the moment, have sufficient votes, more time to make arguments that might convert a majority to their position. If no one seeks to dissuade the majority of the moment, that majority may as well vote and have its way.

A good legislative motto is: When you have the votes, vote!

F.   APPROPRIATIONS ADVOCACY

§ 19–1.   Appropriation procedure.   Legislators carry out the great legislative task of giving and withholding funds for agencies, programs, and private petitioners by procedures that parallel other legislative work.   The final decisions are incorporated into appropriation acts.   These acts may cover a single item, though they usually include a multitude of allocations.   If the bill contains many items, it is called an omnibus appropriation bill. The omnibus bill usually covers one area of government activity, for example, education, and is processed by the appropriations subcommittee that holds decision-making responsibility in that field.

The legal requirements to pass an appropriation act match those of ordinary bills: three readings, majority vote, adequate title, and so on.   A common departure from the ordinary bill-passing procedure is that the appropriation bill is put together and introduced after committee hearings and preliminary decisions on each item.   What items will be in the bill and the dollar figures attached to each are determined in "mark-up" or "allocation" sessions of a subcommittee, using the budget proposals of the executive branch, rather than a bill, to focus attention on relevant questions.

Another departure from regular bill-passing procedure arises when constitutional provisions give the executive the power to veto individual items in appropriation bills.   The power of item veto has less impact than might be expected, however, because each item usually is itself a package of money for several programs. The executive is trapped by the packaging, which puts into most items some veto-proof element.

A distinction must be drawn between mere authorization of expenditures and actual appropriations. Any legislation that establishes a new agency or program, by implication authorizes the expenditure of public money. But actual funding of the program is usually postponed until money is included in an appropriation bill. This protects the prerogatives of the appropriations committee by keeping money decisions in its hands and away from the education or welfare or highway committees. Those committees process the bills that authorize the programs and are often captive of education, welfare, or highway lobbies. A full appreciation of the power of appropriations committees comes with the realization that, while authorization of any continuing program occurs but once, the spending level for that program is set annually or biennially thereafter by an appropriations committee. That committee can end the program whenever it chooses by withholding the money necessary to carry out the activity.

§ 19–2. **Subcommittee autonomy.** Division of legislative labor pervades the appropriation process even more than it does other legislative functions. The volume of work pushes decision making out of the full appropriations committee and into nearly autonomous subcommittees. The general rule of appropriation procedure is that subcommittee decisions prevail through final passage. Subcommittees earn deference to their decisions by holding exhaustive hearings. Subcommittee authority is also strengthened by the seniority typically represented in appropriations subcommittee membership. Hard work and experience give each subcommittee such knowledge that it is nearly impossible for other legislators to sustain a challenge to its decisions. Even if non-members could win the debate, its endless labor gives each appropriations subcommittee the privilege, in the eyes of most legislators, to be upheld even in its mistakes. Before any significant decision of an appropriations subcommittee or its parent committee is modified by floor amendment, the decision must be far out of step with the consensus of the house.

After passing each house, an omnibus appropriation bill is sent to a conference committee where differences between the houses are compromised. The compromise is a mixture of splitting the difference in dollar amounts, trading off programs favored or opposed by each house, and considering the merits of the judgments made by the separate subcommittees. Members of the conference committee are drawn from the membership of the standing subcommittees which originally put together the bill in each house.

Obviously, a person desiring to affect appropriation decisions should direct lobbying to the membership of the subcommittee. Given the traditions of subcommittee autonomy, petitions directed to other legislators are generally ineffective.

§ 19–3. **The executive role in appropriations.** The executive's impact on legislation is nowhere more significant than on appropriations. In all jurisdictions, legislatures begin appropriation work with a review of a formal budget proposal by the executive containing detailed expenditure recommendations. The legislative rule of inertia works in the appropriation process, not only to make the appropriations subcommittee dominant on the decisions within its area of jurisdiction, but also to give these early executive department recommendations a pervasive impact on appropriation decisions.

An executive's budget recommendations do not come out of a void. They start with spending requests from the various agencies of government directed to the executive's budget office. These requests are built on past allocations and on an agency's perception of what it dares request. The agency, in effect, puts a cap on its own appropriation, for neither executive nor legislature is likely to recommend more money than the agency seeks. Therefore, a lobbyist asking for money to support a new program or for additional financing to expand an old one must start at the agency.

Appropriation hearings typically involve a dialogue between the subcommittee and the agency that wants the appropriation. The agency witnesses defend the level of expenditure recommended by the executive. Occasionally they may urge allotment of some modest increase over the executive budget. To ask for this larger amount risks executive rancor, for it puts the agency at odds with a budget decision made by the executive who nominally is responsible for all agency policy.

The appropriations committee perceives its job as finding fat in the figures under discussion. It has little outside assistance in this search for extravagance. Without independent information, the committee is hard put to find a reason to cut back on executive recommendations. The committee has even less inclination to increase recommended expenditures. As a consequence, executive budget office recommendations for government expenditures are very significant. Legislative committees make minor adjustments in specific items, but in the main follow executive recommendations.

§ 19–4. **Re-ordering priorities.** A legislature generally makes only minor changes in appropriation recommendations by the executive. And the executive generally recommends only small changes from past appropriations of the legislature. The proposed budget of the executive branch is built on the budget adopted by the previous legislature. Civil servants prepare the budget. It is not done by political agents of the executive. On the rare occasion when the executive breaks from the appropriation patterns of the past to establish new spending priorities, changes are vigorously examined by the legislature.

The most dominant influence on appropriation decisions—whether executive or legislative—is what was done last time. Inertia rules both the executive and the legislature. To re-order priorities—to make spending decisions on a more rational basis than "last time"—is a major challenge to the institutions of government.

§ **19–5. Line-item versus program budgeting.** Recognizing the need to improve executive and legislative appropriation decisions, public officials are experimenting with the governmental budget making process at every level. Most government budgeting examines the items of expenditure to be made by an agency; for example, should an agency have three secretaries, two phone lines, $550 worth of travel, and a new swivel chair? Expenditures are grouped into categories: personnel, communications, travel, supplies, equipment. These line-item categories become the building blocks of the budget.

Under line-item budgeting, legislators look sharply only at new programs. Usually these stand up to examination, for they are likely to be timely responses to real problems. An agency is delighted to help focus legislative attention on the personnel and material required by new programs it wishes to add to its mission. The agency can then quietly continue past programs, even though those programs may no longer be defensible. Re-examining and shrinking old programs is very difficult under line-item budgeting, but to increase appropriations pursuant to a formula based on inflationary costs and increased clientele is easily justified. Under line-item budgeting, once something is started it is almost impossible to scale it down, let alone turn it off. The search for an alternative to the old line-item system has been prompted by the automatic, unrestrained growth of government budgets under that system.

Program budgeting has developed as an alternative to line-item budgeting. In theory, it requires an examination of programs rather than the traditional examination of the objects of expenditure. The decision makers are asked to look at the benefits derived from the service provided and at its cost, instead of looking at the number of employees, the amount of stationery, the kind of furniture, and the miles of travel. Program budgeting—sometimes called zero-based budgeting—facilitates a re-examination of all activities, whether the agency has carried on the program for one or one hundred years. The benefit of each agency activity is measured against its cost; weak programs supposedly will be discarded.

Experience with program budgeting has fallen short of expectations. Agencies of government find it difficult to price programs, and legislative committees find it difficult to verify the integrity of whatever price tags are attached. The habit of appropriations committee members is to look for fat in government budgets. Textbook versions of program budgeting overlook this vital function and, more seriously, fail to take into account legislator habits. No good process has been designed to convert from line-item to program budgeting. The whole effort faces opposition or lukewarm support from the bureaucrats; agencies are not enthusiastic about giving budget bureaus, executives, or legislators real insight into agency operations when the *status quo* is reasonably attractive. The very information that would make program budgeting work well for legislators and the executive is least likely to be voluntarily revealed. Questionable activities are likely to be hidden in a larger agency program. In some jurisdictions inadequate budget presentations have produced such frustration that program budgeting has been abandoned. In other jurisdictions, legislators and administrators are working out modified program budgets with sufficient line-item information to limit frustration while more workable program-budgeting procedures evolve.

A legislative advocate concerned with appropriations must understand the budget format in his jurisdiction. His interest will be a program interest. But if the format of the budget is line-item, the advocate will not be arguing for the program. Rather he will ask for additional employees or equipment, or increased travel allowance so present personnel can better accomplish program objectives. Normally lobbyists are interested in passing, killing, or amending a bill. In the appropriation process, a lobbyist will want to add an item, delete an item, or influence the amount of an allocation. Knowing what figures need to be changed and whether the figures stand for a program, for personnel, or for agency supplies is essential to lobbying efforts.

If he knows nothing else about appropriations, a legislative advocate ought to know that the legislature in this area of its activity, just as in its other tasks, responds to petitions and information brought by outsiders. This is a legitimate subject for lobbying, but it is overlooked by many interest groups. Appropriation lobbying is mostly left to the bureaucrats.

§ **19–6. Fiscal crises.** During the late 1970's and early 1980's tax revenues in many states took some dramatic swings; many states enjoyed budget surpluses, then suffered severe revenue shortfalls followed by another round of surpluses. These swings weakened the pattern of basing each annual or biennial budget on the previous budget. To do so created embarrassing surpluses and taxpayer outrage or, in the next cycle, illegal deficits. Legislative, executive, and budget office reaction to a budget crisis has been a mixed bag of re-examining priorities and of resorting to mindless "across the board" percentage cuts. The reason for formula adjustments is that, crisis or no, legislators have no more time than before to give every program or every line item a fresh evaluation.

One consequence of fiscal crisis is that the fiefdoms of budget makers were temporarily shaken. The problems and the unpredictability were more than appropriations committees could handle, so they lost the confidence of other legislators, all of whom could see that the appropriation specialists were forced to arbitrary cuts because they lacked the informational foundation for more precise reductions.

§ 19–7. **Budget resolutions.** Some legislatures follow a new technique of government budget making—the budget resolution. The idea is to focus on the big picture, then to set a cap on spending before the detailed work of line item and program analysis begins. The explanation reveals the problem; the big picture cannot be determined without having the sum of the parts. But neither can the parts be evaluated without a sense of the whole. It seems there is no right place to start the budget process.

§ 19–8. **Appropriation riders.** Appropriation bills include secondary provisions, called riders, that put conditions on the use of the appropriated funds. An appropriation rider is a legitimate device to implement the legislative power of the purse. Riders tell agencies to "use this money for this activity." That is a reasonable legislative direction.

Unfortunately, legislators misuse appropriation riders. Often a rider is not closely related to the appropriation. It may be a discordant proposition that seeks a free ride. It may implement an idea that could not pass on its own merits. Normally, abuse of the legislative process by combining separate subjects is limited by the bar on double-subject bills, fear that a second subject will threaten a bill's passage, and respect for normal legislative processes. These checks fail, however, when applied to riders on spending bills. First, the substance and title of an omnibus appropriation bill is so broad that innumerable riders fit into it with no double-subject problem. Second, even the most objectionable rider cannot kill a money bill. Third, legitimate riders necessary to condition and control spending are camouflage for non-germane, overreaching riders. The presence of these characteristics make spending bills favorites for those who seek a short cut to the difficult journey of legitimate legislative procedures.

PART II

MAKING A BILL

CHAPTER 5

IDEAS FOR LEGISLATION

A. SOURCES OF IDEAS AND BILLS

§ 20–1. **Power of ideas.** Intellectual inventions—ideas—are the raw material of the legislative institution. Without this raw material the legislative machinery would stop, for it is designed to evaluate, modify, process, and implement ideas. H.G. Wells wrote, "Human history is in essence a history of ideas." More recently Dean Francis A. Allen wrote, "A sound idea has a power of its own." In the long perspective, the dominant force in legislative institutions is the force of intellect.

Our society does not recognize the capacity of legislative institutions to accept and to implement sound ideas. Scholars rarely focus their energies to create the ideas essential to the legislative process. Even when luck causes the intellectual raw material for legislative action to emerge in scholarship, that material is often left to wither far from the legislature "and waste its sweetness on the [academic] air." The mundane-appearing task of turning theories into bill drafts does not get done—

not because it is mundane, but because the task is often beyond the learned or innate skills of the creators of new ideas.

The community, therefore, must bridge the gap between the conceiving of ideas and the writing of legislative bills.

§ 20–2. **Borrowed and model bills.** Since the talent of legal invention, like the talent of mechanical invention, is a scarce commodity, the most efficient mechanism to obtain bills is plagarism. Neither patent nor copyright laws protect legislative invention; and the idea that works well in one jurisdiction is useful to its neighbors—and free. Ideas are indeed borrowed. New proposals spread across the country, popping up in various legislatures in almost random fashion.

Legislatures also obtain a regular supply of significant bills from the National Conference of Commissioners on Uniform State Laws. That organization promulgates a number of uniform acts each year. These acts are drafted, reviewed, and repeatedly redrafted by drafting committees. Committees of the conference often receive staff help from law professors specializing in relevant fields. All 250 commissioners are lawyers—practitioners, judges, and professors—appointed by governors to represent the various states. Since uniform acts generally possess a scholarly and practical quality beyond the capability of any state legislature working on its own, they have achieved wide acceptance. The Council of State Governments, the

American Law Institute, the American Bar Association, and numerous other organizations also produce model acts for legislatures.

Anyone facing a problem that needs a legislative
solution ought to review the supply of uniform and
model acts before trying to invent an original bill.
Even if a uniform or model act or an act from a
neighboring jurisdiction is not totally applicable, it
is infinitely easier to edit and revise a borrowed
bill than to start a drafting job from scratch.

§ 20–3. **Organized interests.** Those private
interests traditionally well represented at legislatures generate a fair share of legislative bills.
These bills arise through the initiative of business
executives, lawyers, and lobbyists. This occurs
even though lobbyists hired by the vested interests
of the community usually find themselves protecting the *status quo*; they resist change by playing
the role of "defensive lobbyists." Lobbyists whose
usual stance is defensive have good reason occasionally to create or seize an opportunity to urge
affirmative legislative action on behalf of a client,
to use their accumulated legislative knowledge and
skills in a positive role. An unmarred record of
opposing change weakens credibility. Furthermore, a client's willingness to pay decent fees depends somewhat on the number of legislative issues affecting the client's welfare. When the
lobbyist persuades the client to take the offensive
by seeking something from the legislature, that
adds to the number of relevant issues. If a re-

quested bill is adopted, the client receives the benefit of a helpful new statute, something more tangible than the lobbyist's usual service of blocking undesired legislation.

§ 20–4. **Political candidates and chief executives.** Public office is won by political campaigns. Successful campaigns include promises of programs for senior citizens, employees, parents, taxpayers, and consumers. Occasionally, a candidate announces a grand title for a program. Once elected, the candidate is forced to invent some substance for that title. The "war on poverty" is one example. Since public attention focuses more on executive than on legislative races, political pressure squeezes more ideas out of executive than legislative candidates. Executive promises to respond to the real and imagined problems of various constituencies must be followed by specific suggestions.

After election, a chief executive faces a constitutional mandate to report to the legislature on the state of the state (or union). This message and the budget message place a post-election burden on an executive to come up with even more ideas. Individual legislators can hide behind platitudes, but the executive is pushed to specifics. So the staff of the executive routinely conducts a search for ideas that can be borrowed. The media also demand that executives make news. The press habitually gives pronouncements by executives prominent coverage, forcing the chief executive into an opinion-molding, leadership role.

§ 20–5. **Legislators.** As politicians, legislators often state their intention to solve a problem. They also claim later that they "authored" specific legislation. Legislative authorship almost always means fronting for the real creators. It means simply to manage or sponsor the bill within the legislature. Political license permits legislators to pilfer the ideas of others. However the victim of the theft ultimately benefits, for when the stolen idea is introduced into the legislature as a bill for an act, it has made a start on the road to becoming law.

Legislators sometimes think up bills on their own, but it is unrealistic to expect legislators, as a group, to be idea inventors. First, and most significant, the inventive legislator is rare. Second, energy put into invention is lost from the legislator's more basic job of judging proposed legislation. Third, perhaps the best use of inventiveness, when it is found in a legislator, is in the creative editing essential to produce good legislative products. The one legislator in twenty who learns to foresee unfortunate secondary consequences of bills and to create amendments to avoid them should allocate available energy to doing that. Most other work done by such an imaginative legislator is a misallocation of a scarce ability.

Fourth, as politicians, legislators face dangers as initiators of legislation. They are restrained by the political hazard that lies in challenging conventional viewpoints. Legislators have little time to defend unfamiliar propositions. Politicians usually design their speeches to confirm audience biases. Therefore, charting new courses and selling innovative programs usually is left to those outside the elected membership of legislative institutions.

§ 20–6. Individuals. Pace-setting legislative bills are a result of ideas and come most frequently from the thoughts of a series of individuals. The first person in the series happens to get a creative thought. Whether the idea will then be caught and turned into a bill is dependent on chance—at least it has been in the past. The problem is that an individual may not possess both the inspiration to create an idea and the skill to turn the idea into a bill. Legal education has failed to teach that it is useful, perhaps essential, to set up a division of labor for the production of bills. The theorists who conceive solutions to the problems of society receive no instruction in marketing their solutions to legislative institutions. Legislative staff members, in turn, are not taught to examine scholarly law journals to find the raw materials for legislation. Rather, they produce pedestrian bills for legislators responding to political pressures. As they work, the bill drafters typically—and unfortunately—are not involved with the intellectual and creative elements in the community.

The consequences of this gap in the idea chain are illustrated by one rare victory over it. Professors Robert Keeton and Jeffrey O'Connell conducted an exhaustive study of auto accident compensa-

tion which led them in 1965 to recommend no-fault
auto insurance; the Keeton-O'Connell recommendation was consistent with another study done at
Columbia University thirty-three years earlier.
The Columbia study was much discussed in academic circles, but the no-fault concept did not
become a legislative issue until Keeton and
O'Connell took one essential step—they included in
their book a draft no-fault bill. The bill gave the
Massachusetts legislature a grip on the proposal.
In less than a year, no-fault auto insurance moved
from ivory tower, through the Massachusetts general assembly, and to the edge of passage in the
senate. Enactment took three more years, but if
the bill draft had not been included in the Keeton-
O'Connell book, the wait in Massachusetts and
nationally might have been years longer.

The legal system must develop legislative solutions to the problems of society. Scholars must
push their ideas beyond neatly researched articles
for prestigious law reviews; they must create ex-
haustively edited legislative bills and deliver them
to legislatures on silver platters. Editors and readers of legal publications must decide that studies of
legislative inventions can be interesting and influ-
ential scholarly work, work which deserves to be
published. Legislative staffs must survey intellectual sources for ideas and must draft bills to bridge
the gap that occurs when scholars fail to turn
theory into legislative proposals.

B. BILL CREATION AS A GOVERNMENTAL PROCESS

§ 21–1. The process of bill making. Bill creation is a complicated process subject to variations at every step. For example, the first step—recognizing the problem—may be the contribution of almost anyone. The second step, deciding that legislation may be the solution, can be the contribution of a politician, a political platform writer, a lawyer, a bureaucrat, a muckraker, a student, a scholar, or a committee of citizens examining the problem area. The third step is conceiving a realistic legislative response. One who recognizes the legislative potential to deal with a problem can also contribute the insight on how it should be done; indeed that insight may cause the first recognition that a legislative role exists. More commonly, invention of a bill is preceded only by the vague comment: "There ought to be a law." However, this observation can set a mind to work and the idea for a bill may follow.

When a legislative response is conceived, the next step is to draft a bill. The inventor may produce a draft, or may order the bill from a drafting specialist. If the request to the professional drafter is made before the idea and response are thought through, the bill produced will be a disappointment. Bill drafters do not turn out invention on order, at least not often. Of course, a near miss is sometimes good enough. An incomplete concept can carry awareness of the problem into the legislative and public arenas where more attention can be given to the search for a better solution. But usually a bill lacking essential insight will not earn attention or a spot on a committee agenda; the competition for committee time is won by bills ready for passage.

This discussion of bill making is out of balance in one respect. It ignores the brute force approach to a legislative problem. Occasionally, an interest group or a legislature under pressure decides to tackle a problem and to devise some legislative action, even if there is no immediately apparent solution. This decision leads to a commitment to assemble resources for the effort. A mechanism is established to seek, shape, solicit, and screen legislative proposals. All ideas which come out of the effort are evaluated. Promising starts are worked over to see if, with modification, they can do the job. Industry—at least the military industrial complex—has discovered that with adequate resources it can accomplish nearly anything. Focused in the same intense way, the legal-legislative machinery can also produce legal progress on order, rather than on inspiration. But such resolve to solve a legal or social problem rarely exists.

§ 21–2. **Legislative studies.** In the past, legislatures have been almost, though not completely, useless as bill creators. That may be changing. In recent years, legislative staff has expanded significantly. Legislative employees are under some bill-creating pressures; their employers expect something out of them. Since the institution works with bills, bills are the most visible work the staff can produce.

Major legislation often follows a course which includes a blue-ribbon legislative commission of some sort, perhaps with citizen members and staff from the academic world. In a handful of states, independent, creative study has been institutionalized by the formation of law revision commissions. Although the commissions work outside the legislature, they remain under its sponsorship. The commissions turn out legislative proposals in the private law area, proposals that meet problems otherwise ignored as the legislature works on public law issues like taxes, appropriations, and government structure.

§ 21–3. **Agency bill making.** Government agencies bring many bills to every legislature. These "department bills" arise out of day to day department activities and out of special studies. The kind of relationship legislators maintain with executive branch bureaucrats depends largely on the size of the legislative staff. Where the legislative staff is still relatively small, the legislature expects executive agencies to prepare bills and to lobby as advocates for the public interest. Rightly or wrongly, agencies are thought to provide a balance to the private interests served by lobbyists from commerce and industry. The legislature treats agency employees as supplementary to or as a substitute for legislative staff.

When a legislature has its own large research staff, that staff crowds executive branch bureaucrats out of the role of neutral advisors to the legislators. Legislators then view the bureaucrats, not as handy representatives of the public interest, but rather as another set of advocates for another kind of interest group. Rivalries among various agencies and between competitive local government units confirm this impression of bureaucrat as petitioner. But even when the bureaucrats lose their aura as *de facto* legislative staff, they have great influence on the legislature as the source of bills, as agenda writers, and as authoritative advisors. The private lobbyist, recognizing the lobbying power of bureaucrats, often starts the appeal for legislation in the bureaucracy and attempts to recruit it as an ally.

C. SEARCH FOR SANCTIONS

§ 22-1. **Means to an end.** Many times in drafting bills, the moment of truth comes when the drafter asks: "How do we make this all mean something in real life; how do we give it muscle?" The drafter may have trouble finding the appropriate sanction to achieve the objective of the bill. The multitude of devices available, both to penalize and to reward, makes selection difficult. The choice is not limited to a single sanction; a small arsenal can be assembled for one bill. For example, to force motorists to purchase no-fault auto insurance, legislators have: imposed criminal penalties on the uninsured, required vehicle owners to submit proof of insurance or a policy number when licensing a motor vehicle, excluded from benefits those who fail to insure, exposed the uninsured to liability for negligence, and authorized revocation of motor vehicle and driver licenses of uninsured motorists. This list suggests the varied characteristics of sanctions.

These sanctions employ steady and intermittent pressures, early and late inducements, positive and negative forces, public and private enforcing agents, and harsh and gentle mechanisms. Some of the sanctions push the citizen to semi-automatic compliance by making non-compliance procedurally difficult (those connected with vehicle licensing). Others punish violation through state action (criminal prosecution). Others use private action (the retained fault lawsuit). Private pressure to conform comes from insurance agent efforts to sell insurance and from peer pressure. Government agency enforcement comes through spot checks of cancellations and claimed insurance coverage on motor vehicle registration applications.

Often, after a sanction is selected, the bill drafter struggles to soften its impact. Sanctions should produce a satisfactory level of compliance, which need not be 100 percent; but they should not punish unnecessarily. With no-fault legislation, for example, other family members do not bear the same exclusions from benefits or exposure to tort liabilities as does the person who should have bought the insurance; some laws even allow the uninsured car owner to collect no-fault benefits after punitive deductions from those benefits. This better serves the objective of compensating everyone, a goal which would be frustrated through the overly severe sanction of denied benefits.

The bill drafter should reduce the cost and inconvenience of a sanction as much as she can without seriously damaging its effectiveness. For example, to require the owner to include an insurance policy number on a license application costs less than to require a document from the insurance company stating that a policy is in effect. It is cheaper in time and money to the state, the motorist, and the insurance industry. Yet the difference in impact between the two is slight.

§ 22–2. **Criminal penalties.** The word "sanction" brings fines and jail terms to mind; yet these are less valuable means to implement legislative policy than other devices. The judicious bill drafter searches for sanctions short of criminality, making prosecution a last resort. A criminal charge is harsh even when it leads to acquittal or brings a suspended sentence. It pushes the defendant to vigorous battle, rather than to the quick and continuing compliance desired. Criminal prosecution is never self-enforcing, although the quality of being self-enforcing is the ultimate virtue in a sanc-

tion. A criminal sanction is also expensive to the
state—in the cost of prosecution, in the cost of
incarceration, and in its destructive impact on the
life of the defendant. In many circumstances the
criminal sanction is recognized by prosecutor,
judge and jury as overkill. When law enforcers
find juries refusing to convict or are themselves
uncomfortable with bringing particular charges,
prosecution under that statute stops; the criminal
sanction then becomes largely meaningless.

Severe non-criminal sanctions can also self-de-
struct. In one state, a statute provided that an
illegal public employee strike automatically disqualified participants from any pay raise for a
year. When a strike did occur, the statutory sanction made a settlement impossible until everyone
agreed the statute would be ignored. The general
lesson is to keep criminal and other penalties realistic, taking into account human nature. The get-
tough penalty seldom accomplishes its objective,
unless the objective is grandstanding rather than
making good law.

When criminal sanctions are used, the legal pattern of the jurisdiction must be followed. Legislatures seek consistency and balance, so the penalty
for violation of a new law must be in line with
penalties for other violations. The penalty must
also fit the jurisdiction's standard classifications of
felony, gross misdemeanor, misdemeanor, petty
misdemeanor, or tab charges. If a bill writer does
not know the habit patterns of the legislature, the

bill may be submitted to the legislative bill drafting agency with the criminal sanctions left open in
order to obtain direction from the specialists. Official bill drafters have technical knowledge and a
sensitivity to the attitudes of their own legislature
on criminal law issues. A non-specialist may draft
provisions out of tune with prevailing legislative
attitudes and create negative reactions to the entire bill.

Criminal sanctions should be drawn with legislative acceptability the primary concern. The penalty actually applied is so much under the control of
judiciary, prosecutors, parole board, and corrections agency that what a statute authorizes is
usually not important, except to put the conduct
into the appropriate level of criminality.

§ 22–3. Civil fines; corporate sanctions. A
civil fine is non-criminal. But the fine is paid to
the state, unlike civil damages which are paid to a
private person. The fine does not brand the offender with the status of felon or misdemeanant,
which gives it significant advantages over criminal
penalties. The civil fine provides the prosecutor
and judge with an especially useful alternative
when commercial misbehavior occurs in a corporate setting. There the civil fine may be levied on
the corporate entity, even when so many corporate
employees participated in the illegal activity that
criminal prosecution of individuals is difficult.

Corporate misbehavior challenges the bill drafter
and the law enforcer in special ways. Penalties on

corporations, if not appropriately limited, spill over onto employees, shareholders, and even onto communities. For example, the power to terminate the authority of a corporation to do business in a state is practically useless because of all the resulting economic impacts. Cancelling a franchise or permit can also close a business and do widespread harm. The bill drafter who is writing sanctions for commercial legislation must focus some attention on the economic impact of the sanction and on the split corporate personality—real people and artificial entity.

§ 22–4. **Use of agencies.** Executive-administrative agencies implement much legislation. To carry out their tasks, agencies use whatever tools are provided in the specific legislation, plus the flexibility inherent in administrative law. Agencies can adjust law and sanctions to the circumstances of particular cases. This power to act on an almost *ad hoc* basis is both the great strength and the great evil of agency enforcement.

Enforcement of anti-trust law is a dramatic example of this flexibility. Anti-trust legislation has remained essentially the same for decades, but anti-trust law as enforced has varied depending on economic conditions and Department of Justice attitudes. The history of anti-trust illustrates that giving agencies discretionary enforcement authority produces a useful power to negotiate agreements with those regulated. The anti-trust division of the Department of Justice has often cajoled mono-

polizers to modify their activities. In tough cases
the department has negotiated consent decrees
foreclosing business activities it viewed as harmful
to the market place. Consent decrees involve en-
forceable promises not to engage in specified practices.

Most agency negotiation is less formal. Since
Congress gave the Products Safety Commission responsibility to define safety standards, the commission has worked extensively with manufacturers.
Working together, they decide what is feasible.
The standards this commission has set represent
much effort to avoid extra cost and economic dislo-
cations to industry, even at the price of slower
implementation and reduced effectiveness.

State and federal environmental protection agencies engage in the same type of bargaining with
various interests to decide what should be done,
when it should be done, what will be done voluntarily, what must be forced, and what alternatives
are available. This negotiation is continual, so
new knowledge can be put into the process and
decisions adjusted accordingly. If legislatures had
imposed specific rules and deadlines, appropriate
adjustments to new facts would be difficult.

The captive regulatory agency is, of course, a
familiar phenomenon. The failure to build into
laws some degree of insurance against agency sur-
render to political expediency is a serious problem.
Too often, legislatures leave the politically tough
work—laying down the law—to an agency. Al-

most inevitably, accommodation occurs between agency and industry. To protect against excessive compromise, a legislature must provide private remedies to back up and buck up the agency. A legislature must also write the law with sufficient courage to set a standard the agency cannot ignore and to limit the discretion of the agency so that it cannot sabotage the legislature's objectives.

§ 22–5. **Licenses, permits, charters, and franchises.** The legal system keeps control of many activities by licenses, or by permits, charters, and franchises granted by agencies or local governments. The agency granting the license may do so on a selective basis to limit participation to qualified persons, to control the intensity of competition, to ration a scarce resource like television channels, or to maintain monopolies when competition does not make economic sense, as with local telephone service. If the license is granted indiscriminately, but for a fee, the purpose may be to limit the number of participants, to raise revenue, to gather information of value to the public or government (for example, building permits), or to keep a record of those in the licensed business (for example, pawnbrokers).

An inherent part of granting licenses is the power to revoke or temporarily suspend them. This sanction is used extensively and effectively. Driver's license suspensions are obvious examples. Other examples are liquor dealer license suspensions as punishments for sales to minors, restaurant license suspensions for sanitation violations, suspension and disbarment of attorneys, and non-renewal of radio station licenses for lack of sufficient public service.

The legal tool of licensing allows an innovative bill drafter much flexibility. For example, to reduce the overpopulation of deer hunters in the woods at one time (overpopulation causes hunters to shoot at one another), several states now issue part-of-season licenses. In one of these states, hunters may choose licenses either for the two opening days, for the following six days, or for the ten closing days. The later periods give the licensee more hunting days, but a depleted and more alert herd. This system keeps two-thirds of the hunters out of the woods (and out of range) during each period.

§ 22–6. Publicity; education; information. Publicity is a significant, but often cruel sanction. It strikes with bare accusation, even with no evidence of violation. Its impact is uneven; one person with a common name or routine job may suffer little from publicity about missteps, while another person may pay severely in public and private life from a similar report. Therefore, lawmakers often try to control the time and extent of publicity to limit its impact. Prosecuting attorneys, police, health inspectors, and other law enforcement agents receive legislative direction to keep their activities confidential. Authorities protect the identity of juvenile delinquents even after a judicial finding of guilt. Officials purge criminal records when specified periods elapse.

While there are valid reasons to limit public information in the interest of privacy, the bill drafter searching for ways to make legislation effective is more likely to authorize or promote publicity than to restrict it. Legislative policy, supported by the dictates of press freedom, requires that prosecutions, convictions and administrative sanctions be public. Publicity can prevent criminal activity by alerting potential victims. For example, when they learn that confidence game operators are active in a community, officials issue press statements describing the scheme. The operators may be scared off or, because of the publicity, citizens may bring enough new evidence to the agency so prosecution is possible.

Legislation sometimes requires private parties to disclose information. The main sanction to regulate the securities marketplace is forced disclosure through the requirement that new stock issues be accompanied by a prospectus and that insider buying and selling be disclosed in periodic reports.

For a period, television stations, under FCC pressure, ran one anti-smoking public service spot for each three or four cigarette commercials. This anti-smoking sanction had a significant impact, judging by smoking statistics. Thereafter, tobacco companies were not entirely unhappy when the FCC adopted a rule against all broadcast advertising of tobacco because the rule ended those effective public service ads.

In 1977, Congress enacted legislation requiring manufacturers of the artificial sweetner, saccharin, to display a specific warning stating that the product had been found to cause cancer. The legislation was a compromise to avoid a total ban on saccharin. Although the effect of the warning on consumers was not as great as expected, the effect on manufacturers was remarkable. Manufacturers have discarded saccharin for a substitute additive which requires no warning label, a result every bit as effective as a total ban.

Further examples of mandatory information disclosure used to implement legislative policy are the cigarette package health warning and other label requirements like ingredient and nutrition information, safety warnings, date coding, and batch identification.

Rights often are conditioned on notice to others. For example, deeds must be recorded to protect property title, prompt notice must be given on workers compensation claims, and financing statements must be filed to perfect security interests in commercial assets.

Freedom of information acts open the activities of government itself to examination and to the sanction of publicity. Finally, legislatures appropriate significant funds so agencies may engage in public education to help citizens make better decisions in areas like nutrition, health care, agricultural practices, and tax return preparation.

§ 22–7. **Impact statements.** One of the newer sanctions—pioneered in the environmental field— is to require preparation of an impact statement as a pre-condition for taking some action. The statement may be reviewed by an agency as part of the approval process for a permit; or the statement might simply be required as a method to force public and private decision-makers to focus on harmful secondary consequences they might otherwise overlook. Since arising as an environmental protection device, impact statements have become a means to direct attention to a variety of other economic and social consequences. This procedure qualifies as a sanction because it influences conduct; it is a legislative device to change the way people think about proposed undertakings.

§ 22–8. **Private rights.** Much legislation creates or modifies rights of private parties one against another. For example, unfair and deceptive trade practices acts give competitors who are injured the right to recover actual damages, to enjoin, and to obtain a variety of other relief. Legislation often authorizes special private remedies. The best known is treble damages, established as an antitrust remedy because the obligation simply to repay an unjust gain is an inadequate deterrent to continuing misconduct. It is much more effective if a plaintiff can say: "Give my money back. Three times!" This sanction is especially effective when the victim's lawyer goes looking for others who also can get repaid three times (less the lawyer's fee).

The triple recovery is based on experience, habit, tradition, and a rough sense of justice. Experience shows treble damages are enough to deter. Legislators are familiar with the sanction. Bill sponsors who seek less are asked to explain why they are so soft on the offender; sponsors who seek more must explain why they want to enrich careless victims and sharpshooting lawyers. It is easier to stick with the familiar remedy. In circumstances where treble damages are potentially out of balance, bill drafters may include a maximum or a minimum on the recovery.

Legislation establishes many rules of law that profoundly influence private rights. For instance, the old evidentiary statute that limited testimony about conversations with dead persons made some contracts not provable and legally worthless. Legislatures have passed guardianship statutes that throw a protective blanket over wards, relieving them of liabilities they would otherwise bear. The legislatively established right to cancel some contracts during cooling-off periods is a powerful rule of private law that controls door-to-door sales practices. Statutes of limitations, as rules of law regulating private relationships, carry out a legislative policy to end old disputes. The bill drafter working on a bill must decide when disputes under the bill should terminate. Since the answer is subjective and varies from issue to issue, shaping a limitation section is one of the most difficult tasks for bill drafters and other policymakers.

§ 22–9. Suggestions on sanctions. A few summary generalizations about sanctions are appropriate at this point.

(a) Use multiple sanctions if possible. Different citizens respond to different kinds of pressures.

(b) To discover the range of possible sanctions, think through the circumstances of the various actors in the chronological order of events. This helps to imagine what would impel a participant to the desired action at each stage, to imagine what vulnerabilities to sanctions exist at different times.

(c) Inventory the public and private agents available and trace through their circumstances in chronological order to discover points at which, with appropriate statutory direction, they may act with most efficacy to achieve the goals of the bill. Since government agencies have imperfections, private sanctions, self-help and self-actuating devices are invaluable.

(d) Examine each bill to find ways to cushion its sanctions. The drafter and sponsor are wise to consider the effect on those who will suffer the proposed sanctions and on the associates of those who violate the legislation. Sanctions should not spill over and hurt the innocent.

(e) Piggyback enforcement on other procedures as much as possible. If some existing machinery can achieve the goal of the legislation, do not create new machinery.

(f) Use affirmative rather than punitive means to achieve legislative goals. For example, free trash collection in a community keeps yards cleaner than relentless prosecution of those who fail to pick up debris.

(g) Do not equate harsh sanctions with effectiveness. A modest penalty regularly imposed accomplishes more than a severe penalty that is ignored.

CHAPTER 6

BILL DRAFTING

A. BILL DRAFTING TECHNIQUES

§ 23–1. **A first draft.** A bill drafting project goes nowhere until some words are put on paper. Bill drafting is hard writing; the intimidating effect of a clean sheet of paper is great. However, things move along when the bill drafter finally realizes the work will likely be rewritten several times and that the many rough spots can be smoothed out later.

The drafting process moves fastest when the copying machine is used to borrow a first draft. In complicated bills the drafter can borrow many sections from parallel legislation. Comparable legislation also provides a check list of what must be included in the draft bill. For example, if the bill establishes a new administrative agency, a check of prior legislation setting up another agency will indicate the need to provide for method of appointment, terms, applicability of civil service rules, salaries, powers, duties, and procedures to be followed. The copying machine helps especially in drafting amendatory bills; merely writing in new words and crossing out old words on a copy of the statute provides a quick first draft.

One way to speed drafting is to view a bill as a collection of separate parts. The easiest provisions can be drafted first. The drafter can delay drafting difficult sections until confidence is bolstered by seeing the shape of the whole bill. As sections accumulate they are put in sequence; the drafter may insert forgotten provisions at any time and rearrange everything when a more logical structure comes to mind. A grand outline is unnecessary, for sections are surprisingly self-contained.

The most powerful section is often the easiest to draft. It will state the rule of law to be imposed, or the mission of the agency to be created, or the newly imposed task to be performed. The detailed and difficult provisions are those that define when and where and to whom the law is applicable. Eventually, the bill drafter produces a product which is—ready or not—turned over to someone else for comment, study, and further drafting. Only the simplest bills should go from the start of drafting to formal introduction with but one drafter.

The struggle for a first draft can be the work of a scholar bringing academic insight into real world terms; it can be the work of a bureaucrat dealing with a problem confronting an agency; it can be a lawyer's draft of a bill responsive to a client's problem; it can be the product of a knowledgeable, career lobbyist putting together a bill for the next legislative session. In any of these instances the bill should be turned over to the legislature's professional bill drafters to be edited before it is introduced.

§ 23–2. Bill drafting office and the last draft. Every legislature has an office created to perform the full range of bill drafting services. Even though that office regularly drafts bills from scratch on request from an executive branch agency or legislator, its most critical responsibility is to put the final technical polish on all bills to be introduced. These offices routinely receive bills drafted by others and are asked to put them in form for introduction. The office may then simply make the style of the bill accord with the detailed technical rules which outsiders cannot be expected to know. In other cases the office may give a preliminary draft substantive review and suggest helpful changes.

These offices process bills when requested to do so by a legislator, so outside interests usually tap into this skilled, free service through the intervention of a legislator.

§ 23–3. Middle drafts; editing. Between the first draft of a bill and the draft prepared for introduction, the drafter often goes through innumerable rewrites. Some sections fall into good form quickly and easily. Other sections cause repeated stumbles; these usually are the critical sections setting out the extent of applicability of the law—the who, when and where. Each redraft stimulates new insights onto the complex issues addressed. Like a musician working over a difficult passage, the bill drafter will draft and redraft a single challenging section in an effort to make it match the precision of the rest of the bill. As it moves through multiple drafts, a bill also tends to grow. Additional problems come to mind and sections are added to deal with them.

The need for new insights and new provisions during rewriting suggests the value of bringing fresh minds to the effort. One person's imagination is not adequate to put together a complex bill. The primary bill drafter should pass it to others for review, comment, and drafting help. These new participants should be asked to discover problems on their own, rather than being directed simply to work on specific known difficulties. This increases the likelihood that the new reader will spot complications the primary drafter has not recognized; discovering the problems in a draft is essential to the business of polishing and refining the bill.

Involving others in the editing of a bill gives them some pride of authorship. When the suggestions of others are added, a part of the bill belongs to them and they are likely to treat the whole bill more affectionately. Political managers of a bill may even invite potential or certain opponents to participate in editing. If opponents can be accommodated early with reasonable amendments, or if they can be convinced of the sponsor's good will, their later opposition is moderated or avoided. Those adversely affected by a bill also read it with their critical faculties stimulated; they spot defects. It helps to learn of their embarrassing insights during private discussion of a proposed draft, rather than at a public hearing. Even if an opponent springs criticism at a hearing, the sponsor can quickly turn the embarrassment around by saying: "I wish you had written me about that problem when I asked for your suggestions in October."

§ 23–4. **Horizontal editing.** A most useful drafting technique is to examine a bill repeatedly from beginning to end, each time editing out only one or two kinds of defects. For example, the drafter during one examination might concentrate on the sequential numbering of the sections and subsections to correct errors which slip into a bill when provisions are eliminated, added, or rearranged. During the same examination the drafter might also check cross references between sections. This technique is called horizontal editing. It recognizes that the mind cannot be alert to everything at once. Looking for a few specific defects helps uncover mistakes which are missed during an unfocused review of the bill.

Horizontal editing works for the most complex and subtle aspects of a bill, as well as for simple grammar and style problems. Even tactical and political difficulties can be reduced by horizontal editing. For example, a major bill might address some secondary problem that is insignificant compared to the bill's main thrust. Reading the bill once with a focus on legislative tactics, and nothing else, might disclose that that one incidental provision will necessitate a referral to an additional and dangerous committee. The sponsor, having discovered the hazard it creates, can eliminate the provision from the draft.

§ 23–5. **How careful a job?** Professional bill drafters face tight deadlines in much of their work; there is competition for their time from other bill requests and other responsibilities. In each drafting effort there comes a time to call a halt, to order up a final draft for those who will carry the bill on to its fate. The bill drafters may have only a faint impression of what that fate will be. The request to draft the bill may come from a weak legislator whose bills are usually ignored. In that case, a quick, superficial draft seems appropriate. However, the idea may be significant. The drafters cannot know who might take up the issue. They also have self respect; to send out a superficial, and therefore defective, draft offends them and may hurt their professional reputation. As a consequence, most legislative drafting offices do average work on almost all bills. Bills headed for oblivion are drafted as carefully as major bills destined for legislative passage. The trivial bill is over-drafted, while the major bills are not drafted well enough. How does this effect the work of legislators and legislative advocates? It means that nearly every bill that is introduced needs editing. Each must be examined carefully, with editing pencil poised.

Drafting resources should be better allocated. The drafters should know if a bill is being drafted to be passed or to start discussion; if they are not told, they should ask. The bill drafting service in Wisconsin has developed a method to better apportion its resources. That office returns preliminary drafts to its clients clearly marked "not ready for introduction." The preliminary drafts reveal tough drafting choices to the bill requester. The client must then help make the difficult choices, drop the project, or ask the drafting service to plunge into the deep water on its own. If the client takes the third road, the agency completes the draft as best it can.

§ 23–6. Format of bills. Bills are drafted in different formats for different jurisdictions. The device used nearly everywhere when an existing statute is being amended is to draw the bill so both the old and the new law appear in the draft. Words, phrases, sentences, and paragraphs to be removed by passage of the bill are marked by ~~interlining~~. Words, phrases, sentences, and paragraphs to be added are marked by <u>underlining</u>. This system permits an easy comparison of present and proposed law. The change can be evaluated with a minimum of explanation by lobbyists. Major legislation almost always involves amendment of old statutory provisions.

The legislative advocate can rely on the drafting office to do the behind-the-scenes detail work. However, the time pressures on the drafting office become intense and, therefore, the closer an advocate brings submitted work to technical adequacy, the better the relationship with that office will be. Official bill drafting agencies prepare staff manuals on drafting which explain format and other technical details. Buying one of these manuals for regular review is a good investment of the lobbyist's time and money. The knowledgeable advocate with manual in hand can take over a share of the agency labor on a given project. That can be vital when it is necessary to beat the clock at the end of a legislative session or before an important committee hearing.

B. MANDATORY PROVISIONS

§ 24–1. **Title.** Most state constitutions require that the subject or object of a bill be stated in its title. In these jurisdictions, a bill without a title is incomplete and invalid. Even in jurisdictions where a title is not constitutionally required, legislators routinely include a title because of rules and custom. Titles alert legislators, lobbyists, press, and citizens to subjects being considered. Titles also identify existing legislation the bill will repeal or amend. Lobbyists carefully check the statute numbers in bill titles to spot assaults on those parts of the law that they are hired to protect.

Titles may be written first—as a theme for the drafter. But the title must then be rewritten when the full content of the bill is known and when all references to existing law can be included. The title must be carefully drawn, for a misleading or incomplete title can make the act or some of its parts invalid. Also, because a title is read by more people than any other part of a bill, its political impact should be carefully considered. The title must be honest, yet put the bill in a favorable light. It should not raise any suspicions or fears not justified by the real effect of the bill.

§ 24-2. **Enacting clause.** All bills include a formal statement like: "Be it Enacted by the Legislature of the Commonwealth of Pennsylvania." The enacting clause is constitutionally mandated in many states. It is now unlikely to be omitted because of modern copying and word processing equipment, but in earlier decades typists and scribes occasionally forgot the critical line. In some jurisdictions, such an error makes the bill invalid. To give this legal effect to a mechanical error is barely defensible. The enactment clause requirement is the basis for one rare, but amusing, legislative tactic. Some legislatures actually permit a foe to move to strike the enacting clause from a bill. If the motion carries, the bill is killed.

§ 24-3. **Effective date and time.** When the legislature changes the law, that change must take effect at a specific moment in time. That moment is determined by a provision in the act or by a general rule applicable to all legislation in the jurisdiction. Most legislatures have adopted a provision on effective dates as part of a general act on statutory construction. The most common of these rules is that a bill is effective the day following adoption unless the bill specifies otherwise. In other states, the general rule is that bills take effect on one specific date (some weeks after the projected adjournment of the session), unless the bill provides otherwise. Appropriation bills take effect at the start of the next fiscal year.

When an effective date is included in a bill, it should be expressed as a specific calendar date, rather than as a time interval after adoption. If the effective date is expressed as an interval, readers are forced to find out when the executive signed the bill (an inconvenience) and then calculate what day it takes effect.

The obligation of the legislative advocate, staff member, or legislator is to provide a sensible effective date by asking this set of questions on each bill: Can the bill be effective at once or is lead time necessary for public education or for preparatory work by agencies or others? How much lead time is necessary? Should different parts of the bill become effective at different times?

The time of day a law takes effect is also significant. A nearly insoluble problem arises if a bill is made effective at the moment of signing. Both the time the act was signed and the time of events affected by the act (for example, making a contract) may be hard to pinpoint. Many statutory construction acts make laws effective at 12:01 a.m. It is presumed that all events on the effective date occur after that hour.

§ 24–4. Amendment and repeal sections; implied amendment and repeal. To the extent that one act is inconsistent with another, the latter act prevails. This allows legislatures to amend and repeal by implication; that is, legislative acts may gloss over past legislation and impose a new rule, yet leave the old, dead law on the statute books. Lawyers and other citizens may then be surprised to find that a statute, apparently relevant to some significant situation, has been superseded. Such negligent legislating leaves statute books in semi-chaos, full of inconsistencies that can be sorted out only by finding the date of each enactment and giving effect to the words last adopted. Sometimes a number of amendatory laws may have to be examined in detail to discover when the inconsistency came into the law.

Another rule of statutory interpretation creates a presumption against implied repeal; it provides that inconsistent provisions are given effect if they can be reconciled in any way. Courts resist implied repeal. Judges try to find some way to give effect to any statute that has not been repealed. The practice is justified because a legislature can strike from the law any provision it wants to terminate. In theory, the rule against implied repeal pushes legislatures to clean out obsolete sections of statutes. In reality, legislators are unaware of and unmoved by this subtle rule of interpretation. But legislators, staff, and lobbyists in every jurisdiction would improve the law substantially if they worked conscientiously to keep statutes free of superseded provisions.

It is difficult to draft bills that repeal or amend all inconsistent statutes. First, the drafter must find the inconsistencies, then decide whether to repeal or rewrite. Often an inconsistent provision cannot be repealed, either because parts must continue in effect or because circumstances not covered by the new law must remain under the old. The bill drafter then must define the boundary lines of applicability between the old and new rules—a hard job. The task usually arises when the new bill is nearly complete. The drafter, eager to get on to the next project, is sorely tempted to take the easy road and rely on repeal by implication to dispose of the inconsistent provisions.

One middle road is available. When a semi-inconsistent provision turns up, the drafter can decide whether the old or the new law should have priority. Then the following useful phrases can be inserted: "notwithstanding the provision of" and "subject to the provisions of." The effect is to alert anyone who reads either section to the presence of the other section and to indicate which is to be applied when they overlap.

Of no use—prima facie proof of incomplete work, in fact—is the phrase: "other law to the contrary notwithstanding." The rule that makes the last act effective in cases of inconsistency does the same thing, so this phrase is redundant at best. If the bill drafter knows or thinks contrary law exists, she should locate that law, then repeal or amend it.

C. SOMETIMES USEFUL PROVISIONS

§ 25–1. **Statutory construction act.** A number of legal rules are, in effect, incorporated into each act adopted by a legislature. Most states have codified these rules into a statutory construction act. Included are canons of statutory interpretation, effective date provisions, definitions of standard terms, miscellaneous directions to bill drafting agencies, and a variety of other provisions. Anyone working with a legislature should become familiar with its statutory construction act.

Some of the provisions are stunning on first reading because they are so basic, like the provision: "Words of one gender include the other genders." This sentence is statutory law in at least 45 states. It also is section 4 of the Uniform Statutory Construction Act. Other particularly useful provisions of that act, which parallel provisions in effect in many jurisdictions, are:

Section 3. The singular includes the plural, and the plural includes the singular.

Section 5. Words in the present tense include the future.

Section. 6. The work "week" means 7 consecutive days.

Section 8.

(a) In computing a period of days, the first day is excluded and the last day is included.

(b) If the last day of any period is a Saturday, Sunday, or legal holiday, the period is extended to include the next day which is not a Saturday, Sunday or legal holiday.

(c) If a number of months is to be computed by counting the months from a particular day, the period ends on the same numerical day in the concluding month as the day of the month from which the computation is begun, unless there are not that many days in the concluding month, in which case the period ends on the last day of that month.

Section 11. A quorum of a public body is a majority of the number of members fixed by statute.

Section 24. The repeal of a repealing statute does not revive the statute originally repealed or impair the effect of any saving clause therein.

§ 25–2. Non-retroactivity and savings clauses. The Uniform Statutory Construction Act contains two provisions dealing with the problem of retroactivity.

Section 14, a non-retroactivity clause, reads:

(a) A statute is presumed to be prospective in its operation unless expressly made retrospective.

Section 25, a savings clause, reads:

(a) The reenactment, revision, amendment, or repeal of a statute does not, except as provided in subsection (b):

(1) affect the prior operation of the statute or any prior action taken thereunder;

(2) affect any validation, cure, right, privilege, obligation, or liability previously acquired, accrued, accorded, or incurred thereunder;

(3) affect any violation thereof or penalty, forfeiture, or punishment incurred in respect thereto, prior to the amendment or repeal; or

(4) affect any investigation, proceeding, or remedy in respect of any privilege, obligation, liability, penalty, forfeiture, or punishment; and the investigation, proceeding, or remedy may be instituted, continued, or enforced, and the penalty, forfeiture, or punishment imposed, as if the statute had not been repealed or amended.

(b) If the penalty, forfeiture, or punishment for any offense is reduced by a reenactment, revision, or amendment of a statute, the penalty, forfeiture, or punishment (if not already imposed) shall be imposed according to the statute as amended.

Common law bars retroactive effect in most cases and canons of construction presume an intent of non-retroactivity with or without statutory affirmation of the principle. Sections 14 and 25 simply codify common law. Although having two sections implies some difference between the non-retroactivity and savings clauses, they are two sides of a single coin. One covers additions to statutory provisions; the other covers repeals or subtractions from the statutes. But both do the same thing; that is, they apply old rules to the past and new rules to the future. It does not make any difference whether the change occurs from striking out words, adding words, or substituting words.

§ 25–3. **Severability clauses.** Legislatures at one time faced a judicial attitude that if any part of a legislative act was invalid the entire act would fall. This rule caused legislatures, first, to include severability clauses in most acts, and later, to include general severability rules in statutory construction acts. The uniform act contains the following typical provision:

Section 16. If any provision of a statute or the application thereof to any person or circumstance is held invalid, the invalidity does not affect other provisions or applications of the Act which can be given effect without the invalid provision or application, and to this end the provisions of the statute are severable.

This provision in general law makes severability clauses in individual acts unnecessary. Courts interpret severability clauses to accord with the basic rule of statutory interpretation, that the intent of the legislature controls. Severability saves that which the court believes the legislature wants saved, but no more. Courts did much the same with the old presumption against severability; they permitted litigants to argue that the legislature intended to keep in effect those portions of an act that were not inextricably interwoven with invalid provisions. History shows severability clauses only change the initial presumption, shifting the burden of persuasion as to what parts of an act can stand alone. Shifting that burden makes severability sections worthwhile, but it seldom changes the outcome of a case.

§ 25–4. **Purpose clauses.** Opinion is divided on whether introductory purpose sections improve or harm legislation. They are defended on the basis that an opening section stating a bill's objective helps a first-time reader understand a bill. However, the reader must study the bill itself to evaluate what its working sections really do. Purpose clauses are also defended on the ground that they aid in statutory interpretation. To a court looking for legislative intent, a purpose clause may seem useful. But opponents and proponents of a piece of legislation insert qualifications and limitations in its working provisions, not in its purpose clause. Therefore, to decide tough questions of meaning, courts and agencies must look to the substantive provisions of a law (and the requirements of justice in the case before them), rather than nonfunctional purpose clauses.

Sponsors of legislation often insert a purpose section in the draft bill to gain the political advantage of a public relations message. If that is the objective, the purpose section can be stricken as unnecessary when the bill moves close to final passage. This keeps the statute books shorter and deprives courts of purpose-section sermonettes to use as crutches when they interpret the law. After a bill is passed, most purpose clauses are seldom read anyway.

§ 25–5. **Short titles.** When a bill establishes a separate program or set of rules, an identifying name is useful, like: "This act may be cited as the Uniform Marital Property Act." The short title is adopted along with the substantive rules of the act. Statute indexes usually include a list of short titles or popular names of acts; these provide a quick way to locate the statute.

Short titles have political value; the name gives a proposal a bit of personality and individuality. It also gives a bill a handy identifier which helps in the legislative process and with the media. However, a short title usually is appended only to a bill of real substance. If a bill drafter puts one in a trivial bill, it may bring ridicule to the measure and harm its prospects.

§ 25–6. **Headnotes.** Headnotes are the bold-face captions which flag the substance of each separate section of bills and acts. Headnotes should not be confused with the short titles, which apply to a series of sections and are part of the act.

The statutory construction act in each jurisdiction determines whether headnotes are part of the law or only an editorial device. Generally speaking, headnotes are not part of the law. Some acts are exceptions to the general rule, however. The Uniform Commercial Code, for example, was written with the headnotes as part of the law. Therefore, even if the usual rule in a jurisdiction is to ignore headnotes in statutory interpretation, the rule does not apply to the UCC, for UCC headnotes contribute to the act's meaning, along with all its other words.

D. DEFINITIONS

§ **26–1. Power and utility of definitions.** A legislature may make a term in an act mean anything it wants. If an act says: "For the purposes of this act 'up' means down," then *up* does mean *down*—although that is not a helpful definition. Used properly, definitions are powerful tools to make bills shorter, more understandable, and more precise. However, this tool is overused, misused, and abused. Bill drafters can greatly improve or damage their work through definitions.

Definitions are placed at the beginning of a bill, but they should be written last. Ambiguities are discovered when a complete draft is under review. Only then does the need for various definitions become clear. Even then, all alternatives to using a definition should be considered. Before adding definitions, the drafter should try to rewrite the ambiguous provision, using modifiers and qualifying sentences. If these additions make the section too complex, the drafter is forced to divide the provision into parts and to treat some of the problems separately. The drafter should first try a substantive provision which tackles the issue directly, for example, "This act does not apply to proprietary trade schools." As a second choice the drafter can turn to definition, for example, "The term 'college' means . . .".

The bill drafter usually inserts a definition to achieve clarity. The drafter does this when no word, even with the help of modifiers, expresses an idea with sufficient precision. Obviously the drafter should use the best natural word and its statutory definition should add to or change its dictionary meaning as little as possible.

The bill drafter can also shorten a bill when one reasonably accurate term can be defined and substituted for a long or awkward enumeration that would otherwise be repeated several times in the bill. Defining *person* to make it cover almost all legal entities is the classic example of a definition that saves words.

§ 26–2. **Avoid substantive rules.** One reason to hold off writing definitions is to reduce the temptation to insert substantive rules into definition sections. Rules should be straightforward commands, and not buried in definitions. Yet bill drafters regularly misuse definitions by putting substantive law into them. Bills drawn in this style confuse the reader. A definition must never encompass the central idea of a bill; that leads to unfathomable complexity. Terms used in the definition then need definition, and the drafter ends up with three or four definitions modifying the main definition. Worst of all, when the drafter puts the heart of the bill in a definition, what is written later as the main substantive section is secondary and has meaning only if the reader plugs in the definition. It is nearly impossible to edit the mess. Usually, an expert drafter can repair a definition-bound bill only by taking it apart and putting it back together in a wholly different format.

A bill drafter can avoid the hazard of substantive rules in definition sections by using cross references between substantive sections instead of definitions. For example, a bill may use an applicability section to specify those persons subject to the rule of the bill. The section laying out the rule itself then may say: "Those persons described in [the section on applicability] shall . . .". Both sections are full of substance, and neither masquerades as definition.

§ 26–3. **Means, not includes.** Definitions should tell a reader what the defined terms mean. Most times a bill drafter should write a definition with the verb *means*—and write it tightly enough so it says what is intended. A bill should say, for example: "College means . . .". If the definition does not cover everything included in the meaning, the use of *means* is misleading. To remedy the problem, the drafter should either rewrite the definition or not define the term at all. Only when the purpose of the definition is to add some marginal idea to the natural meaning of the term should the drafter say "College includes . . .". If the intent is to take marginal things out, say: "College does not include . . .". *Includes* and *does not include* appropriately replace *means* in definitions only if the purpose is to rely primarily on the natural meaning of the term while sharpening the edges.

§ 26-4. **Other rules about definitions.** While the main imperative on definitions is that they should not include substantive provisions, there are other important rules:

Natural meanings. Defined terms should have natural meanings. Readers neglect to check back to definitions, so any unnatural meaning may be missed. Unnatural meanings are unnecessary because the English language has words which alone or in combination come close to almost any intended meaning.

Bound by definition. Once a term is defined, the draftsman must live with that definition. Whatever the context, the defined term carries its statutory definition, rather than Webster's. One routine item for bill editing is to find each sentence in which the defined term is used and to read the full definition into it. If the definition does not fit perfectly, a different word must be substituted for the defined term in that sentence or a modifier must be added.

Juxtapose definitions. If a defined term is used only once in a bill, its definition should be relocated in the section where the term is used or the definition should be eliminated and the idea the definition was to convey should be incorporated into the text. The drafter should not hide the definition at the beginning of a bill if it can be placed where the reader will more likely see it.

Avoid excessive use. The final rule is to strike every unnecessary definition. A reader expects a definition to change the normal meaning of the defined term. If it does not, the definition adds confusion to the bill, not clarity. Since definitions modify the natural meaning of terms, a defined term is dangerous to readers who overlook the definition.

E. COMMON DRAFTING ERRORS

§ 27–1. **Horizontal editing again.** A bill drafter cannot avoid errors in initial drafting; they must be found and corrected with editing. Drafters produce adequate bills on complex subjects only through repeated review of the bill, each time focusing on one or two kinds of likely problems. Each bill should also be reviewed by more than one bill drafter. The initial drafter, even one who edits expertly, overlooks some defects. An error spotted by a reviewing editor is often one of several

of the same type. Each mistake serves as a guide
for further productive horizontal editing.

Another reason to search for defective writing in
bills is that drafting errors are symptoms of policy
weakness. Writers make grammatical errors
when they lack a focus on underlying policy. For
example, if the verb is singular and the subject is
plural, the drafter usually had no firm focus on
who the subject should be.

The following sections treat bill defects that are
appropriately the focus of horizontal editing.

§ 27–2. Shall and may; should and must.
Shall is the most powerful word in the legislative
arsenal. It must not be squandered by misuse.
Shall must not be wasted by being used to put
verbs in the future tense. The future tense is
seldom needed in statutes, for a legislative act
applies to the ever-present present. The novice
bill drafter finds it unnatural to write in the present tense while thinking about the future. But
once the drafter learns to think in terms of the
time when the statute is read, the present tense
comes easily. Then those invaluable *shalls* are
saved for their proper use.

Shall is a word of command. The proper use of
shall is to give an order. If the intent is to give
permission, the word *may* is used. Between intent
to command and intent to give permission, there is
a middle ground, direction. In everyday speech,
the auxiliary verb *should* is used to direct the
person to do something. Unfortunately, statute

style has barred the use of *should*. Statute style also has barred the use of *must* as the imperative verb. This left drafters with *shall* to denote both commands and directions. Within the past decade, some jurisdictions have modified these style rules by permitting the use of *must*. Consequently, not all bill drafters are stuck using a single word to denote two different types of instruction. However, in most cases, the distinction between commands and directions must still be made through the context in which they are used.

Editing bills for *shall*, *may*, *must* and *should* produces more corrections of substance than any other single horizontal editing effort. Defensive lobbyists attack the *shalls* in bills to protect their clients from legislative intrusion. The skilled drafter follows the lead of these professionals by focusing on each *shall* and *may* to see if the bill needs a muscular *shall* inserted in a key spot or if the bill antagonizes with an offensively commanding *shall* where a *may* would suffice.

A bill editor doing horizontal editing can conveniently combine a review for one other bill weakness with a review of *shalls* and *mays*. Often when a sentence must express a negative, the negative is inaptly inserted in the subject by the one small word *no* at the beginning of the sentence: "*No* drafter shall . . .". It is clearer to insert the negative in the verb phrase immediately after *shall* or *may*; for example, "A bill drafter shall *not* hide the negative."

§ 27–3. **Or, and, and/or.** *And* is conjunctive; *or* is disjunctive; *and/or* is not used in legislation drafted by those who have self-respect, training, and iron wills. Since *and* can be both conjunctive and disjunctive, *and/or* is unneeded. If ambiguity persists, the context must be adjusted or some phrase used to make clear whether "any or all" or "one or more" is the intended meaning.

The difference between *and* and *or* may have serious substantive consequence. Perhaps because the words are so small, their significance is often missed until horizontal editing focuses attention. One example makes the point: "To qualify, a person shall be an owner of valid record title (and) (or) be in possession of the property." Which word is right? Either makes legal and grammatical sense, so the choice depends on the purpose of the legislation.

§ 27–4. **Misplaced duty.** Statutes are bossy; they give orders. But writers of bills regularly forget to direct the orders to someone. For example: "School buildings shall have fire alarms." It is difficult to hold a building accountable for its failure to have an alarm system, but this provision places the duty on the building. The problem is not simply one of style; it is often difficult for a drafter to determine who should have responsibility. In this example, the school board, the school superintendent, the local fire department, the state fire marshall, the school architect, the electrical contractor, or the general contractor might be assigned responsibility. Until the writer of a bill focuses on who must carry out the legislative purpose, a key part of writing the law has been omitted. To work, the law must give orders to and impose sanctions on some human. For example: "The school superintendent shall arrange for installation and maintenance of fire alarms in all school buildings."

§ 27-5. Jargon. A mental quirk of many bill writers compels them to fill their bills with *such.* *Such* usage offends readers not brainwashed to think *such* words belong in *such* writing. A bill drafter can take out almost every *such:* by deleting some; substituting *the, this,* or *these* for others; and inserting honest words that contribute legal meaning in place of still others. To use *such* is bad bill drafting.

Professor Reed Dickerson in Legislative Drafting (a short and useful book) lists additional forbidden words:

above (as an adjective)	said (as a substitute for "the," "that," or "those")
aforesaid	
afore-mentioned	same (as a substitute for "it," "he," "him," etc.)
and/or	
before-mentioned	
herein	to wit
hereinafter	whatsoever
hereinbefore	whensoever
provided that	wheresoever

Professor Dickerson did not exhaust the available examples of bill drafting jargon. But to present even this short list may do as much harm as good. It would be better if bill writers were not exposed to the words in the first place.

To eliminate jargon, an editor looks for words and phrases that say in stilted ways what should be said simply, that say indirectly what should be said directly, and that say with technical words what should be said with everyday vocabulary. The bill writer who uses legalistic words wants to make the bill sound legal, but she loses the virtue most desired—clear meaning. A good bill drafter aims at a style of writing worthy of her brightest non-lawyer acquaintance.

§ 27–6. **Parallelism.** A bill drafter must struggle to maintain a consistent grammatical style (parallelism) throughout a list of items or ideas. To do so, one must develop consistency in thought, for grammatical breakdowns occur when items in a list are thought of in different ways. For example, a list of duties falls apart grammatically if the duties are not imposed on the same person, if some are conditional and others are absolute, if some are active and others are passive, if some are procedural and others are substantive, if some are affirmative and others are negative. The reviewing editor who finds a mixed-up list in a bill can invariably improve the substance of the bill by putting the list into a consistent grammatical form.

§ 27–7. **Lists and modifiers.** Bill drafters often create ambiguity when a list of items is followed by a modifier. The reader may be uncertain whether the modifier applies to the whole list or only to the last item. For example, consider this clause: ". . . subject to deeds, mortgages, liens, and financing statements *when filed.*" Do all have to be filed or only financing statements? The drafter can avoid the ambiguity by repeating the modifier or moving it so it unmistakably applies to all items. ". . . subject, *when filed,* to deeds, mortgages . . .". Or, if the other meaning is intended, the modified item can be moved to the beginning of the list along with its modifier. ". . . subject to *financing statements when filed,* deeds, mortgages . . .".

§ **27–8. Cross references.** Among the drafter's tools, few aid the reader more than cross references. These road signs tell the reader which sections take precedence (notwithstanding section ___), which are subordinate (subject to section ___), which must be read together (as provided in section ___), which offer alternatives (unless section ___ is applicable). Cross references allow a drafter to simplify the complex. For example: "this act applies to the persons specified in section ___, in the circumstances specified in section ___ at the times specified in section ___, and subject to the exclusions in section ___."

Cross references cause more mechanical mistakes in statutes then anything else. The final chore in bill drafting is a miserably boring check for accuracy in the use of these useful phrases.

Invariably, adding or deleting subsections or sections throws off the cross references. Only a careful last minute review of each referenced section avoids error.

§ 27–9. **Grammer.** Good legislative drafting varies little from other good writing; it requires adherence to the basic rules of grammar. Basic grammatical rules of style particularly applicable to statutes are: use the present tense, use the indicative or imperative mood rather than the subjective, use the active voice rather than the passive, use the singular in preference to the plural, and use the third person. Because ambiguity is the great fault, the bill drafter must adhere infallibly to one standard grammar rule: make the antecedent of every pronoun unmistakable. Edit every bill horizontally matching pronouns and antecedents.

To avoid ambiguity, bill drafters avoid one technique of good style. Synonyms cannot be mixed in a bill to achieve variety of expression. In statutes different words are presumed to convey different meanings. Consistency cannot be sacrificed to achieve a more interesting style. For example, if *bank* and *banking facility* are both used in an act, the reader appropriately expects a different meaning for each term. For one meaning, the drafter must use only one term.

F. TACTICAL DRAFTING

§ 28–1. Involve opponents. Sponsors can help pass their bill by bringing opponents into the drafting process so completely that the foes voice all their questions, objections, twits, and rages while the bill is being written—prior to the time the legislative committee gathers to consider it. An invitation to participate in drafting disarms potential opponents. The foes can hardly refuse the invitation, for a refusal shows an intransigence not in accord with the compromising spirit of legislative institutions. Nearly every significant bill eventually forces a collaboration of its sponsors and those who originally wanted the bill to disappear. Therefore, wise sponsors start early to listen, to bargain, and to accommodate.

Supporters of a proposal usually need an official arena in which to meet with likely opponents to go over a preliminary draft. An executive-agency invitation extended to probable opponents is especially difficult to ignore. At an agency-sponsored meeting, a preliminary bill draft will focus discussion on the precise solution offered, will bring to mind the alternatives available for each provision and will narrow differences. A draft prevents diversionary and pointless arguments over principles; it gets the participants working on actual words and concrete ideas.

If sponsors have enough endurance, they can sometimes pass a bill by having so many drafting sessions and so many rewrites that opponents lose interest, wear out, or decide opposition has reached a point of diminishing returns. The name of this game is "Wear the bastards down." Of course, opponents must win some concessions along the way so they have a basis to rationalize giving up the fight. Otherwise they may get as stubborn as the sponsors.

§ **28–2. Limit scope.** A bill should be drafted so that on introduction it ruffles as few feathers as possible. If, from the beginning, the drafter of a regulatory bill limits coverage to the prime targets, a smaller corps of opponents will show up. Once a group has lined up in opposition, it is hard to get that group out of the line-up of opponents. Even a tactical amendment to cut the group out of the bill cannot entirely erase its suspicions. Lobbyists threatened by a bill also may agree at an early date to stick together to the end, even if some of their clients are later amended out of the bill's coverage. The excluding amendment does not help the bill's passage as much as leaving the group out in the first place.

Furthermore, the late appearing exclusion is no compromise to those left on the hook. When opponents see that other targets of the bill have won exemption while they still bear the full impact of the bill, they make the effective point that their clients are being discriminated against. The best compromise leaves those subject to the bill semi-molified and convinced that the bill sponsors acted as fairly as possible in pursuing their objective. A bill may be intentionally drawn to allow room for this kind of compromise; that is, it may be made unnecessarily strong so as to establish a tougher starting point for bargaining. The idea, then, is to leave room for effective compromise with those subject to the bill's provisions. The negative side of that strategy is that initial opposition may be more intense.

§ 28–3. Intentional vagueness.

Some provisions of a bill can be drawn (1) to offend little, but also to gain little for its sponsors, (2) to achieve 100 percent of the sponsor's objective, though to do so will spark vigorous opposition, or (3) to finesse a critical issue by leaving it up in the air. Which choice should a sponsor select? The first makes the job of passing the bill easier, for opponents are less aroused; most of the battle is left for a later day. The second choice gives a sponsor some trading stock for compromise and, if the bill is passed with the particular provision included, the victory is more significant. But the sponsor runs the risk that the tough bill will not pass. The third choice makes the bill incomplete. It will bother those who want the legislature to deliver certainty in the law. And when the issue is later decided in another arena, such as a court or agency or trade association, or by subsequent legislation, the issue that has been sidestepped may be resolved against the sponsor. On the other hand, vagueness may cause those affected to overlook some hazard in the bill

or to decide they are willing to gamble on ultimately winning the finessed decision. The sponsor then
faces milder opposition and a simpler legislative
battle.

There is no one correct choice, but the third
option, intentional vagueness, serves legislatures
well and often. It may be adopted consciously,
occur by oversight, or turn up as a compromise
during negotiation on the bill. Legislators eagerly
duck tough questions if answering them threatens
the passage of a bill for which a consensus has
developed.

G. PACKAGING BILLS

§ 29–1. **The strategy of bill packaging.**
Some proponents of legislation proceed with an
attitude that style rules or custom or fate dictates
the general shape of each bill. They carelessly
leave important tactical decisions to neutral bill
drafting technicians, decisions that will control, for
example, whether the bill will be long or short,
whether it will amend the current statute or replace it with entirely new language, and whether it
will address problems comprehensively or piece-
meal.

The wisest advocates do not take for granted the
shape of their bills. They turn their thoughts to
legislative strategy early in the drafting process.
They make tactical decisions on how their proposals will be packaged, decisions that in many cases
will profoundly effect the likelihood of success or

failure for that legislative undertaking. The following sections discuss some of the packaging
choices available to the legislative advocate.

§ 29–2. Housekeeping bills and woodchucks.

A favorite legislative line is: "This is just a housekeeping bill." That tells legislators to let down
their guard, to relax, to trust. It says, this bill is
routine business, just fixing up loose ends. The
"housekeeping bill" may be pages long. In the
honest housekeeping bill, section after section im-
proves grammar and style, corrects obvious errors,
adjusts agency fees to inflation, and so on. The
bill may extend the coverage of successful programs and rules slightly beyond their original limits. It may take account of new technology. It
may shift responsibility from agency to agency. It
may adjust state law to changes in federal law.

But deep in a housekeeping bill some section
may insert into the statute a few words with substantive implications worthy of careful thought.
The housekeeping bill may hide—innocently or
deceitfully—the wolf in sheep's clothing. (In some
states victims of these provisions of hidden substance call them woodchucks, but terminology varies.)

Over the long haul, legislative tacticians do best
by packaging legislation in honest bills, bills without hidden impacts. Earned trust passes bills.
Therefore, the sponsor of a housekeeping bill must
keep it honest. Sponsors must also bear in mind
the danger that someone may find a "woodchuck"

in what was intended as a perfectly innocent provision. Faced with a provision that might be perceived as not entirely technical, the sponsor should offer the cautionary note that: "There is a little substance in Section 10, but the rest of the bill is pure housekeeping."

When sponsors have both substantive and technical objectives, they often do best to separate the provisions into two bills—one for noncontroversial housekeeping, the other for those provisions that have policy implications. The technical provisions are offered, and in large part accepted, on faith; the sponsor then concentrates educational and persuasive work on the substantive half of the two-bill package. The package almost always seems less weighty than one all-purpose bill because it puts less burden of study on legislators. The wheat of substance, concentrated in a relatively short bill, is conveniently separated from the chaff of technicality. The single bill, in contrast, forces readers to watch out for substance in every section of a much longer bill.

§ 29–3. **Department bills.** The department bill carries an aura of innocence much like the housekeeping bill, but that aura comes from the bill's origination in a public agency, rather than from its lack of substantive significance. Legislators approach a bill generated by a department of government with a different set of suspicions than are turned on a bill brought to the legislature by a private interest. Legislators expect bureaucrats to act in the public interest because that is what the bureaucrat is hired to do. Agency officials often advise legislative committees, playing a role much like regular legislative staff. This leads to the kind of trust that translates into a presumption of good intention when the legislature examines the bill offered by that department. A legislature looks with a different mind set at bills brought in by banks, by labor, by truckers, or by utilities. The advocate for those interests has a responsibility to act honestly, but legislators know that honesty does not preclude pressing for special favor and privilege.

The private lobbyist can occasionally take advantage of the trust between legislature and agency by persuading an agency to include in a department bill provisions of value to the lobbyist's clients. The agency more or less fronts for the private interest. Regulated industry, and the regulator, together tell legislators that the bill is "wholly in the public interest." This severely tests the legislative capacity to make a critical assessment of the bill. To package a long-sought change of law in the homey wrapping of a department bill is a lobbyist's dream.

§ 29–4. Codification and recodification bills. Legislators accept pretty much on faith bills that purport simply to clean up the form of some part of the law or to incorporate case law into statutory form. These extraordinary "housekeeping" bills that codify or recodify the law usually come from non-political institutions like law revision commissions or from ad hoc drafting groups manned by legislative staff or academic reporters. All participants swear off private interest and political machinations, and success usually follows the drafting effort when that pledge is kept.

This does not mean that codification and recodification bills do not make substantive change in the law. A significant share of law reform comes by reworking and rethinking a subject area during the process of codification or recodification. The change seems more academic than political, but it is change nonetheless.

§ **29–5. Crusher bills.** One kind of bill, much like a codification bill but with huge measures of acknowledged substantive change, is primarily the product of one organization—the National Conference of Commissioners on Uniform State Laws (NCCUSL). The Uniform Commercial Code is the ultimate example.

The UCC, having been worked out with the nation's leading commercial interests, was delivered to state legislatures by those interests in 1952 with the request to pass the lengthy bill without changing a word. The Pennsylvania legislature acquiesced in 1953, but the New York legislature balked and other legislatures simply watched and waited. The New York legislature finally passed the UCC in 1962, after several years of intense study conducted by its Law Revision Commission and after putting on the substantial amendments recommended by that commission. The NCCUSL incorporated the New York amendments into the official UCC and thereafter other legislatures fell into line by adopting this revised draft. Fell into line with what? With the local commercial establishment, with the dominant commercial state of the nation, with the Philadelphia lawyers who had first embraced the act, and with the NCCUSL (a familiar source of acts on obscure and complex topics).

The UCC, nearly 100,000 words long and of exceeding complexity and subtlety, was beyond the institutional capacity of legislatures to rework in any detail. This bill and others like it are "crushers." Any legislature will either ignore a crusher bill, or pass it, depending on external advocacy. The job of measuring the merit of the proposal is candidly delegated to other institutions. Such delegation is practical and appropriate. It saves legislative energy for more political work that must be done within the legislature itself—work that cannot be delegated.

Every few decades most bodies of statutory law reach an age where their maturity begins to show. Even a flexibly written and hugely successful statute like the Uniform Commercial Code has attracted the rewriters. At the instigation of the same interests who promoted the initial drafting of the code, the NCCUSL redrafted Articles 8 and 9 of the Code in the 1970's. Year by year since then various legislatures have enacted these articles in

their revised form. In 1985 the NCCUSL promul-
gated a Uniform Personal Property Leasing Act, a
supplement to the UCC, to plug the gap in commercial law created by the burgeoning leasing industry. The NCCUSL has now commenced a rewrite of UCC Articles 3 and 4 to take account of
the substitution of electronic fund transfers for
checks.

What does this history mean to a legislative
advocate? It means some legislative objectives can
be successfully packaged in huge bills.   It also
means the lobbyist concerned about commercial
law over the coming decade must keep an eye on
what the caretakers of the UCC are doing. The
legislative deliberations of greatest relevance to
many commercial lawyers occur in the committees
of the NCCUSL. Experience shows that the legislatures likely will accept verbatim the NCCUSL
redrafts of the UCC articles. Commercial interests
resist efforts in the legislature to undo these packages, for legislative changes take out of the quasi-
academic world and put into the political arena
issues that the commercial community prefers to
thrash out in the safer environment of a three to
five year drafting effort by the NCCUSL.

A bill does not have to reach the dimensions of
the UCC to be a crusher. Often using the extra
long bill pays dividends. When a bill reaches a
certain length, it intimidates the legislators. They
look for a consensus among the interest groups
affected instead of giving the bill meaningful inde-

pendent review. With no one raising objections, most legislators happily skip serious study of even a ten page bill. They take it on faith.

Long bills are highly efficient, measured by the effort expended against the results achieved. However, measured by the amount of thought brought to bear on each legal change, long bills are less likely to produce sound legislative judgments. Sponsors often do well to use long bills, but those legislators and others sitting in review of the bill should allocate study time according to its substance. This would lead to more study for most multi-page bills. Legislators habitually give the one-paragraph bill many times more attention per word than they give to longer bills. Logically a bill with twenty-five substantive sections should get as much deliberation as twenty-five single-section bills, but legislatures do not work that way.

When a long bill is being reviewed, attention lags before review is complete. Since almost everyone reads bills starting at section one, closing sections are rarely read with the attention of a fully alert mind. The sponsor may take advantage of this fact by hiding a sensitive or unpopular section near the end of a bill, rather than putting it where logical organization dictates. Sometimes an alert reviewer finds the most significant provision in a bill in its last or next to the last section, where the repeal of some significant statute will appear.

§ **29–6. Omnibus bills and the package of bills.** An omnibus bill gathers somewhat related, but separate, provisions into a single bill that is not quite either codification or housekeeping. Legislatures use omnibus bills most notably to structure appropriations into packages covering a distinct subject area, a package that can be conveniently processed by one appropriations subcommittee. Other legislative efforts are also sometimes combined into larger bundles appropriately called omnibus bills.

The omnibus bill device can best be understood by contrasting it with the tactical alternative—a series of separate bills. When political pressure creates a legislative desire to respond to a problem, the response can be in one grand bill or in a series of bills clustered around that problem. An example is a major campaign for tax reform. One assumption is that tax revision will come in a single bill, or not at all. The strategy, then, is to construct an omnibus bill that will sufficiently satisfy all the disparate forces for change so they will unite to overcome the separate constituencies opposed to closing each of the targeted loopholes.

Proponents of tax reform could adopt quite a different legislative strategy. The tax revision program could be divided into five, ten, twenty or more separate bills to be enacted by Congress *seriatim*. The hope would be to pass each bill with votes of legislators generally favoring tax reform, yet allow each member of Congress to cast a *no*

vote on the act or acts in the package most offensive to the groups with which the congressman is
allied. The legislative war might thus be convert-
ed into several dozen divide-and-conquer
skirmishes.

In choosing between the package of separate bills
and the omnibus bill, a sponsor must evaluate the
support and opposition to each separate objective.
He must determine whether combining the
changes builds a consensus of support or accumu-
lates opposition. He must decide whether lukewarm legislators will take the bad with the good in
the omnibus bill or reject the good because of the
bad. He must also look ahead to judge whether
some of the toughest pieces of the program can
pass in the future without the attraction of the full
package. The efficient use of the sponsor's time is
also a consideration. Handling a number of small
bills is more work than handling the same program in a single large bill.

The opportunity for double-dealing is clearly
higher when action is taken piece-meal, rather
than in one fell swoop. A few pieces will be lost if
isolated from the "package." But maybe the
pieces that cannot carry themselves on a separate
vote should be lost, for the separate bill strategy
allows the legislative process to focus sharply on
the merit of each piece of the package rather than
confronting each member with an "all or nothing"
choice.

§ **29–7. Half-step bills.** On many problems, political timeliness and legislative desire to act outrun the intellectual raw material available. This situation may arise when a rule of law must be changed before any substitute is ready for legislative enactment. To respond, the legislature may pass a half-step bill, one which cancels the old rule, leaving it to commerce or the judiciary to fill the newly created blank in the law. In one jurisdiction, for example, a statute established the rule that in the sale of real property the only implied warranty was a warranty of good title. When the legislature later wanted to open the way to warranties of fitness for the use intended, it felt unready to spell out the types of properties and sales to be included, the remedies, the circumstances in which there would be a right to contract out of implied warranties, and the obligation of a buyer to inspect the property. So the bill as adopted simply repealed the prohibition on warranties. The effect was the same as if the legislature passed an act that provided simply: "In the sale of real property, warranties in addition to a warranty of good title may be implied to the extent appropriate." This bill removed the barrier of the old law and allowed the courts to develop incrementally the specifics of a new and better law.

A common legislative response to a problem, when no legislative solution is known, is this simplistic, half-bill approach: the legislature describes the problem, it declares the problem will be met, and it establishes an agency to do the job. At one time or another legislatures have, for example, dumped environmental protection, energy management, and mass transit into the laps of agencies to which they gave little direction and few resources. Constituents could not say the legislature ignored the problem, although that is about what it did. Sometimes this abdication of legislative responsibility may even work.

§ **29–8. Trailer bills.** Almost invariably when a legislature first passes a major bill it drops a few stitches. Agencies and lawyers and businesses discover these mistakes as they prepare to live under the new legislation. The dropped stitches must be picked up in the next legislative session in a special kind of housekeeping bill. Legislators view these bills as so inevitably necessary that they pass easily, although the institution may fight over what will be included. One name for these follow-up bills is "trailer bills."

The phenomenon of the trailer bill reveals another tactic relevant to bill packaging. Bills establishing large new programs often include an effective date that puts off the start of the program for many months. The delayed effective date is a particularly effective way to deal with technical objections and claims of infeasibility. The sponsoring organization promises to prepare before the distant effective date a faultless trailer bill to cure all claimed defects. The program, in effect, is offered as a two-bill package, the initial bill which is being harshly examined and a yet-to-drafted trailer bill of pledged perfection.

PART III

PERSPECTIVES ON LEGISLATIVE POWER

CHAPTER 7

LEGISLATIVE POLICY MAKING

A. SOURCES OF LEGISLATIVE POWER

§ 30–1. **The republican system.** The republican system of government (representative democracy) is the form of the federal government and is imposed by the United States Constitution upon the states as a condition of membership in the union. In a republican system, legislative power resides in an elected representative body. Legislative power is the authority to make public policy through the enactment of statutes. Each legislative body derives its power from the constitution of the jurisdiction it serves.

§ 30–2. **Congress has delegated powers.** The federal Congress possesses only those powers that have been delegated to it by the states through their ratification of the United States Constitution and amendments to it. The tenth amendment to the Constitution reads: "The powers not delegated to the United States by the Constitution nor prohibited by it to the states, are reserved to the states, respectively, or to the people." This amendment makes it clear that Congress possesses only delegated powers. Accordingly, each act of Congress must be founded on some power granted in the United States Constitution.

Congress has found legal justification for nearly anything it has wanted to enact. This fact is largely attributable to another clause that dramatically expands the granted powers of Congress. Article I, Sec. 8, clause 18, says Congress has the power "To make all laws which shall be necessary and proper for carrying into execution the foregoing powers, and all other powers vested by this Constitution in the government of the United States, or in any department or officer thereof." Courts have grown accustomed to finding most acts of Congress "necessary and proper" to implement some granted power, notably the commerce clause.

§ 30–3. **States have residual power.** State legislative power is residual; it differs fundamentally from congressional power which is delegated. State constitutions contain a provision creating a legislative branch. Having once established a legislature, a state constitution need go no further; all the legislative power of the state naturally falls to that institution. Any additional words regarding legislative power either act to limit the legislature in some way or are superfluous. A state constitution is consulted to find limitations on legislative power. It is not necessary to have an affirmative grant of power as authority for any specific piece of legislation.

§ 30–4. Local units have delegated powers.

Legislative power also resides in municipal councils, school boards, county commissioner boards, and boards for other units of local government. Like Congress, local units of government possess only those powers delegated to them. Select powers, out of the full set of state sovereign powers, are given to local units either by the state constitution or through legislation delegating responsibility for policy making on certain issues. Each local ordinance or resolution, like each act of Congress, must be based, therefore, on a specific grant of power.

B. CHARACTER OF LEGISLATIVE LAW

§ 31–1. Statutory law.

Lawmaking is a partnership of legislature and court. Rules of law, whether made by court or legislature, represent public policy. Legislatures continually make and remake legal rules as they work to shape public policy to reflect current knowledge and values. The dynamic character of legislative lawmaking challenges lawyers to aid both clients and the public by participating in the legislative process, rather than simply accepting legislative law as is.

Still, a lawyer advising clients on what the law is must turn to the statute books, not to a bill drafter. No matter what field a lawyer works in, legislative law is dominant. In commercial law the Uniform Commercial Code is the primary source of legal rules. Consumer protection acts are significant in affecting the operation of the marketplace. The law of marriage and divorce comes from the legislature. Legislation provides the basic rules for criminal law, probate administration, securities and corporate law, debtor's and creditor's rights. Benefits under welfare programs, medicare, workers compensation and vocational rehabilitation are set and administered pursuant to legislative action. The more specialized fields of law—labor law, local government law, patent law, bankruptcy law, antitrust law—are built primarily on legislation. Federal and state administrative procedure acts provide the foundation for the processes of administrative law. Even in the ancient field of property law, recording acts, condominium acts, and acts modifying old common law principles in landlord-tenant relationships significantly affect the law.

This list of legal fields dominated by legislation establishes that legislatures are the pre-eminent lawmaking institutions of our society. The proposition stands even omitting the pervasive impact of tax legislation on personal and business activities.

§ 31–2. **Statutory rule equals case rule.** Despite its omnipresence in daily life, many lawyers carry a distorted impression of legislative law. Practitioner and scholar view rules made by legislative bodies as different from rules derived from appellate court precedents; they view legislation as more authoritative, more rigid, more meddlesome, less lawyerly. A sounder understanding is Judge Vinson's ". . . the law is all the law there is, the law is more for the parties than for the courts, the people will rely upon and adjust their behavior in accordance with all the law *be it legislative or judicial or both*." (Warring v. Colpoys, 122 F.2d 642 (D.C.1941)).

Judicial and legislative law speak to society with equal authority. Both are backed by sanctions, both are subject to change to account for new conditions and new wisdom, and both are forward looking in their impact. In addition, the law from each institution is often modified by the other. Lawmaking is indeed a partnership of court and legislature.

§ 31–3. **Relative lawmaking advantages of legislatures and courts.** Legislatures make broad general rules that carry the law in new directions. Legislatures, through the process of codification, also organize and streamline the law, thus simplifying it. In these tasks, legislative bodies possess significant advantages. They have extensive resources available for research and broader input from experts in the community. Several volumes of background material may be produced on a single legislative proposal.

To the judicial system falls the task of lawmaking in the context of actual fact situations. A court makes law with hindsight. Lawmaking by judicial precedent, our system of common law, has demonstrated the great capacity of courts to recognize what is just in the context of a particular controversy. Making a fair rule for the case at hand produces a just precedent for the future.

In the partnership of court and legislature, the judicial branch refines the generalizations of the legislature, fills in the blanks in legislative enactments, and incorporates into the lawmaking mechanism the basic values embodied in constitutions, which on occasion are overlooked amidst the pressures of legislative conflict.

Historically, our nation has devoted greater intellectual energies to the judicial lawmaking function. Society has allocated inadequate intellectual resources to the legislative branch. The partnership could work better if more effort were given to improving the quality of legislative lawmaking.

§ 31–4. **Rigidity of statute law.** In the partnership of court and legislature, the legislature contributes the most dramatic changes in the law, but it also has a stultifying effect on specific rules. The rigidity of statute law arises from the tendency of the legislature to ignore a field of law once it has enacted a basic code in the area. The work of past legislatures in the fields of property law, probate law, commercial law, patent law, bankruptcy law, securities law, and other private law fields is not reexamined with appropriate regularity. Those who seek to reform old legislative enactments in the private law area, which is largely nonpolitical, must struggle to get the attention of the legislature. That attention is more likely to go to the issues of appropriations, taxation, and government operation.

The rigidity in statutory law is a product of the legislature's policy-making sovereignty. When a statute is enacted, courts are restricted in their authority to impose a conflicting policy. A court may find itself forced to adhere to the statute even though this produces an unjust result. In other words, when the legislature has acted in a field of law, the judicial system may be foreclosed from the law reform that would otherwise come through judicial decisions. Legislative action in a field theoretically reduces by half the opportunity to reform the law and forces on courts the policy judgments of a legislative body even when those judgments have become obsolete. The converse is not the case. If a judicial decision has left a defect in the law, that defect is concurrently subject to either legislative or judicial correction.

Courts quite effectively escape this theoretical trap. Using constitutional principles, courts set aside a share of legislative errors. Courts also choose to misread statutes to produce justice in the cases before them; the result is that they modify statute law to accord with current knowledge and necessity. If judges fully appreciated the obstacles to legislative reform of private law, they might provide even more imaginative statutory interpretation to strengthen the lawmaking partnership of court and legislature. Lawyers, as advocates in court, ought to encourage this progressive treatment of legislative acts.

§ 31–5. A proposal for judicial power to modify statutes. Dean Guido Calabresi of Yale, bothered by statutory rigidity, has proposed that courts take to themselves the authority to modify statutes that no longer "fit the legal landscape." The title of his 1982 book, *A Common Law for the Age of Statutes*, catches the gist of what he proposes. Critics of Calabresi's suggestion say it is undemocratic, that he asks courts to usurp legislative authority.

A bill I drafted in the mid 1970's and introduced in the Minnesota senate offers an alternative way to give courts a common law function in this age of statutes. When passed, my bill will accomplish Calabresi's purpose, while avoiding the charge of usurpation. By enacting the bill a legislature will authorize courts to modify, in the interests of justice, any statute (1) more than 20 years old and (2) within the category of private law. With the bill, a legislature, in effect, requests courts to help with the impossible chore of bringing old statutes up to date.

The Minnesota senate passed the bill in 1982. In both 1985 and 1986, the Senate committee again recommended that the bill pass. However, the Senate leaders did not schedule the bill for floor action after it lost in a House of Representatives Committee by a single vote. These affirmative

Senate actions, though they have not yet made the bill law, demonstrate that legislators find the idea of judicial repair of old statutes acceptable. At least, they find it acceptable after it has been carefully explained to them.

C. FORM OF LEGISLATIVE LAW

§ 32–1. **Acts and session laws.** A bill which makes its way completely through the legislative process is filed by the chief executive with the secretary of state. The filed copy, called the enrolled bill, is the most authoritative record of statutory law. After the annual or biennial legislative session, each jurisdiction publishes books of session laws in which acts appear as chapters, numbered in the order they were filed with the secretary of state. These volumes are entitled "Laws of (State) 19__." The session laws of the United States are entitled "United States Statutes at Large, _____ Congress, First (or Second) Session." At the municipal level, ordinances are generally filed with a city or village clerk and published in a legal newspaper. Copies of single acts or ordinances are available from various offices.

§ 32–2. **Compilations.** A shelf of books containing the laws enacted by each legislative session since the founding of a state includes all the statutory law of that jurisdiction. But to make legislative law usable, someone must publish it in a form that groups together by topic all currently effective provisions. For example, provisions relating to

traffic laws, no matter when passed, must be included in one chapter and placed in logical order.
The publication containing general and permanent
statutory law of the jurisdiction arranged by subject and reflecting all legislative changes up to the
date of publication is called a statutory compilation. Only seventeen states publish official compilations. In thirteen of these states, publication is
done regularly every few years by an officer of the
state with the title Revisor of Statutes or Code
Revisor.

A significant benefit of official compilation is
that the legislature may amend the law by reference to the compilation. The procedure followed
in states without official compilation is to refer in
amending legislation to the original enactment and
to all subsequent amendments by session law number. When the amendment is to a provision of the
law which has been frequently changed, the result
is a bill nearly impossible to understand. Despite
obvious advantages, universal acceptance of regular official compilation has been blocked by two
obstacles. First, a large investment is necessary to
produce the initial compilation; and second, a substantial annual appropriation is required to maintain an office of the professional quality needed to
keep the compilation up-to-date session after session.

§ 32–3. **Annotated statutes.** Private law
book publishers produce compilations to make the
statutory law readily available in states with and

without official compilations. Lawyers, courts, and legislatures treat these unofficial compilations as the source books for the statutory law of the state. The unofficial compilations take on the character of official compilations in everyday life.

To make their compilations more useful, private publishers add annotations referring to relevant judicial precedents, law review articles, attorney general opinions, and legislative histories. Annotated statutes are a primary tool for legal research in states both with and without official compilations. Sets of annotated statutes are published for all fifty states, the District of Columbia, Puerto Rico and the Virgin Islands. The United States Code Annotated is the comparable publication covering the acts of the United States Congress.

§ 32–4. Law revisions. From time to time legislatures undertake law improvement efforts called law revisions. A law revision is a single act by which the legislature repeals and reenacts the entire statutory law on a particular topic or on all topics. If the act covers all the legislative law of the state, it is called a bulk revision; if it covers one subject, it is called a topical revision. Revision starts with a compilation. The compilation, rather than merely being published, is brought to the legislature as a bill which the legislature affirmatively enacts. The pre-existing acts from which the compilation is constructed are repealed. The adoption of revised laws is the essential first step in instituting a system of official continuous compilation. But even if a jurisdiction misses the opportunity to begin official compilation, the housekeeping involved in the adoption of revised laws is probably essential at least twice each century.

Law revision can be substantive, or it can be limited to organization and style. If substantive, a revision updates the rules of the substantive statutory law. Often, though, the effort is limited to improving the form of the law by eliminating duplicate and obsolete provisions and by organizing the acts adopted by the legislature over the years into orderly chapters, sections, and sub-sections, without changing their substantive effect.

§ 32–5. **Codification.** The activity of codification complicates the vocabulary of legislation. Codification is distinguished from law revision because it always involves substantive change in the law and because it not only reworks the jurisdiction's statutory law but also puts into the statutes relevant rules of law derived from judicial precedent. A code is a systematic and comprehensive statement of all the principal rules of law in a particular field, which statement is then adopted as an act of the legislature. States have made great achievements in law improvement by codification because the process blends the output of both lawmaking institutions in society—the judiciary and the legislature. Examples of significant codifications are the Uniform Commercial Code, corporate codes, probate codes, criminal codes, motor vehicle codes, and administrative procedure acts.

The drawbacks to codification are that it is so often badly done and it contributes to the rigidity of the law.

CHAPTER 8

RUNNING GOVERNMENT

A. LEGISLATURE AS OPERATOR OF GOVERNMENT

§ 33–1. Creating and financing government agencies. A constitution provides the broad charter for the organization of government. The task of completing the organization falls to the legislative branch. The executive branch agencies are created by legislative acts. Reorganizing and updating these agencies is a constant legislative activity. In addition, the legislature usually has responsibility for creating the judicial tribunals, including municipal, probate, juvenile, county, family, general trial, and appellate courts.

After it establishes the structure of government, the legislature must appropriate funds to keep the machinery operating. Budgets of executive-administrative agencies depend upon legislative appropriations or upon fees authorized by legislation. Within the legislative institution, the appropriation task consumes more energy than any other. The power of the purse insures that bureaucrats of the executive branch, over time, are extremely sensitive to the opinions of the legislative branch. In a power struggle between the elected executive and the legislative branch, the government bureaucracy is as much an ally of the legislature as of the executive. The executive may claim loyalty from appointed agency heads, and those who hope for future appointments, but the legislature has as allies the career employees who are permanently dependent on appropriations.

§ 33–2. **Structuring and overseeing local government.** State legislatures not only create and fund state government, they also dictate the pattern of local government organization and finance. The form and power of municipalities, the role of counties, the method of school district organization all depend upon legislation. Special service districts and regional government agencies arise out of legislative decisions. Programs of state aids (state taxes re-distributed to local governments) provide significant municipal and school money. In addition, local taxing power comes from legislative authorization and is subject to whatever restrictions the legislature imposes. Substantial portions of the work of every state legislature involves structuring and overseeing local government.

§ 33–3. **Legislative oversight.** The legislature carries an obligation to oversee the work of government agencies. To increase public confidence and regain control of its creations, the legislature has attempted through legislative oversight to increase its control over agencies. Legislative oversight is a generic phrase describing attempts to ensure that administrative agencies perform their functions adequately and within the parameters of the enabling legislation.

The primary objective of legislative oversight is to make the bureaucracy sensitive to the public's concerns by holding the agencies politically accountable for their actions. Many techniques are used to keep agencies to their intended subordinate power positions. A basic oversight function occurs during the appropriation process, when the performances of agencies are examined and evaluated. However, oversight is not all concerned with money. Hearings on proposals to change missions, to reorganize departments, and to alter procedures enable legislatures to examine the performance of agencies. Senate confirmation of executive appointees also provides an occasion for legislative oversight; the appointees may be examined about their attitudes on the agency's mission and their plans to accomplish the objectives of the agency.

Legislative oversight may occur when a legislator provides service to constituents. After receiving a complaint, a legislator contacts the agency for an accounting of its actions. Agency performance may improve as a result. Unfortunately, the agency is more likely to respond simply by accommodating the interests of the person who contacted the the legislator; the underlying practices which led to that person's dissatisfaction may continue. Though the legislator's immediate problem of an unhappy constituent is met, the legislator usually lacks the sophistication, the energy, or the motivation to challenge the underlying deficiencies. In fact, when a legislator's contact with the agency leads to favored treatment for a constituent, the intervention promotes *ad hoc* decision-making and weakens total agency performance, rather than improving it.

§ 33–4. **Legislative veto.** A widely used method of Congressional oversight has been the legislative veto. A legislative veto is a statutory device which subjects agency proposals and decisions to additional legislative consideration. The legislature may disapprove agency action by a committee, one-house or concurrent resolution. Since its first use in the Legislative Appropriation Act of 1932, the legislative veto as a method of oversight has been surrounded by controversy.

The legislative veto circumvents traditional bill passing procedures by failing to satisfy Article 1, section 7 (and state equivalents), which require presentment of legislative action to the executive for approval. This creates a separation of powers problem. In the case of committee and one-house resolutions, they also fail to satisfy Article 1, sections 1 and 7 (and state equivalents), which require both houses to pass legislation.

The technique has been defended on the ground that the veto is not a legislative act and that, therefore, it is not necessary to follow constitutionally established bill-passing procedures. In Immigration and Naturalization Service v. Chadha (103 S.Ct. 2764 (1983)), the Supreme Court determined that exercise of the legislative veto provision of the Immigration and Nationality Act was, in effect, a legislative act; its use affected the legal rights, duties and relations of persons outside the legislature. Based on this determination, the Court invalidated the provision on the grounds of bicameralism and separation of powers violations. Declining to limit the scope of its opinion, the majority theoretically invalidated all federal legislative veto provisions. Practically speaking, the precedential value of *Chadha* remains to be seen. So far, Congress has not systematically repealed legislative veto provisions, notwithstanding the *Chadha* decision. Some states, too, will continue to use the legislative veto notwithstanding *Chadha*, for the Supreme Court interpretation of the federal constitution does not bind the states in their interpretaion of state constitutions.

B. LEGISLATURE AS ALLOCATOR OF RESOURCES

§ 34–1. **Money and public policy.** Whether expressed as reordering of priorities, meeting public needs, saving the taxpayers' dollars, or any of the other taxing-spending phrases of politics, decisionmaking on public spending is a significant legislative function. In 1973, an estimated 33 percent of the gross national product was expended at the direction of national, state, and local legislative bodies. Legislative bodies continue to control the spending of roughly a third of the gross national

product. The public policy ramifications of the
decisions behind these expenditures are profound.
Major social impacts arise from both spending and
taxing.

A common criticism of legislative performance is
that legislatures fail to give appropriate energy,
courage and long-range perspective to how society's
resources are used. In fact, money issues—levying
taxes and making appropriations—come close to
dominating legislative work. But little external
help is offered, except that motivated by direct
selfish interest. Inevitably, responsive legislatures
fail in the face of imbalanced advocacy. They
cannot carry the burden of appropriation decision-
making without the wise guidance of the entire
community.

§ 34–2. Appropriations. There are a myriad
of policy judgments involved in decisions that allocate resources. Are schools to be financed locally
or through state aids? Will rich school districts
offer better programs or will all districts be given
resources to provide equal opportunities? Are public colleges to be financed at a level which allows
modest tuition and quality education, thus squeez-
ing private colleges to a smaller share of the educational market place? Are student aids to be provided to subsidize private colleges indirectly? Are
public institutions for the retarded and the mentally ill to be financed at custodial levels, or will
appropriations include funds for training and for
treatment? Are appropriations going to be made to

preserve nature areas? Will public resources be made available for playgrounds, parks, zoos? Will the quality of these facilities be good or bad? Are public resources to be directed at speeding the automobile from home to job or for mass transit? Will public funds go to train police or to produce a corrections system designed to pull the apprehended criminal from a criminal life style? Will health money be spent on treatment or on preventive medicine, public health, and medical research?

§ 34–3. **Taxation.** Every dollar appropriated by legislative bodies is extracted from the public through tax legislation. Tax policies have significant potential for social engineering. For example, the level of death taxes affects the degree of concentration of wealth. Selective excise taxes penalize the product taxed. Taxes on business, passed on to consumers as part of the price, produce a regressive tax structure. Reliance on income taxes creates a tax structure less attractive to the wealthy.

Policy choices in the income tax law also involve social engineering. Examples are special treatment for capital gains, deductions for charitable contributions, exemptions for senior citizens, credits for dependent children, investment credits, and depletion allowances.

The hardest fought battle in the average legislative session occurs on the omnibus revenue-raising bill. The public policy made in that bill may be short term, or it may set a pattern of taxation that

will continue for decades. Either way, the decisions involve millions of dollars. While the bill is
written and re-written, those who will have to pay
calculate the cost. As tax legislation is negotiated,
lobbyists for tobacco, liquor, mining, retail, whole-
sale, utility and manufacturing industries lose a
great deal of sleep as they play their separate or
cooperative roles in influencing the final bill.

C. LEGISLATURE AS INVESTIGATOR

§ 35–1. **The tool of investigation.** The legislative investigation is a basic means for carrying
forward legislative work. The investigation may
be a straight-forward hearing (an ordinary step in
the legislative process) or it may be a strong pursuit of new information relevant to policy making.
Legislators use investigation in lawmaking, resource allocation, and government operation.

Legislative investigation also has a function of
its own—public education. The massive records
developed by congressional committees can lead to
decisive turns in public policy. They provide the
raw material for reporters, editorial writers, muck-
rakers, scholars, and the policy formulators from
business, labor, and agriculture organizations.
Legislative investigations have revealed abuses
that had not been exposed in any other arena.
Hearings on the Wall Street abuses which contributed to the great depression are an example of an
investigation that led directly to a new body of law,
the Securities and Exchange Act.

§ **35–2. Investigative abuses; some safeguards.** Like any other power, the legislative power to investigate can be abused. To many people, these investigations are synonymous with witch-hunts. Finding scapegoats is a classic political technique in both totalitarian and democratic societies. Legislators are politicians and an investigation is a way to use the scapegoat device, if a legislator is so inclined. The best safeguard against abuse of the power to investigate is good sense and responsible attitudes in the legislature. There also are constitutional due process restraints. The leading case is Watkins v. United States (77 S.Ct. 1173 (1957)) which laid down the following rules for the protection of any person caught up in a legislative investigation.

- The investigation must relate to a subject upon which the legislature can act.

- The resolution authorizing the investigation must define with specificity the scope of the investigation.

- The proceedings must accord with defined standards of due process.

- The legislative right to be informed must outweigh a witness's right of privacy.

- The privilege against self-incrimination must be respected.

- Unreasonable search and seizure is prohibited.

- The freedoms of speech, press, religion, or political belief and association cannot be abridged.

In evaluating legislative investigations, it helps to recall that witch-hunting Senator Joseph McCarthy, after his abuse of the investigative power, was brought down by that same power in the Army-McCarthy hearings of 1953.

§ 35-3. **Legislature versus executive.** A legislative investigation may conflict with a claim by the executive that confidentiality is necessary for the executive branch to perform its functions effectively and efficiently. Operation of the executive branch requires some confidentiality of internal advice and discussion (work product) and protection of sources of information. Courts are reluctant to enter into disputes between executive and legislative branches over the issue of executive privilege. Such disputes are usually left to the political process for resolution.

In United States v. Nixon (94 S.Ct. 3090 (1974)), the court ruled that judicial intervention was appropriate; it went on to rule that claims of executive privilege by President Nixon had to give way to the need for evidence when what was involved was "due process of law in the fair administration of criminal justice." But dicta in the opinion emphasized the significance of executive privilege. Therefore, as precedent, the case may weaken the legislative branch in its capacity to investigate the executive.

Political reality, of course, deters executives from non-cooperation and may prove to be more compelling than any legal refuge gained from *Nixon*. Further, that case is not likely to be a popular citation for public relations aides seeking to protect the reputation of any chief executive—president, governor or mayor.

CHAPTER 9

LIMITATIONS ON POWER

A. PRACTICAL LIMITATIONS ON LEGISLATIVE POWER

§ 36–1. **Legislative frustration.** A legislature at work is conscious of legal limitations on legislative power, but is more conscious of real-life restraints on what it can do about the problems of society. Public disillusionment with the institution is often based on a misunderstanding of what the legislature can accomplish. Failures are blamed on an absence of good intentions, rather than on an absence of practical ideas. While critics condemn the lack of response to particular problems, those same critics fail to help the legislature overcome barriers to effective action. Legislators are frustrated by their inability to meet society's expectations and also by the public cynicism that greets this inability.

§ 36–2. **Political reality as a limitation.** Most legislators do not walk the corridors of capitols trembling with concern over their next campaign. But they do worry. Most legislators trim their sails on some issues. The sail trimming, coupled with the fact that members usually hold the same biases as their constituents, means the institution seldom acts on a controversial issue until a consensus develops in the general public. The conservatism of public opinion acts as a significant limitation on the actions and power of legislatures. This political reality stymies the usefulness of the institution for those who would strike boldly in new directions. Groups frustrated by this characteristic do not admit that it is actually political responsiveness which defeats their objectives. They blame instead legislative stupidity, unresponsiveness, or venality.

This raises a fundamental issue of political theory: the validity of Edmund Burke's view of the legislator as a delegate using "his unbiased opinion, his mature judgment, his enlightened conscience" free of dictation from his constituents. Burke provides the material for rich theoretical discussion. But the practical conclusion relevant at this point is that legislators (and a legislature as a whole) follow Burke—when they dare.

§ 36–3. **Inadequate sanctions.** Even if the legislature wants to act and has a favorable political climate in which to act, it may not be able to solve a problem. A legislator must include an effective sanction to make an enactment a law, rather than a platitude. "If wishes were horses, beggars would ride." And, if wishes were more than wishes, statutes would stop the writing of bad checks, would move public school teachers to more inspired service, would free citizens from their dependence on nicotine, and would keep rain from being acidic and from falling on parades.

The failure of prohibition between 1919 and 1933 is a memorable reminder that a legislature may be unable to force people out of their usual pattern of behavior. Citizens cannot be coerced to virtue. Legislating morals may serve as an expression of community consensus, but legislators and legal scholars have not discovered sanctions to push people into conduct they are not ready to follow. When legislatures attempt to dictate morals, the law is embarrassed by non-compliance. Law is also weakened, because the dignity and legitimacy of compliance are vital to its strength.

The American Bar Association has recommended repeal of statutes against victimless crimes. Whether there are victims or not may be the practical key to whether state intervention on moral issues is wise. Prohibiting an activity when no one else is affected has little consequence except to reduce respect for the law. On the other hand, the law can tackle conduct based on the deepest prejudices and most established conventions when that conduct hurts other citizens. Dignity and legitimacy are present when the law seeks to protect those who need protection, and no amount of evasion of the law can take that dignity away. Many who urge repeal of victimless crime laws at the same time support anti-discrimination legislation. In the first case, violation of the law makes repeal sensible; in the second case, violation reveals a social defect and makes its proscription necessary, even when sanctions are inadequate.

§ **36–4. Inadequate legal mechanisms.** Legislative policy must be implemented through the executive and judicial branches of government. Closely coupled with the inadequacy of sanctions is the absence of legal mechanisms in the other branches to enforce sanctions or otherwise accomplish the objectives of legislative policy. The deficiencies and handicaps of those who must enforce the law—inherent or arising from inadequacies of talent or will—undercut legislative policy objectives. Prosecutors often are unwilling to charge and juries are unwilling to convict. Administrative agencies are reluctant to act when there is significant resistance. Agencies and courts cannot discover facts necessary to support enforcement action. Bureaucratic red tape and arbitrariness, weak executives and prosecutors, court delay, and the co-opted regulatory agency explain why legislatures cannot effectively harness the power of society to produce the results sought through legislative enactments.

§ **36–5. Inadequate financial resources.** Since money is required to achieve many legislative objectives, limited financial resources preclude legislatures from doing many things they would like to do. Health care, education, highways, welfare, consumer protection, scientific research, historic preservation, environmental protection, and all the other state programs add up to a huge financial burden. On top of this are the costs of national defense and such local government programs as police and fire protection, water and sewer service, and traffic regulation.

While the public supports these objectives and supports legislators who pass programs to achieve them, taxpayers also resist increased taxes. The voting public exerts constant pressure to hold down taxes. Legislators convert that pressure into legislative resistance to expenditure. For their own political survival they must necessarily say "no" to some expenditures. A legislature leaves some problems untreated as it responds pragmatically to the political pressures to limit tax burdens.

§ 36–6. **Inadequate knowledge, imagination, wisdom.** "Knowledge is power," according to Francis Bacon. The legislature, together with other human institutions, struggles along with imperfect knowledge. Because of this limitation, it can never exercise its full theoretical potential. Legislative ignorance arises, in part, because the legislature does not receive information which exists elsewhere in the community. Facts may not reach the legislative body because they are purposefully held back, because no interest group communicates them, because there is no appreciation of their potential value to the legislature, or because citizens lack knowledge about how to provide the information in usable form.

Legislatures also share the ignorance of the rest of society. What doctors do not know about health hazards, what environmentalists do not know about environmental impacts, and what economists

do not know about economic interrelationships is
not known by the legislature either.

Another intellectual deficiency of legislatures is
lack of imagination. Americans have a history of
mechanical ingenuity; their inventions have
changed the economic life of the world. Invention
has a role in the legislative process; somebody has
to work out legislative solutions to recognized problems. Until the ingenious idea comes, however,
the legislative institution cannot act effectively, no
matter how clear the necessity for action may be.
It often appears that our legal inventions do not
match our scientific and mechanical developments.

Finally, there is the element of wisdom. The job
of the legislature—passing judgment on proposals
for legislation—requires common sense and a long
perspective. This quality of wisdom is not universal in or out of legislative bodies; legislatures are
human institutions with human failings.

§ 36–7. Time and pay. Limitations arising
from intellectual failings are compounded because
of time pressures. Legislators are universally
over-burdened with legislative and political responsibilities. When a session adjourns, legislators
look back on dozens of decisions which required
more study and thought than they were able to
give to them. Every legislator at every level is
reminded of this time pressure by the stack of
reports not read, by the bills voted on without
adequate study, by the agencies whose functions

are not understood, and by the public institutions not visited.

Most state constitutions limit the length of legislative sessions, although recently periods of meeting have been extended dramatically. Between 1960 and 1974, states with annual sessions increased from twenty to forty-two. By 1985 only six states retained the biennial session. Official times for meeting tell only part of the story because interim work through special commissions or standing committees can produce year-round legislative activity. The real limit on time is the salary level. Legislative work must compete for time with career and family obligations. When legislators are paid part-time salaries, they give part-time service. Generally states do not pay legislative salaries that justify full-time vocational commitments from individuals with the level of ability required to be excellent legislators. Unfortunately, when full time salaries are paid, some candidates seek, win, and retain the office for its economic value, rather than to serve the community.

B.   LEGAL LIMITATIONS ON LEGISLATIVE POWER

§ 37–1. **Bill of rights limitations.** Constitutions, especially bill of rights sections, limit legislative power. Bills of rights, both state and federal, have a significant impact on legislative life. They are an invaluable bulwark against the more irrational proposals made to legislative institutions.

For example, the provision that private property cannot be taken without just compensation frustrates many legislative aspirations. The provision protects property owners from overreaching laws by forcing upon legislatures the difficult task of appropriating funds to acquire park land, confiscate billboards, save redwoods, obtain highway rights-of-way, clear slum property and achieve many other valuable goals. The requirements of due process of law and equal protection are also pervasive obstacles to inappropriate legislative action.

Prohibitions on *ex post facto* laws and bills of attainder are provisions aimed directly at legislative action. An *ex post facto* law makes conduct criminal or increases the applicable penalty after the conduct has occurred. Bills of attainder are legislative pronouncements of guilt, inappropriately imposing a sanction on identified individuals without judicial process.

§ 37–2. General constitutional limitations. The following are examples of common constitutional restraints on legislative power beyond bill of rights limitations. Each may or may not exist in a state.

(a) Special legislation. Special legislation is often barred by a generality like: "No special legislation shall be passed where a general law may be made applicable." In other states the limitation prohibits particular types of special legislation or combines a general limitation and more precise proscriptions. These limitations respond to a timeless problem in all state legislatures—the practice of passing acts applicable to specific localities or to limited circumstances. This practice leads to ill-considered policies, favoritism, legislator domination of local government, and waste of legislative energies.

(b) **Taxing power.** The authority to impose taxes is limited by state constitutions in a variety of ways. These may be sound, simple requirements that taxes be uniform on the same class of taxpayers. Or they can be complex, detailed provisions establishing special taxation for railroads, extractive industries, motor vehicles, forest products, newly-established business, homesteads, or eleemosynary institutions. Any tax bill passed by a legislature must be written with these limitations in mind.

(c) **Dedicated funds.** Proceeds from particular taxes may be dedicated by a constitution to specific uses. Sometimes the rationale is that the tax is primarily a user fee, as is the case when motor vehicle and gasoline taxes are dedicated to road building. Other times the repercussions from a new tax are cushioned by dedicating the proceeds to a politically attractive use like reforestation. A legislature at a later date may want to use the funds for a more timely and appropriate purpose. If there is a legislative consensus to bypass the constitutional limitation, the legislative craftsman may be able to label as reforestation some activities which are only marginally related to forests. Technical ingenuity and judicial reluctance to set aside actions of the popularly-elected legislative branch usually permit the legislature to have its way. But it is difficult to build a legislative consensus in the face of restrictive constitutional provisions, so these restrictions may have a greater political than constitutional law effect.

(d) **Debt limits.** Legislative profligacy has led to constitutional restrictions on the legislative power to incur debt. These limitations may be expressed in dollar figures. Where this is the case, the provisions are repealed or evaded as inflation makes them absurd. In other jurisdictions the use of borrowed funds is restricted to capital expenditures, or an extraordinary vote within the legislative body is required to incur debt.

(e) **Grandfather provisions.** When state constitutions were written, particular aspects of the *status quo* occasionally were protected. University or college charters, state capital locations, or county lines may have constitutional status. Decades after their adoption, these "touch-me-not" provisions may conflict with desired legislative policy. Again, drafting ingenuity can achieve many legislative objectives while avoiding direct conflict with the literal words of the provision.

(f) **Mandated programs.** State constitutions may require the legislature to maintain a militia, to establish public schools, and to carry out a variety of other programs. If a recalcitrant legislature ignores a constitutionally imposed obligation, the legal system provides no sanction to force its implementation. However, the constitutional provision does give legislative strength to those who support the mandated program. When the constitution imposes the obligation to implement a program on an executive branch official, a mandamus action may be brought to require its implementation. But the official and the court will be stymied if the legislature fails to appropriate money to meet the obligation.

Whether or not a program is constitutionally mandated, the appropriation power gives the legislature a means to cut it off if it chooses. Even if the provision of the constitution includes dedicated appropriations from state revenues, the level of expenditure must be left to legislative discretion. The legislature can respond with a dollar-a-year program.

§ 37-3. **State boundary.** A multitude of activities legislatures would like to regulate occur beyond their separate territorial jurisdictions. These events may involve drinking or marrying or contracting at an age lower than is permitted in the home state. They may involve statutory authority for the organization of corporations under a set of rules contrary to the policy of the home state. Conflict with the policies of other states is an everyday limitation on many business-climate issues. Not being able to control public policy in other jurisdictions, a state must continually act with one eye on the realities of interstate competition that its domestic businesses face, including the costs of unemployment compensation, workers compensation, pollution control, minimum wages, taxes, and neglected public services.

§ 37–4. **Past and future as limitations.** The law assumes that citizens will rely on existing rules of law in the conduct of their daily affairs. Once a day has passed into history, lawmakers are restricted in their freedom to reach back to change those rules. This restriction on retroactive legislation is strongest in criminal law because the bill of rights prohibits *ex post facto* legislation. In other areas of the law, changing a rule after the fact gives unfair advantage to one party and thus deprives others of property or contract rights without due process of law.

A legislature is also limited in its power because it cannot deny to a later legislature the power to change the law. Each new legislature starts with the full authority possessed by any of its predecessors. It may repeal, amend, or extend any act of a past legislature, provided it does not give the change retroactive effect. This point is generally reduced to the truism: "No legislature can bind its successors." Few propositions of the law are so simple yet so basic. In the legislative institution, the future always belongs to the future.

C. STRUCTURAL LIMITATIONS ON LEGISLATIVE POWER

§ 38–1. **Federal supremacy.** Article Six of the United States Constitution provides:

This Constitution, and the laws of the United States which shall be made in pursuance thereof, and all treaties made, or which shall be made, under the authority of the United States, shall be the supreme law of the land, and the judges in every state shall be bound thereby, anything in the Constitution or laws of any state to the contrary notwithstanding.

This is the supremacy clause. It means a state legislature must always take into account policies adopted in Washington. Two issues arise when state action is in apparent conflict with federal law. The first is whether or not the congressional action falls within the powers granted to Congress. If Congress exceeded its authority, the congressional act is invalid and, despite the supremacy clause, has no priority over state action. The second issue is whether or not Congress intended its policy to supersede state policy. Congress often acts without intent to preempt state policy making, or with an intent to preempt on a limited set of issues. The congressional intent may be that state and federal policies should coexist.

In deciding preemption questions, the relative merit of the conflicting congressional and state legislative policies is not at issue. A congressional act may be extremely unwise compared to the state act, but the federal act and policy will control nonetheless if congressional intent is to preempt. Occasionally, when it acts on a problem, Congress provides explicitly that its action does not preclude state action in the area. This permits using the states as testing grounds for alternative policies. Even with such a provision, some degree of pre-emption may be unavoidable as the law is applied.

§ 38–2. **Separation of powers.** A fundamental principle of constitutional law is that one branch of government cannot exercise the powers of the other branches. In most state constitutions, the provision which grants legislative power to the legislature also grants judicial power to the judiciary and executive power to the executive.

In theory, the separation of powers doctrine requires the legislature to do its own lawmaking. The legislature cannot delegate the job to administrative agencies or to the electorate through referenda on issues. The restriction on the power to delegate shuts off some options for carrying out legislative work. However, the complexities of society have created a need for substantial delegation and the doctrine against delegation is now tattered. Nonetheless, it has continuing significance which is discussed in §§ 48–1 to 48–4.

The separation of powers doctrine also denies the legislature authority to take on responsibilities which belong to the judiciary or the executive. For example, the power of appointment is an executive function. A legislature cannot create an office and then fill it by legislative selection. If it did so, the appointment would invade the prerogative of the executive and be invalid. Except in cases of impeachment, the legislature would also intrude upon the power of the executive were it to assume a power of indictment. The legislature also cannot act as a judge of cases and controversies, for adjudication of disputes is assigned to the judiciary.

Coupled with separation of power are checks and balances. These contemplate some involvement by each of the branches with its coordinate branches. As to the judicial power, for example, judgeships are created by the legislature and the executive appoints persons to judgeships. As to the legislative function, the executive may veto legislation. And by making budget proposals, the executive influences the legislative power of the purse. At the same time, the legislative appropriation power intrudes upon internal operations of both the executive and judiciary. Legislatures set salaries and they structure and restructure the other branches. Senates hold power to reject executive appointments. Finally, the judiciary may set aside actions of the other branches which are substantively or procedurally unconstitutional.

§ 38–3. **Federal courts versus state legislatures.** The separation of powers principle contemplates a system of checks and balances. Each branch holds some power over the others. However, the supremacy clause gives all branches of the federal government primacy over any branch of state government. This produces a serious breakdown in the theory of balanced power. When federal judges, enjoying lifetime tenure and independence from political pressure, take action that conflicts with policies set by a state legislature, the state legislature has no responsive check or balance. The state holds little countervailing power and no power of retaliation.

The issue is not academic. Federal courts have exercised jurisdiction to set aside state policies on corrections, welfare, and the care of the institutionalized, ordering fundamental revision of spending priorities by declaring programs in these areas inadequate to the point of illegality. Federal courts have also repudiated state policies for financing education when those policies produced unequal tax burdens in different communities or unequal benefits for students in various localities.

Federal courts in these cases disrupt the states' power to allocate public resources; they set aside basic state policies on where tax money is to be spent. The circumstances that cause federal courts to overturn legislative policy may be a consequence of inadequate lobbying at state legislatures. If stark errors in legislative judgments give apparent validity to court intrusions on state policy, such misjudgments would not occur if citizens petitioned the legislature as ardently and as effectively as they petition the courts.

Of course, in taking on these spending issues, courts do not face the burden of balancing competing requests for resource allocations; that balancing is an important part of the legislative agenda. In striking balances between competing interests legislatures may, in fact, have been making defensible allocations of limited resources.

With changes in the judiciary during the Reagan presidency, the trend toward review of state programs by the federal judiciary based on equal protection and unusual punishment grounds has declined. If the courts had continued to invade legislative perogatives by providing judicial relief to those petitioners frustrated by legislative decisions, the courts soon would have been deluged by plaintiffs asking them to overturn legislative policies, especially appropriation policies. If convicts, mentally ill and retarded persons, top female athletes, and students in poor districts receive federal court help to obtain an increased share of state appropriations, are not mediocre athletes, average and gifted students, and the unemployed entitled to seek similar assistance?

The courts must limit their intrusions to instances of gross legislative error or they will be crushed by the weight of petitioners unhappy with legislative decisions. A line of judicial restraint must be maintained to protect the courts from countless lawsuits by the forces that now contend for appropriation priorities in the legislative arena.

D. DIRECT DEMOCRACY

§ 39–1. **Initiative and referendum.** The constitutions of twenty-one states establish an initiative process allowing citizens to propose legislation by signed petitions. The initiative in the United States grew out of the progressive movement of the early 20th Century. The objective was to create a means to bypass what were perceived to be corrupt legislatures.

Legislation initiated by voter petitioners may go directly to an election day ballot for approval or it may go first to the legislature and on to voters only if the legislature fails to approve the initiated measure. Each state constitution determines whether the issue must be submitted directly or indirectly, or the constitution may allow the petitioners to choose. Submission of an initiated proposal to the electorate is called "referendum."

Voter referenda are not limited to voter initiated measures. A few state constitutions require a referendum on a legislatively adopted act whenever a sufficient number of citizens petition for the opportunity to reject the act. And in a few states the legislature itself may ask that an act by placed on the ballot for voter approval or rejection. Referenda are used in every state to ratify amendments to the state constitution. Amendments are submitted for voter ratification after a legislative vote calls for their submission or, occasionally, after a constitutional convention proposes them.

§ 39–2. **The evils of initiative.** The initiative process leaves little room for a relentless focus on words; but such a focus is at the heart of the traditional legislative process. Initiative and referendum slight the deliberative thought that should be the essence of any lawmaking process. The zealous citizens who circulate initiative petitions rarely draft the law they propose with sufficient care. Certainly they give inadequate attention to avoiding unintended consequences and to moderating the deleterious effect of their proposal on the institution or program that is the target of their petition drive. The initiative and referendum process provides little opportunity in its later stages to correct the initial drafting errors, in stark contrast to the refining and correcting of bills that dominates ordinary legislative proceedings. The initiative provides almost no means to hear and to accommodate dissenting views—to compromise.

Initiative is not a liberal procedure, but is rather a harsh method by which a bare majority or a passionate minority seeks to impose its will on the entire community. The initiative process bypasses the mechanisms by which deliberative, representative legislative bodies moderate proposed legislation.

§ 39–3. **The evils of referenda.** The referendum presents its own set of problems, whether it is part of the initiative-referendum process or a separate device. Fundamentally, referenda cause law approval to turn on public relations and advertising campaigns, rather than on conclusions drawn from the deliberations of an institution designed to make considered judgments. The availability of a referenda mechanism as a ready alternative undermines the ordinary legislative process by giving legislators a means to pass the buck for policy making onto the voters. This weakens legislatures, for no institution is strengthened by allowing it to sidestep difficult work.

Referenda impose on voters burdensome issue decisions; these ballot questions draw the electorate's attention away from its great responsibility to choose the best public officials from overly long lists of candidates. Political energy is diverted from candidate campaigns to electioneering for referendum issues.

The legislative and political costs of initiative and referendum are not balanced by significant benefits. The whole scheme changes the law very little over the long run, for the legislature mirrors informed public opinion on major issues. In time, the public gets from its legislatures what it sensibly demands. The political responsiveness of legislatures makes initiative and referendum unnecessary.

Opponents of initiative and referendum sought to invalidate the processes on the ground that they violated the mandate in the federal constitution that every state be guaranteed a republican form of government. The legal challenge failed, but it helped slow the adoption of these approaches to direct democracy.

Use of referenda as the means to ratify state constitutional amendments has one indisputable justification—there is no viable alternative. The campaigns for ratification often turn on advertising techniques and have some of the other evils of the referendum process, but voters at least know they are working on the fundamental government charter, rather than on ordinary legislation. Voters are therefore less likely to yield to political fads and moods of the moment. Furthermore, voter approval of constitutional change maintains the consent-of-the-governed character of the constitution.

CHAPTER 10

THE STRUGGLE FOR LEGISLATIVE POWER

A. APPORTIONMENT

§ 40–1. Effect of malapportionment. As the decade of the 1960's began, the great power of legislatures was to a disproportionate degree held by rural America. A few hundred voters chose a legislator in some country districts, while the constituency of another legislator in a suburban community of the same state numbered hundreds of thousands of citizens. Furthermore, some legislative districts in the thinly populated commercial and industrial sections of central cities were appropriately called "rotten boroughs." The malapportionment was reflected in Congress as well. In state after state the rural bias that arose from malapportionment produced legislatures which consciously favored rural constituents by putting small-population congressional districts into rural areas and large-population districts into urban areas. Consequently, malapportionment affected the substantive law produced by both Congress and state legislatures. Outnumbered urban legislators could not force legislatures to give attention to urban problems. Those problems were swept under the rug.

§ **40–2.** **One person, one vote.** In 1964, the
United States Supreme Court held that state legislative districts must be drawn to provide equal
representation to all citizens. Apportionments
which failed to achieve this equality were declared
defective and inoperative. Ultimately, where legislatures failed to apportion equitably, courts drew
the district lines. The one person, one vote requirement was also extended to Congressional districts.

The reapportionment decisions, capped by Reynolds v. Sims (377 U.S. 533 (1964)), are probably the
most significant in the court's history. If a trans-
fer of power from one set of individuals to another
is revolution, the years immediately following
Reynolds v. Sims witnessed one of the greatest
revolutions in world history. In state after state,
legislative power balances shifted from rural to
urban constituencies. By the end of the decade,
problems of urbanization were no longer pigeonholed; instead they were pushed onto legislative
agendas. Once on the agenda, the problems received conscientious attention from all legislators,
for the problems were then recognized as legitimate legislative concerns.

A short term by-product of one person, one vote
was an improved quality in legislative members.
Eliminating over-represented districts forced pairs
of incumbent rural legislators into contests against
one another where the election rule was survival of
the fittest. Metropolitan America benefited not

only from additional representation of its own, but also from more competent and broader-minded rural legislators.

§ 40–3. **Gerrymanders and other offenses.** The drawing of boundaries for legislative and Congressional districts offers further opportunities for inequities. The gerrymander—drawing irregular district boundaries to concentrate or dissipate political strength—has a long history. If used to the detriment of a racial minority, the gerrymander will fall to judicial challenge. As this book goes to press, the Supreme Court has not yet invalidated a gerrymander to achieve simple partisan advantage.

Concentrating or dissipating the voting strength of particular groups is most easily accomplished through the combination of gerrymander and multi-member districts, rather than through gerrymanders alone. Where courts have drawn boundaries, they have provided that each legislator must run in a single-member district. The courts have not yet invalidated a legislatively adopted plan because it allowed legislators to run at large in multi-member districts, but if evidence is presented showing that a multi-member district was established to discriminate against a racial minority, a challenge will certainly succeed.

The struggle for legislative power through districting has been fought in both courts and legislatures. As the accumulation of judicial precedents has made the ground rules for apportionment more definite, legislatures have picked up the apportionment burden. Once rural/urban equality was achieved, it was no longer an impossible task for the legislature itself to maintain fair representation. Consequently, the judicial role in apportionment is shrinking.

Some legislatures have created outside groups to draw district lines. Districting is difficult for a legislative institution, since it sets party against party and colleague against colleague. Every member is directly affected by the provisions of an apportionment bill, so on this issue the usual division of labor does not work. Delegating the task of drawing district lines to non-legislative commissions has growing support because so much legislative energy is squandered in drafting and considering reapportionment bills. The price paid for this delegation is reduced continuity in legislative membership. Commissions without legislator members naturally have been less concerned with protecting incumbents.

B. THE CONDUCT OF ELECTIONS AND CAMPAIGNS

§ 41–1. **Election law.** Strict rules on the conduct of elections are necessary because elections serve to allocate and reallocate power, a function that much of the world accomplishes through revolution and insurrection. Detailed statutes set the rules to be followed by the agencies that establish voting precincts, arrange polling places, buy voting machines, accept candidate filings, prepare ballots, supervise voter registration, choose election judges, and generally operate the machinery by which elections are conducted.

Other detailed statutes regulate campaign practices. These "fair campaign practices acts" commonly define as campaign sins misrepresentation, anonymously produced pamphlets, the wining and dining of voters, and a variety of other "corrupt practices." They also provide sanctions to be applied against transgressors, ranging from misdemeanor to felony penalties and, if the offender is the election winner, disqualification from office.

§ 41–2. **A decade of campaign reform.** If elections substitute for revolution as the means of allocating government power, then it ought not be surprising that those who lust for power throw the force of their financial resources into election battles. Campaign contributions are made to influence who wins office. Some seekers of power also contribute to influence the attitude with which winners of elections conduct their offices. Occasionally, contributions are made with an explicit and corrupt understanding that there will be a *quid pro quo*. Many citizens believe that the financing of politics undermines legislative ethics.

The 1970s, both before and after the Watergate revelations, brought several changes in the law relating to the financing of campaigns. One change at both national and state levels attempted to bring "clean" money into politics through public funding. The objective was to equalize political opportunity and to reduce the distortions of public policy that result from conscious or subconscious *quid pro quo* relationships between campaign contributors and public officials.

Attacking the other side of campaign funding, legislation imposed limits on the amount that any individual donor could contribute to a candidate. The objective was to put a cap on the political impact an individual could have, no matter how rich. Next, extensive disclosure obligations were imposed on campaign committees. Candidates were required to show how contributions were spent. They were also required to disclose who contributed and how much.

§ 41–3. **An evaluation of campaign financing reform.** Reformers intended these changes— public funding, contribution limits, and disclosure requirements—to have an impact on politics, they wanted government to change how elections were carried on. Therein lies the source of great difficulty. Campaign reforms, although in many ways desirable, keep running up against the obstacle of the bill of rights. Almost any regulation of elections imposes direct or indirect restrictions on the power to participate in the election process. The founding fathers intended elections to be a check on government. But campaign finance reforms put government into the election process. This seems inherently to conflict with the great political reasons for freedom of speech and the right to freely associate in common effort with like minded people.

The Supreme Court addressed these tensions in Buckley v. Valeo, (424 U.S. 1 (1976)). That case invalidated all ceilings on campaign spending as unwarranted restrictions on first amendment rights of free speech. To limit political spending, according to the Court, is to limit political speech. Any restriction on political speech carries a heavy burden of justification, and to reduce the cost of elections was not a sufficient justification. However, the *Buckley* Court found a sufficient justification for limiting contributions made to candidates and for mandatory disclosure of the names of contributors and the amount of their contributions.

Constitutional issues aside, a decade of experience invites an evaluation of the practical impact of these campaign reforms. Clearly "nonpolitical" money inserted into the political arena distorts the marketplace economics of election funding. Good economics applied to political funding says money should be available only to candidates realistically contending for an office or carrying a political message worth dissemination. A subsidy should not continue simply because government mindlessly allows its funds to be used to carry all messages proferred, even those that cannot sustain themselves in the private marketplace of ideas. Nonselective expenditures promote the destructive factionalism of splinter group politics, diluting support for the major parties and reducing the level of consensus. Yet, it is obvious that public funding should not be based on a government decision that a certain political orthodoxy should be heard.

Finally, contrary to the intended purpose, disclosure requirements have strengthened the public attitude that politics operates on *quid pro quo*'s. News reports continually match office holder actions to lists of campaign contributors. If something is said often enough, and if it has any credibility, it will be believed by many. This *post hoc, propter hoc* conclusion has damaged politics immeasurably. It also ignores the reality that contributors are more likely to have sought out candidates with compatible political philosophies than to have arranged *quid pro quo* deals. That recipients of contributions subsequently behaved in office in a way consistent with the views of their contributors can validly be interpreted as showing officeholder adherence to long held political values, rather than showing their crass allegiance to political fund raisers.

§ 41–4. **Proposals and prospects.** The campaign finance laws adopted up to now may simply give the illusion of reform. Certainly they have not reduced the levels of distrust and disillusionment. If there has been failure so far, what new approach might be attempted?

Maybe we should go back to basics. The electorate, of course, always carries the burden of ensuring honest politics. No matter how politics is

funded, the responsibility rests with voters, to select for office those candidates with the character
and the ability to act in the public interest. Perhaps there are ways to increase the public capacity
to fulfill this responsibility.

Modern technology (particularly television) has
increased the cost of politics. The high cost is,
however, not nearly so much a result of the rivalry
among politicians as it is the result of the kind of
advertising used. The most expensive advertising,
whether political and commercial, is that which
consumers cannot avoid. The billboard, the large
and startling print ad, the individualized computer
letter, and, above all, the television spot devour
money. Further, the price of political advertising,
and therefore of political campaigns, is set by the
rates on the commercial soap and beer advertising
that must be preempted during campaign periods.

Ironically, the most expensive advertisements
contribute least to the fund of political information
and understanding in the electorate. Political
campaigns have value only as they aid the voters
to make wise choices; they are justified primarily
by the facts, the logic, and the insight delivered to
election-day decision makers. There are two poles
of political advertising; the first based on substance and message, the other based on slogan and
image. The former is the type of political speech
that it is vital to protect. The latter is more akin
to the "jingle-ism" of commercial advertising.

It would be desirable to limit this type of political merchandising so that campaign resources can be better spent actually informing the electorate. Restricting this type of advertising may well be justified by the important government interest of promoting an informed and rational electoral process. Limits on the most expensive and intrusive advertising devices would force voters to invest more of their own energy in searching out political information. The media, the politicians, and the conscientious part of the electorate would adjust to the new reality. If there were some fall off in voting percentage among those voters who are moved to vote only by mindless television appeals, nothing important would be lost.

C. LEGISLATOR ELECTION CHALLENGES

§ 42–1. **House judge of own members.** When the election of an individual to a legislative body is challenged, the issue is judged by the house involved. The historical basis for this practice is the English parliament's need to insulate its members from the king. If the right to sit in parliament had been a judicial issue, the king's judges would have had power to exclude the king's adversaries from membership. To protect itself, parliament seized the power to admit or exclude its own members.

Election contests brought to the legislature involve the questions of, first, who received the most votes and, second, whether or not the election was conducted in accord with the fair campaign practices act of the jurisdiction. While legislatures may use other tribunals for preliminary fact-finding, and even to recommend judgments, the ultimate decision rests with the legislative body. Given party and factional divisions, a legislature's judging of election contests is not above suspicion. Like redistricting, judging election contests could be carried on more efficiently and fairly outside the legislature. Unlike redistricting, legislatures have not surrendered the ancient prerogative of self-judgment. Nor have courts, except to a limited extent, taken over the task.

§ 42–2. **Exceptions.** The sovereignty of legislative bodies to judge their own membership was qualified by the United States Supreme Court in 1966. In Bond v. Floyd (385 U.S. 116), the action of the Georgia House of Representatives excluding Julian Bond from its membership was reversed by the Supreme Court on the basis that the exclusion violated Bond's freedom of speech. Three years later, in Powell v. McCormack (395 U.S. 486 (1969)), the Supreme Court ruled that Congress could exclude Adam Clayton Powell from membership only upon a finding that he failed to meet the constitutional qualifications for membership in the House of Representatives. Constitutional qualifications for office are very limited, usually including only age, residence, citizenship, and a willingness to take an oath to uphold the federal and

state constitutions. *Bond* and *Powell* taken together add up to a rule that a legislative body may not
violate an individual's right to a seat in the legislature nor his constituency's right to have him there.
Exclusion must be based on the candidate's failure
to meet the constitutional qualifications for the
office or on defects in the election. *Bond* and
Powell establish judicial review only when there is
exclusion, and then only if the exclusion is alleged-
ly based upon unconstitutional foundations.

Legislative bodies have a separate power to expel
from membership one whose corruption, disorderly
behavior, or other misconduct makes continued
membership inappropriate. This power to expel is
not conditioned on failure to meet the legal qualifications to hold the office. Whether it may be
subject to free speech limitations, as is the right to
exclude, has not been judicially tested. Expulsion
normally requires an extraordinary vote comparable to the vote required to remove a judicial or
executive officer through impeachment.

PART IV

IMPACT OF CONSTITUTIONS

CHAPTER 11

CONSTITUTIONAL TESTS OF LEGISLATION

A. JUDICIAL REVIEW OF CONSTITUTIONALITY

§ 43–1. Source and reason for the power. Courts and legislatures are coordinate, equal branches of government. Yet courts have assumed the power to declare legislative acts invalid. The power is not explicitly granted in the United States Constitution nor in state constitutions. Whether courts possessed this power of review was in dispute until authoritatively established in Marbury v. Madison. (1 Cranch 137 (1804)). Justice Marshall's reasoning in *Marbury* (at 177) was:

It is, emphatically, the province and duty of the judicial department, to say what the law is. Those who apply the rule to particular cases, must of necessity expound and interpret that rule. If two laws conflict with each other, the courts must decide on the operation of each. So, if a law be in opposition to the constitution; if both the law and the constitution apply to a particular case, so that the court must either decide that case, conformable to the law, disregarding the constitution; or conformable to the constitution, disregarding the law; the court must determine which of these conflicting rules governs the case; this is of the very essence of judicial duty. If then, the courts are to regard the constitution, and the constitution is superior to any ordinary act of the legislature, the constitution, and not such ordinary act, must govern the case to which they both apply.

In his masterpiece essay on constitutional law, Judge Learned Hand said of *Marbury*:

For centuries it has been an accepted canon in interpretation of documents to interpolate into the text such provisions, though not expressed, as are essential to prevent the defeat of the venture at hand; and this applies with especial force to the interpretation of constitutions, which, since they are designed to cover a great multitude of necessarily unforeseen occasions, must be cast in general language, unless they are constantly amended. If so, it was altogether in keeping with established practice for the Supreme Court to assume authority to keep the states, Congress, and the President within their prescribed powers. Otherwise the government could not proceed as planned; and indeed would almost certainly have foundered, as in fact it

almost did over that very issue. (The Bill of
Rights, 1958, at 14–15).

§ 43–2. **Judicial restraint.** Judicial review is
a sensitive issue; even a century and a half after
Chief Justice Marshall's court exercised the power,
Judge Hand still had to lend his mightly mind to
its defense. Justice Brandeis, in a concurring opinion in Ashwander v. TVA (56 S.Ct. 466 (1935))
observed that the court throughout its history "frequently called attention to the 'great gravity and
delicacy' of its function in passing upon the validity of an act of Congress." Brandeis then listed the
methods the court uses to restrain itself in the
exercise of the power to overrule a decision of a
coordinate branch. He included the following:

(a) The court will not pass on constitutionality in
a non-adversary proceeding.

(b) The court will not anticipate a question of
constitutional law in advance of the necessity of
deciding it.

(c) The court will not formulate a rule of constitutional law broader than is required to decide the
case before it.

(d) The court will not pass on a constitutional
issue if there is present some other ground upon
which the case may be disposed of.

(e) The court will, if possible, construe a statute
to avoid the constitutional question.

(f) The court will not decide a constitutional question except upon the challenge of one injured by it.

(g) The court will not decide a constitutional challenge to a statute by one who has availed himself of its benefits.

§ 43–3. Presumption of constitutionality. Another restraint on the judicial review power is a presumption of constitutionality. Because of this presumption, those who challenge statutes must overcome strong intellectual, emotional, and political forces which incline a court against striking down a statute. The basis for the presumption is an assumption that a legislative decision to pass an act includes a determination that the act is constitutional and that, as a consequence, a court puts itself in conflict with a conscious decision of the legislative branch if it finds an act unconstitutional.

§ 43–4. Severability. When a court believes a statute is invalid and cannot find a way to avoid deciding the issue, it may still exercise restraint. It can escape direct conflict with at least some elements of the statute if it severs invalid parts, leaving only the remaining, valid parts in effect. Appellate court opinions fail to reflect the full extent that severability rescues portions of statutes under attack. Parties fighting over one section ignore other parts of the statute and, unless prompted by the litigators, courts forget to say that

their decision does not affect the validity of those
sections of the act not relevant to the case.

A court's opinion must be discounted if it implies
that a statute is invalid in all respects and in all
applications; some of the act still may be effective.
A lawyer attacking a statute can make it easier for
the court to rule her way by explicitly limiting the
challenge to that portion of the statute which damages her case and by urging that the rest of the
statute be left in effect. The lawyer thus reduces
the stake for the court that is asked to negate
legislative policy.

§ 43–5. **Effect of a declaration of invalidity.**
Even though a court says a legislative act is invalid, the act remains on the statute books; a court
cannot repeal legislation. For example, in 1923
the United States Supreme Court declared all minimum wage laws unconstitutional; in 1937 the
decision was overruled. This meant that the minimum wage law of the District of Columbia, dor-
mant from 1923 to 1937, was suddenly in force as if
newly adopted, even though it was seriously out of
date. Therefore, when one of its acts has been
struck down, a legislature should be aware that the
act has not been repealed, only shelved either in
whole or in part. What, then, should the legislature do? It may rewrite the act to repair whatever
created the constitutional problem. If repair is
impossible or inappropriate, it may repeal the act.
In any event, it should not leave the act on the

statute books to trap those who fail to notice a
decision holding the act invalid.

B. LEGISLATOR'S DUTY TO UPHOLD
CONSTITUTION

§ 44–1. **Oath of office.** State legislators begin
their terms of office with an oath to uphold the
constitutions of the United States and of their own
jurisdiction. That is the only official promise they
make. With respect to the federal Constitution
the oath is required by clause 3 of Article VI.
Drafters of state constitutions inserted similar provisions. Constitution writers clearly intended to
impose a responsibility for adherence to the constitution on all officials, including legislators.

However, as legislators consider bills, those without legal training, and some with law degrees as
well, feel inadequate to make decisions on constitutionality. Many are therefore unwilling to face up
to constitutional issues. But legislators, no matter
how insecure, should not quickly relinquish these
questions to courts. Judges have no monopoly on
the ability to read or to think through the basic
propositions contained in a constitution. In addition, legislators who hesitate to make judgments on
constitutional questions regularly make other decisions for which they have as little training, experience, or information.

§ 44–2. **Practical reasons for legislators' duty.** For two practical reasons, legislators must not
renege on their oath to uphold the constitution and

on the obligation to make decisions on constitutionality. First, courts adhere to a presumption of constitutionality. Judges are reluctant to hold an act unconstitutional because of the belief that the legislature has done its share of the job; they assume that an invalidating decision contradicts a prior, thoughtful conclusion arrived at by a coordinate branch. If legislatures shirk this responsibility, the judicial presumption has no factual basis. The law over time rejects presumptions that are false. If legislators value this one, as they should, they must protect it by fulfilling their obligation.

Second, when a legislature passes a statute, citizens order their affairs on the belief that the act is constitutional. Because of its provisions, people act in ways they would not act if the statute had not been passed. Persons adversely affected by the law must either suffer its effects or bring a lawsuit to present the issue of unconstitutionality to a court. Litigation is expensive in time, money, and energy. A legislator does an injustice by making any citizen choose either to sue or to suffer. If a legislator believes a bill is unconstitutional, but casts a vote to pass it anyway, the vote imposes unfair burdens.

§ 44–3. Temptation to defer on constitutional questions. A realistic examination of legislative performance on constitutional issues must include political considerations. If public opinion runs strong, and especially if the constitutional issue is close, political expediency may cause a legislator to vote for a bill even when believing it to be invalid. That this happens does not mean the action is justified.

In one circumstance, a legislator can legitimately vote for a bill though she thinks a court is likely to declare it unconstitutional. That circumstance occurs when the legislator believes the court to be wrong and her own interpretation to be consistent with the intent of the writers and ratifiers of the constitution. The legislator, by acting on her own convictions, challenges the court to rethink its conclusions. This independent, but honest, legislative judgment is precisely what the presumption of constitutionality contemplates.

C. MAJOR FOUNDATIONS FOR CONSTITUTIONAL CHALLENGE

§ 45–1. **Constitutional pegs.** A constitutional challenge to legislation must be based on some specific provision of the constitution; there must be a peg on which to hang the attack. A few towering propositions underlie most constitutional assaults on legislation, primarily procedural due process of law, equal protection, and the fundamental freedoms of the first amendment. These basic, giant, ever-expanding principles of constitutional law encompass such dynamic values in our legal system that they dominate judicial review. They are discussed in the next few sections, as is the discredited doctrine of substantive due process.

§ 45-2. Preferred freedoms. When a statute (or an official administering the statute) abridges one of the liberties that courts embrace with special fondness, the flag goes up and the act is in legal trouble. Preferred freedoms include those specifically named in the constitution (religion, speech, assembly, petition, contract, press) and others necessary to exercise the enumerated freedoms (privacy, personal autonomy, symbolic speech, association).

Passing an act that infringes on one of these freedoms does not usually reflect a problem of legislative motive as much as it reflects legislative inability to imagine in advance the way legislation will affect specific circumstances. Harsh consequences to individuals are lost from view during legislative deliberations focused on the search for the "greatest good for the greatest number." Of course legislatures are not without sin. Thomas Jefferson and his allies insisted on the first ten amendments to the constitution, the Bill of Rights, with the knowledge that government—even republican government—would on occasion abuse individual citizens. Legislatures, responsive to majority pressure or to pressure from passionate minorities, at times lose sight of the fundamental rights of individuals.

§ 45-3. Equal protection. Justice Holmes once said of challenges based on the equal protection theory, "It is the usual last resort of constitutional arguments to point out shortcomings of this sort." That was in 1927. Today, the equal protection argument is among the most attractive and frequently used tools to protect individual rights. It is particularly appealing because the challenge leaves the government with a choice; either abandon the action or adjust it so that similar individuals are treated in similar manner.

When legislators allocate burdens and benefits, lines of demarcation are necessary; some persons must be included and some excluded. An equal protection challenge to legislation forces an examination of the boundary lines between those included and those excluded from the act. An equal protection analysis determines whether the legislative classification constitutes an invalid discrimination. One of two tests is applied in these cases, a minimum rationality or a strict scrutiny standard.

From 1937, when the Supreme Court first applied the minimum rationality standard to an economic due process case, through the 1960's, equal protection challenges were analyzed under this two-tier system. Economic and social welfare classifications received a minimum rationality analysis. But the courts applied a higher "strict scrutiny" standard to analyze classifications infringing on the exercise of fundamental rights and those based on "suspect" criteria. The court determined what was suspect based on whether the classification exhibited an inherent likelihood of being arbitrary and against public policy.

Justice Thurgood Marshall found the two-tier analysis unsatisfactory for several reasons. He said it is unrealistic to insist on a dichotomy when what actually exists is a spectrum of suspiciousness. Existing alongside the spectrum of suspiciousness is a spectrum of justification for the classifications. According to Marshall, the court needs to subjectively balance the inequities of a particular legislative classification against the policy justifications for that classification.

Currently, the majority of the Supreme Court employs a modified two-tier analysis. Fundamental rights classifications and those based on suspect criteria (race and national origin) continue to be analyzed under a strict scrutiny standard and economic and social welfare classifications still receive a minimum rationality review. The modification has come with the court's recognition of "near suspect" classifications. Like suspect classifications, what falls into the new category is up to the court. So far, the court has employed an intermediate standard of review—more than minimum rationality, but less than strict scrutiny—when analyzing classifications based on alienage, legitimacy, or gender characteristics.

§ 45–4. **Procedural due process.** Due process undergirds judicial review of any legislation which establishes legal procedure. A court may find unconstitutional procedures in the whole thrust of a legislative act or in its application to a specific situation. In either case, a ruling of unconstitutionality forces the legislature to repair the act.

Among the main elements of procedural due process are reasonable notice, an opportunity to be heard and to present evidence, and a fair tribunal. In criminal cases, procedural rights also include representation by counsel, speedy and public trial, confrontation of witnesses, and jury trial. Bills must provide the essentials of due process, either in the bill or in its statutory and real life context. A particularly useful way to avoid due process defects in a bill is to incorporate by reference another statute which has already been tested and approved.

§ 45–5. Substantive due process. Legislation is also subjected to due process review in its substantive aspects. Economic substantive due process was the judicial weapon used against the New Deal programs in the 1930's and against earlier legislative efforts to regulate business. The concept of economic substantive due process originated with Allgeyer v. Louisiana (17 S.Ct. 427 (1897)) which held that state legislative restrictions on foreign insurance companies infringed "the liberty of contract."

Over a number of decades the courts aggressively protected business from legislative regulation. For example, in 1905 laws setting maximum hours for work were held invalid; and in 1923 the court held that both federal and state legislation setting minimum wages deprived business of liberty without due process of law. The court also used substantive due process to overrule state legislation on yellow dog contracts, price fixing, and arbitration of wage disputes.

This form of aggressive economic substantive due process was overturned in West Coast Hotel Co. v. Parrish (57 S.Ct. 578 (1937)) and has been shunned by the Supreme Court since then. Commentators now recognize that courts utilizing the doctrine of substantive due process had set themselves up as super legislatures. The legal community generally and appropriately condemns the theoretical base for that judicial domination.

Substantive due process may, however, be making a comeback, but not in its economic aspect. The abortion and birth control decisions, based on substantive rights of privacy or self-determination, are viewed by some commentators as substantive due process decisions. Privacy has been labeled a liberty which cannot be taken without due process of law, just as freedom to contract was so labeled in *Allgeyer.* Cases have also held that incarceration and mental commitments not followed by minimally adequate treatment or by efforts at rehabilitation deprive convicts and mental patients of due process. The difference from the old substantive due process is that courts now are protecting personal liberty, not economic liberty.

Today legislation which clashes with individual rights is suspect, whereas legislation regulating the economic affairs of the community is not. Judicial

second guessing of legislative policy involving economic judgments earned such a bad reputation in
the first four decades of the 20th century that it is
not likely to be revived in the foreseeable future.
But a new substantive due process protection of
individual rights regarding care and treatment,
privacy, travel, association, and self-determination
has become a significant judicial check on legislative policy.

§ 45–6. **Ebb and flow of preferred pegs.** Legal history shows an ebb and flow in the impact of
constitutional provisions. At various times, the
changing personnel of the court finds different
principles more congenial to its way of thinking.
In 1949, Justice Jackson persuasively endorsed
equal protection as a judicial rein on legislative
action to substitute for the rein of substantive due
process. Jackson said:

> The burden should rest heavily upon one who
> would persuade us to use the due process clause
> to strike down a substantive law or ordinance.
> Even its provident use against municipal regula-
> tions frequently disables all government—state,
> municipal and federal—from dealing with the
> conduct in question because the requirement of
> due process is also applicable to State and Feder-
> al Governments. Invalidation of a statute or an
> ordinance on due process grounds leaves un-
> governed and ungovernable conduct which many
> people find objectionable.

Invocation of the equal protection clause, on the other hand, does not disable any governmental body from dealing with the subject at hand. It merely means that the prohibition or regulation must have a broader impact. I regard it as a salutary doctrine that cities, states and the Federal Government must exercise their powers so as not to discriminate between their inhabitants except upon some reasonable differentiation fairly related to the object of regulation. This equality is not merely abstract justice. The framers of the Constitution knew, and we should not forget today, that there is no more effective practical guaranty against arbitrary and unreasonable government than to require that the principles of law which officials would impose upon a minority must be imposed generally. Conversely, nothing opens the door to arbitrary action so effectively as to allow those officials to pick and choose only a few to whom they will apply legislation and thus to escape the political retribution that might be vested upon them if larger numbers were affected. Courts can take no better measure to assure that laws will be just than to require that laws be equal in operation. (Railway Express v. New York, 69 S.Ct. at 466 (1949)).

Justice Jackson's opinion displays great respect for legislative prerogatives and an understanding of the need to avoid, if possible, conclusive confrontations between court and legislature. He suggested a variety of judicial restraint that uses a review that says: "You cannot do it that way" rather than "You cannot do it at all."

Jackson's preferred judicial tool of equal protection shaped many of the powerful public policy decisions of the Warren Court. The old economic due process doctrine was not revived by the activist Warren court. Instead, legislative policy was subjected to meaningful review under the equal protection clause. Other review of legislative action by the Warren court was consistent with Jackson's preference for review of means rather than ends. the Warren court used procedural due process review more than any previous court.

The procedural emphasis still prevails. It is so strong, in fact, that some writers contend it verges on substantive review. In a recent example, the Burger court held that the absence of any procedure to overcome factual presumptions on residence invalidated distinctions between residents and non-residents. Some scholars believe the clause offended against was the equal protection clause, rather than the due process clause. This residency case demonstrates how one clause overlaps others and how, in the review of legislation, they may be combined to produce something more far-reaching than any clause standing alone.

CHAPTER 12

CONSTITUTIONAL RULES AIMED AT LEGISLATURES

A. SPECIAL LEGISLATION

§ 46–1. **The vice of special legislation.** Most state constitutions prohibit special legislation, but local bills are passed nonetheless. Special legislation uses up legislative energy in bits and pieces, leaving the institution less able to deal with general legislative business. Fortunately, procedural shortcuts, primarily consent calendars for noncontroversial bills, keep the actual effort spent on bills relating to single governmental units far below that which is assumed by observers who merely count the number of local and one-situation bills introduced or passed. Procedural shortcuts, however, sometimes result in ill-considered policy decisions. If a bill applies to a single unit of government and has the support of the governing body of that unit, the legislature gives the bill only superficial attention; policies may be adopted that would never be approved if the issue were examined for statewide application. As a consequence, the legislature fails to establish responsible and uniform statewide regulation of local government units and, through special acts, it creates preferential and prejudicial discrimination between communities.

There are two checks on local special bills that are more effective than constitutional prohibitions. One is a critical legislative attitude toward special legislation. The other is the adoption of statewide legislation that provides adequate powers to local units, making special legislation unnecessary. With good general law, a presumption arises within a legislature that communities do not need special treatment. Local bills then are viewed suspiciously and become as difficult to pass as general laws. Legislators, are then more willing to tackle a problem of local authority by offering a general, statewide bill.

§ 46–2. **Bogus general legislation.** The constitutional prohibition on special legislation often is stated: "No special law may be enacted where a general law could apply." Such a provision has little meaning because any rule can be drawn to apply statewide. The provision also is impractical because it interferes with legitimate special legislative treatment of special problems. This prohibition is evaded by cloaking special laws in the garb of general legislation. A special bill for one local unit is drawn so it appears to apply to any units meeting specific criteria. The criteria actually limit its applicability to the one community the sponsors intend to affect. Population is the most common bogus criterion since it is handy to use. Because courts have not developed general rules that separate unnecessary special acts from those which are useful, courts have often deferred to the legislature by upholding these spurious classifications.

Using artificial, general-law classifications to camouflage local legislation creates two special problems. First, it may not be obvious which community is affected. Persons who do not have the identifying codes do not know that a law for a county of "more than 40,000 population and between 425,000 and 450,000 acres" applies to Able county and no other. The target county is semisecret. Second, at the next census Able county may change population and no longer fit the description; but some other county, one that wants nothing to do with the special law, may fall into the class. Until the code based on population is changed in the old act, Able county will be without its accustomed special authority.

The vulnerability of special legislation to shifting application as population changes is a result of the judicial requirement that classifications must be open. Open means other units must come under the law if at any time they meet the criteria in the law. This is necessary to protect the charade that the act is general legislation. If the class is fixed by the facts as of some point in time, the class is closed. The class then is stripped of the presumption that it is an honest classification related to a legitimate legislative purpose. Instead it is held to be descriptive of the target community. As such, it is an invalid special law.

B. NON-RETROACTIVITY

§ **47-1. Unfairness.** Were a legislature to change the law applicable to any specific situation after the fact, it would be acting unfairly and unconstitutionally. Retroactive legislation deprives someone of the benefit of vested legal rights—property, contract, or whatever—without due process of law. The doctrine prohibiting retroactive legislation is built on the due process clause.

Constitutional principles aside, it would be disastrous to allow legislatures to resolve existing legal disputes by changing rules to suit legislative petitioners. Both the sense and reality of justice would be shattered if private affairs were decided in the political arena with new rules established for old facts. Legislators know this; the rule against retroactivity is rarely questioned by legislators. The rule is followed instinctively, even by those who never receive a formal explanation of the principle.

§ **47-2. Curative acts.** Despite the nonretroactivity rule, legislatures may pass retroactive legislation that is valid in those few circumstances where it is fair to do so. Since the prohibition on retroactivity is based on unfairness, the bar does not apply if justice is served by giving an act retroactive effect. An act to cure an obvious mistake in the law or to correct a procedural error is called a curative act. If a curative act is attacked on the basis of its retroactivity, its validity depends somewhat on whether the challenger relied on the former law. However, reliance and change of position based on the old law does not make curative legislation automatically invalid; the test is justice. The usual presumption of constitutionality applies to curative acts; legislative conduct with curative acts is cautious enough to support the presumption.

Any act intended to reach back in time to correct errors of the past must be clearly drafted to indicate the retroactive intention, for there is a strong presumption that legislation is intended to have only prospective effect.

§ 47–3. Procedural—substantive distinction.

When an event occurs, its legal consequences are decided by the law then in effect. The rights of the parties are not vulnerable to subsequent modification of the law. However, the method by which the vested rights of the parties to the event are adjudicated may be changed. If a legislature or court fashions a new mechanism to more efficiently and fairly adjudicate disputes, pre-existing disputes ought to be determined under the new and better procedure. In short, the rule against retroactivity applies to the substantive law, not to procedural law. It is often said that procedural law can be changed retroactively, but this is inaccurate. What is meant is that newly adopted procedural rules may be used for processing old conflicts. In a literal sense, a procedural change can

never be retroactive, since a new procedure can
never be used yesterday.

§ 47–4. **Ex post facto criminal laws.** The
procedural-substantive distinction is modified in
criminal prosecutions.   Retroactive changes in
criminal law are barred as *ex post facto* laws (after
the fact laws).   The prohibition of *ex post facto*
laws applies to all changes detrimental to the
defendant, whether in procedure, in the substantive elements of crime, or in the punishments that
may be imposed after conviction.   The law takes
the position that a defendant has a vested right in
any beneficial procedure.   Since the state is a
party to the prosecution, and also makes the procedural rules, it is prohibited from changing those
rules to the detriment of a criminal defendant.

§ 47–5. **Bills of attainder.** Bills of attainder
are legislative acts which: (1) punish (2) specified
persons (3) without a judicial proceeding.   The
prohibition on bills of attainder is based partly on
the problem of retroactivity and partly on separation of powers.   The separation of powers element
is that the legislature does not hold power to act as
judge of cases.   The retroactive element is that a
legislature cannot impose sanctions upon past behavior.   Close questions arise as to whether an act
is a bill of attainder if it limits those who may
enjoy some right or privilege.   If those disqualified
are few in number and the basis for disqualification is past activity, the bill may slip over into the
bill of attainder class.   For example, in United

States v. Brown (85 S.Ct. 1707 (1965)) the court
held invalid as a bill of attainder a congressional
act that barred persons who had been members of
the Communist party from labor union office.

C. DELEGATION OF POWER

§ 48-1. Traditional rules on delegation.
Discussion of legislative power to delegate responsibility to others—and the limitations on that power—requires walking a tightrope between what
courts say and what they do. Legal theory on
delegation is unsatisfactory, so judicial action is
unreliable. Courts long ago constructed an elabo-
rate body of law restricting the power to delegate.
Without expressly overruling these rules, courts
have side stepped them for years. But the problems and evils of delegation are so severe that the
current anarchy in the field is not likely to continue. Also, courts continue to apply some basic
portions of the early body of law, partly as form
and partly as substance.

The law started with the proposition that legislative power had to be exercised by the legislature,
not delegated to others. As society grew increasingly complex, it became necessary to delegate a
good deal of legislative work in order to keep the
essential legislative task manageable. Legislatures responded with more and more delegation;
courts responded with almost complete acquiescence. Courts surrendered—almost.

The next generation of cases said the legislature must lay down standards to control the use of whatever power was delegated. Legislatures responded by stating standards like: just and reasonable, for the general welfare, to prevent unfair competition. Again, the courts surrendered. Today courts accept these meaningless phrases as adequate standards.

There is still validity to the original reasons for prohibiting delegation and, later, for requiring standards. First, legislators must be accountable for public policy. Delegation to administrative agencies or subordinate units of government interferes with that accountability. Second, the law must be accessible to citizens. Legislation enacted without detail or standards produces law hidden in the labyrinth of informal agency behavior. This delegated law is not published or even written down.

§ 48–2. **Professor Davis' suggestions.** Professor Kenneth Culp Davis proposed a response to the conflicting currents around the delegation doctrine. In discretionary Justice (Tulane Press, 1971) Davis developed this view of delegation: legislatures will delegate, courts will allow delegation, agencies will accept delegated power and exercise it arbitrarily unless checked in some way, courts and legislatures and executives do not now check agencies, and something new is needed to deal with the problem.

Davis offered this resolution. Courts should let legislatures delegate and insist on meaningful standards for the exercise of delegated power. But courts should permit the standards to be spelled out over a period of time by the agency to which the delegation is made, rather than force the legislature to spell out the standard at the beginning. Further, Davis said that courts should require the agency to record and maintain as open precedents the facts found and the rules applied in its cases, require the agency to explain deviations from its established precedents, require the agency from time to time to codify in general rules its accumulated precedents, and allow a party to defeat an agency action by showing in court that the agency is not keeping its rules up to date or not maintaining and following its established precedents.

The attractiveness of the Davis proposal is that it does not expect the impossible from the institutions of government. Legislatures are permitted to use administrative agencies in the rough way they are inclined to; that is, the agency is sent out into the real world to slay the dragon, even though the legislature does not know the exact nature of the dragon or precisely how it is to be slain.

Davis' proposal gives a court some materials with which to review the work of any agency. These materials are agency precedents including explanations, agency rules, and the record in the specific case under review. The court, with these materials, need not defer blindly to agency expertise. The court can force an agency to lay out its policies for the public to follow or to challenge. The legislature can also better oversee agency performance by examining the agency's precedents and regulations. When the legislature knows agency policy, it has the ability to dissent; it may then pass an act imposing a different policy. Under current practice much agency policy is hidden from everyone—courts, legislature, public, and the agency itself.

Whether the Davis proposal will be accepted broadly is still uncertain. What is certain is that there will be agency resistance to it. The proposal is intended to limit agency power, and it does so by imposing new chores on them. Bureaucrats will protest; they will also claim great new costs in an effort to defeat any legislation imposing the Davis theory. However, courts can adopt much of his approach to judicial review of agency actions without legislative action.

§ 48–3. **Incorporation by reference.** The useful drafting technique of incorporating other documents into a bill by reference occasionally runs afoul of the non-delegation doctrine. The problem occurs when any future change in the incorporated material will result in a change in the bill itself. This gives those who can amend the incorporated material the additional power to change the legislation. For example, if future changes in federal income taxes are incorporated in a state income tax law, the legislature is delegating to Congress the power to amend state tax law. Many jurisdictions prohibit this. If future changes in the National Electrical Code are incorporated into a state's statutes, power to make the law is delegated to the American Standards Institute, which writes that code. This delegation is prohibited. The prohibition does not bar incorporation of any edition of the National Electrical Code published prior to the incorporation. Congressional acts may also be incorporated by reference if future amendments by Congress are not included. But a legislature cannot give a blank check to another institution to change the law of the state.

This does not prevent other institutions from affecting a state's law. For example, most states have soldiers and sailors acts which are effective only in war time. Congress declares a state of war. This is not a delegation of power to Congress. Rather, the effectiveness of the statute is conditioned on "a fact of independent significance." Congress controls that fact; it does not control the law.

Non-delegation does not bar incorporation of other acts of the same legislature—including future amendments. Since amendments come from the same institution, power is not surrendered to others. Incorporation of other statutes is an immensely valuable drafting strategy. It permits the bill drafter to borrow provisions that have already been legislatively examined. Therefore, the policy judgments represented in the incorporated sections need not be reexamined closely by the legislature. Incorporation also makes a bill shorter, which means there is less to explain. It is less intimidating.

There are, however, negative aspects to incorporation. The legislature does not reexamine incorporated language, which means any defect continues on, now with an impact in two places. The imperfection might have been noticed and corrected had it been copied and put into the new bill verbatim, rather than incorporated. Also the extent of incorporation may be obscure. One statute may not fit perfectly into another, yet incorporation assumes it does. Serious ambiguity results from a misfit incorporation. A bill drafter must examine the effect of inserting a provision into a law for which it was not drawn. The new bill must also indicate whether future amendments to the old statute are included in the incorporation. Generally, they are included under the provisions of the state's statutory construction act.

§ 48–4. **Voter referenda prohibited.** The nondelegation doctrine extends to the electorate as well as to agencies. Except in the jurisdictions that by constitution authorize submission of legislation to the electorate for ratification, legislatures cannot duck responsibility for lawmaking by referring the decision to the voters. The suggestion for such referral surfaces regularly when an issue is controversial, even where such action is constitutionally invalid. Politically it appeals to many legislators to "let the people decide." The doctrine of nondelegation bars legislators from yielding to that temptation.

D. TITLE AND DOUBLE SUBJECT

§ 49–1. **Double subject.** State constitutions commonly contain a provision like: "Each bill shall have a single subject which shall be expressed in its title." This provision prohibits throwing disparate provisions together in one bill, either arbitrarily or for calculated tactical advantage. The single subject rule imposes an external discipline on the legislative process. Combining unrelated ideas in one bill precludes a clean decision on the merits. Each provision moves to passage under the protective cover of the others, rather than winning approval on its own. Congress is under no such constitutional restraint, although the rules of House and Senate attempt to limit multi-subject bills.

The double-subject prohibition is stronger in theory than in reality. Courts tolerate the legislative practice of enacting multi-subject bills because judges appreciate the necessity to combine legislative business into packages. It is impossible to put each separate legislative idea into a separate bill. The waste and confusion would be monumental if that were tried. What courts have demanded— sporadically—is an effort at reasonably honest packaging. They require that the multiple objectives of a bill not be discordant. If a common element links its provisions, the bill is upheld. A bill for enactment of revised laws (a reenactment of all the statutory law of the state) has a single subject. The enactment of a three hundred page bill significantly modifying all the commercial law of a state (the Uniform Commercial Code) is upheld, since there is a unity of subject with its broad reach.

Courts are less tolerant if they detect a union of private interests within a bill. Special interest legislation gets a more suspicious double-subject examination, for a merger of self-seeking petitioners is the evil at which the double-subject rule is primarily aimed.

§ 49–2. **Title.** The title requirement has its separate purpose, but is irrevocably wedded to the double-subject prohibition. By simple craftsmanship, the writer of a bill can cure a double-subject problem by drafting a title that covers everything in the bill and shows a unity in its provisions. Some unifying factor can almost invariably be found. In addition, a title that states a single subject, but fails to cover the entire content of the bill, provides a way for a court to cure a double-subject defect. Parts of the bill not reflected in the title can be severed by the court as invalid under the title requirement. Then the rest of the bill has a single subject and can be upheld.

The purpose of a title is to give both public and legislators notice of the contents of the bill. The test of a valid title is honesty, rather than completeness. The most terse title is legally adequate, even one simply listing the number of a statute amended by the bill. Only if the title misleads the reader about the contents of the bill are portions vulnerable to attack. Well-drafted bills adhere to more stringent standards than those imposed by courts. Legislators like helpful titles. Also a candid, comprehensible title wins votes, for it suggests that the bill has the same characteristics. Requirements and styles vary somewhat from state to state, but the following guides for bill drafters are appropriate for most jurisdictions:

(a) State a single subject before using a conjunction, otherwise the title suggests a double subject.

(b) After stating a single general subject, list the main provisions of the bill, not omitting any provision with as much significance as those mentioned. These provisions ought honestly to alert the reader to the substance of the bill.

(c) Say "providing penalties" if criminal provisions are included.

(d) Enumerate all prior legislation which is amended by the bill.

(e) Enumerate all prior legislation which is repealed by the bill.

PART V

STATUTORY INTERPRETATION

CHAPTER 13

FUNDAMENTALS OF STATUTORY INTERPRETATION

A. LEGISLATIVE INTENT AND STATUTORY INTERPRETATION

§ 51–1. Statutory interpretation defined. A person engages in statutory interpretation by reading a legislative act to determine its meaning. Legitimate interpretation requires an honest and intelligent effort to understand the intention of the legislature. Commentators generally identify two separate ways to look for legislative intent. The first is to focus on the plain meaning of the words used; the second is to examine the purpose of the enactment.

Legislatures stumble, as do all others who try to communicate information and ideas; ambiguity, vagueness, omission, and mistake find their way into statutes. Therefore, the reading of statutes is not an exact science. There is much room for deliberation, for disagreement, and for doubt even though the words have been invested with the

293

authority of the legislature. Actually, readers relentlessly look for ambiguity, vagueness, omission, and mistake in statutes precisely because the details of statutes have real life significance.

§ 51-2. The rule of legislative intent. The basic rule of statutory interpretation is that statutes are to be read to further the intent of the legislature. In the governmental scheme of separation of powers, the legislature has the policymaking prerogative. When a legislature has established a public policy, all the rest of the community, including the judiciary, is to follow that policy as it is expressed by the words of the statute. But determining legislative intent is often difficult, so formulae, canons of construction, practical guides, and folklore have grown up around it.

§ 51-3. Purpose approach. The purpose approach to finding legislative intent is thought of as more modern than the plain meaning approach, although its roots extend to Heydon's Case (76 E.R. 637, (1584)). Heydon's Case directed courts to ask what was the law before the act, what was the mischief or defect to be corrected, what was the remedy designed to cure the defect and what was the true reason of the remedy? "And then the office of all the judges is always to make such construction as shall suppress the mischief, and advance the remedy and to suppress subtle inventions and evasions for continuance of the mischief . . . and to add force in life to the cure and remedy according to the true intent of the makers of the act, *pro bono publico.*" In short, the purpose approach calls for reading a statute to accomplish the objectives of the legislature. To state the proposition is to reveal some circuity underlying the rule, for how is the objective of the legislature determined?

§ 51–4. **Plain-meaning approach and golden rule exception.** The plain-meaning approach, usually considered contradictory to the purpose approach, looks at the words enacted by the legislature and gives them their natural and normal meaning. Legislative battles focus on what the words of the statute shall be. Since the job of the legislature is to enact words, courts cannot ignore the words chosen. The plain-meaning rule recognizes that certain sets of words are by enactment sanctified with the policy-making authority of the legislature.

It would be impossible to dissent from the plain-meaning approach if everyone read words to mean exactly the same thing, if drafters worked flawlessly, if legislators knew precisely what they intended to say, and if humans could imagine all the future cases that might arise under any legislative enactment. But humans fail at each of these tasks. To deal with reality, courts have engrafted the golden rule exception to the plain-meaning approach. This exception provides that the literal meaning is followed only until it leads "to any absurdity or manifest injustice." Thus courts and all others engaged in statutory interpretation are instructed to follow the words until the words lead to unjust results, then depart from the literal meaning to the extent necessary to yield fair and sensible decisions.

§ 51–5. A legislature's attitude. Minnesota's statutory construction act reflects typical legislative feeling about how the verbal handiwork of a legislature ought to be read. It includes these two sections (adopted in 1941 and unchanged since then):

645.16 LEGISLATIVE INTENT CONTROLS. The object of all interpretation and construction of laws is to ascertain and effectuate the intention of the legislature. Every law shall be construed, if possible, to give effect to all its provisions.

When the words of a law in their application to an existing situation are clear and free from all ambiguity, the letter of the law shall not be disregarded under the pretext of pursuing the spirit.

When the words of a law are not explicit, the intention of the legislature may be ascertained by considering, among other matters:

(1) The occasion and necessity for the law;

(2) The circumstances under which it was enacted;

(3) The mischief to be remedied;

(4) The object to be attained;

(5) The former law, if any, including other laws upon the same or similar subjects;

(6) The consequences of a particular interpretation;

(7) The contemporaneous legislative history; and

(8) Legislative and administrative interpretations of the statute.

645.17 PRESUMPTIONS IN ASCERTAINING LEGISLATIVE INTENT. In ascertaining the intention of the legislature the courts may be guided by the following presumptions:

(1) The legislature does not intend a result that is absurd, impossible of execution, or unreasonable;

(2) The legislature intends the entire statute to be effective and certain;

(3) The legislature does not intend to violate the constitution of the United States or of this state;

(4) When a court of last resort has construed the language of a law, the legislature in subsequent laws on the same subject matter intends the same construction to be placed upon such language, and

(5) The legislature intends to favor the public interest as against any private interest.

What has this legislature been saying through the years? First: pay attention to the words we write (the plain-meaning approach in the second paragraph of § 645.16); second, but don't make us look ridiculous by giving absurd meanings to our enactments (the golden rule exception in § 645.17(1)); and, finally, we want to achieve our policy objectives (the purpose approach in § 645.16(1), (2), (3), (4), and (6)). A critic might conclude that the legislature enacting these provisions does not know its own mind. A more accurate view is that the legislature, seeing merit in all the rules, invites readers of its statutes to pursue the task of statutory interpretation with wisdom and understanding, using each of the approaches as appropriate.

B. INTERPRETING WITH AN EYE TO THE BILL PASSING PROCESS

§ 52–1. **Intent comes from the process.** Some commentators have denigrated the idea of legislative intent because legislatures are thought always to act with a variety of individual intents. The idea of a group intent seems to be just another legal fiction. Reality is, in fact, that a legislature usually acts with what is close to a single intent. Legislative acts come from the community. Lobbyists bring petitions in the form of specific bills prepared for formal introduction. The legislative process is largely a ratification of winning petitions. Most legislators on most bills share a common intent simply to give the author and the sponsoring lobbyist what they are asking for. The

intent of the proponents of the bill quite legitimately can be accepted as the legislative intent.

But intent also comes from a bill's opponents.
Amendments to a bill may be approved by a majority of the body even when bitterly opposed by the
bill sponsors. A controversial bill usually makes
its way through a legislature only after the institution inserts significant compromises to accommodate opponents and lukewarm supporters. When a
court, agency, or lawyer later interprets an act, the
limitations that the opponents demanded and won
are just as much a part of the legislative intent as
is the goal of the sponsors. Discussion of legislative intent often treats the process as if a legislature passes bills without dissent. In reality, legislatures struggle to balance the request for the bill
as introduced with petitions for changes in its
sections, phrases, and words.

The reader of an act, therefore, should think of
the words of the statute—those words acquiesced to
and those won through amendment—as expressing
the relevant intent. That is not just a legislative
intent; it is a community intent. Lobbyists—and
the law office staffs that back up lobbyists—give
pending bills a vigorous reading. These agents for
the constituent groups of the community puzzle
over how each provision might be read, what its
effect might be. They then decide whether to
acquiesce or whether, instead, to object and to seek
modification of the bill through amendment. The
reader must presume that the community took

note of all the words written, and that it took
account, also, of words that could have been included, but were not. The reader must presume also
that lobbyist silence was acquiescence in the act as
adopted.

**§ 52–2. Look at the session law, not just the
compilation.** Interpreters of legislative law often
make the mistake of only examining a law as it is
expressed in official or unofficial statutory compilations. The interpreter of a statute who wants to
take full account of the bill passing process must
read the statute in its session law format. The
session law shows precisely what the legislature
and lobbyists had before them. It shows the <u>un-
derlining</u> and ~~interlining~~ that legislators studied to
discover precisely how the bill changed existing
law. Session laws also include the title, an important part of each legislative act. A reader cannot
fairly determine legislative intent without examining the bill title.

Further, because a section in a statutory compilation is often derived from an original enactment
and a series of separate amendatory acts, the legislative intent underlying the section will have been
built act-by-act over time. Intent, then, sometimes
has to be discovered piecemeal out of those separate acts. A reader may be able to uncover the
reason for the most puzzling incongruities in a
section of the compiled statutes by looking at all
the separate acts from which the section was compiled. Some errors arise because rules permit

amendatory bills to be drawn without reproducing all sections of the prior law. Only sections being amended must be included. The omitted sections gave the amended provisions their original context. Without that context before them, legislators permit ambiguity to slip into the law. The reader then cannot sort out the mess without examining each session law from which the compilation has been assembled.

C. READERS OF STATUTES AND THEIR ATTITUDES

§ 53–1. **The reader's bias.** A person rarely dips into a statute book without having some business in mind. Most readers approach a statute with either hope or fear; hope that it will authorize some contemplated conduct or fear that it will bar planned action. The interpreter of a statute reads it to discover: What does this legislative enactment prohibit us from doing? Permit us to do? Direct us to do? Compel us to do?

Even if the reader of a statute is at first largely neutral about its meaning, reading a statute will likely stir reactions of enthusiasm or displeasure as the reader's sense of logic and justice and efficency—and of opportunity—is satisfied or offended. The reader will develop a preference for one meaning or another, and end up asking: Can I read the statute this way, or am I stuck with another meaning?

The reader of a statute, then, usually has a mind set and is likely to find a legislative intent shaded toward the desired meaning.

§ 53–2. **Find meaning of statute, then apply it.** Some commentators view statutory interpretation as a two step process. The first step is to assign meaning to the words and the second is to apply the statute to the situation at hand. As a generalization, this approach overlooks the reader's bias discussed in the previous section. Most readers find it psychologically impossible to assign a meaning isolated from the situation that brought the reader to the statute in the first place.

The one clear virtue of viewing statutory interpretation as a two step process is that the second step lays bare the active role the reader plays in giving life to statutes. The reader of statutes, whether bureaucrat, lawyer, business executive, judge, or scholar, can fairly be viewed as a delegate of the legislature, a delegate who is expected to make each act fit into present circumstances in a way that furthers the legislative purpose. This often requires readers—and not just activist judges—to do some creative lawmaking.

§ 53–3. **Attitudes toward legislative supremacy.** An interpreter of a statute, recognizing that it is both legitimate and necessary to make some law during interpretation, must also recognize that her freedom in reading the statute is limited. The reader must ask two questions: To what extent ought my view give way to the legislative choice?

And, to what extent ought I supplement the words of the statute to serve what I perceive to be the broad legislative purposes?

As these questions reveal, the fundamental issue of statutory interpretation is a question of attitude. Each reader conducts the business of interpretation in a swirl of emotional and intellectual attitudes that arise from the reader's personal assumptions about the quality and legitimacy of the legislative institution. One reader's reaction to an obvious ambiguity might be disdain for the legislative "clowns" who produced such a flawed product. That reader likely will resolve the ambiguity with an attitude of lawless superiority, without a sincere effort to discover actual legislative purpose. Another reader might react to the same ambiguity with the assumption that the defect is in the reader, rather than in the act. This reader will engage in a frantic search for a legislative message, a message that is not there. Still another reader might assume the legislature simply overlooked the ambiguity, or that the legislature consciously left the act vague as part of legislative consensus building. Either of these last two assumptions lead to the attitude that on that precise point the legislature has delegated lawmaking responsibility to the reader.

Even without a patent ambiguity to seize on, some readers take an arrogant attitude toward the makers of statutes. These interpeters of statutes do not cleave to republicanism, believing instead in a government of philosopher kings, or of the elite, or of the masses. When reading the words that have been made into law by the processes of representative democracy, these individuals are not gripped by the same emotional bond others of us feel. Unrepublican views affect how one thinks about legislatures, and, therefore, how one interprets legislation. For faithful interpretation, each reader of a statute must suppress authoritarian, elitist, and anarchical inclinations. Every reader should be inhibited by a respect for the legislature's inherent authority to have its way—to rule—in our system of representative democracy.

§ 53–4. **Legislative imperfection.** To put the task of statutory interpretation into proper perspective the reader should accept with sympathetic understanding the reality that legislatures are fallible institutions. Statutes are not the product of months of work by a single brilliant individual who polishes it by rewriting. Legislative acts emerges from the hubbub of legislative struggle, from the drafts of beginning lawyers, from the work of lobbyists who are casual about clarity but forceful about policy, from the chaos of adjournment deadlines. A legislative act comes from committee effort, another reason to expect the communication to be a bit self-contradictory. Eugene O'Neill dramas confuse; so do statutes. No one should be surprised.

§ 53–5. **Aged statutes.** One problem in finding legislative intent arises because some statutes are old. The intent of a 19th century legislature may be difficult to translate into an intent that fits today's world. It does not work to interpret a statute in the context of its passage, rather than in the context of the changed world. If readers refuse to adopt statutes to new technology and new customs and new ways of doing business, each legislature will be forced constantly to repair the work of the past; none of the essential updating of the law could be left to the judiciary and others. Treating statutes, as well as constitutions, as living documents is an economical use of resources.

§ 53–6. **With an eye to the legislature.** In some circumstance the reader must operate as if the legislature itself were looking on, checking to see that the statute is given an acceptable meaning. For example, if a government department does not like what it finds in a statute, the department may ask: What deviations from what is clearly written in the statute will the legislature tolerate? What can we get by with without offending our legislative friends? Without energizing our legislative foes? If we read the statute as we would like to, will the legislature rein us in by amending the act? Or will it cut our budget?

In other circumstances parties know that if they commence a lawsuit on a point of statutory ambiguity, an amendment to the statute will quickly be adopted to resolve the ambiguity and moot the dispute. The usual concern about how a court might read the statute is then largely irrelevant.

D. CANONS OF STATUTORY CONSTRUCTION

§ 54–1. **More for writers than readers.** The following rules of statutory construction, although formulated for use in the context of interpretation, are more valuable to the writers of bills than to the readers of acts. For the writers of statutes, the canons provide discipline and a firm logical base for drafting. If writers use the logic of the canons, they make future interpretation of their words easier. But if writers forget the canons and readers remember them, trouble is certain.

The reader must be flexible, practical, tolerant, helpful, and realistic about the imperfections of legislative work. Because rules are overlooked at the bill-writing stage, rules can never be applied neatly to the interpretation of legislation. Legislative purpose and the need for justice in the case at hand are better guides to how a statute should be read then all the canons of construction multiplied ten times. Canons are, however, valid signposts that sometimes help the reader interpret statutory words more sensibly.

§ 54–2. **Strict or liberal interpretation.** A largely meaningless provision in many acts directs that the act be given a liberal construction to implement its objectives. Inclusion of the clause suggests that the purpose approach be used to extend the applicability of that particular act. In many jurisdictions the liberal construction canon appears in the general statutory construction act, which means it applies to every act passed by the legislature. The legislature then intends to change slightly the basic approach to statutory interpretation in that jurisdiction. What is to be changed is an historical attitude that legislation should be resisted, that "Statutes in derogation of the common law are to be strictly construed." With or without the boilerplate provision calling for liberal interpretation of statutes, the antagonism to legislation expressed in that old rule no longer pervades the law.

Penal and tax statutes are, however, given a strict interpretation. Strict interpretation, on these two kinds of statutes, means that ambiguities are decided against the state; it does not mean that the words are read literally. Here the principle of strict construction is related to the rule of contract law which holds that ambiguities in contracts are resolved against the party who wrote the contract. The state writes penal and tax laws, so it loses on all ambiguities. Strict and literal are therefore not synonymous in statutory construction, although confusion of the terms is common.

§ 54–3. **Intent to change law; whole statute given effect.** It is presumed under the canons of construction that a legislature does not go through the work of passing an act without intending to change the law. Courts reading statutes struggle to find in each act a modification of prior law, even if by its terms the act seems to do nothing. A corollary rule is that courts are to give meaning to every provision of the act. These canons of construction force participants in the legislative process to resist the apparently meaningless bill and the apparently empty provision. These two rules also show more distrust of courts than other rules of construction; the rules imply that courts would like to give effect only to those provisions or acts of which they approve.

Under these rules, when statutory provisions appear inconsistent, the reader must read one as an exception that prevails over the other more general provision. Therefore, a special act overrides a more general act and a specific provision prevails over a general provision. When acts are so inconsistent that both cannot be given effect, the later act, since it is the more recent expression of legislative will, supersedes the earlier act.

The presumption of intent to change the law does not apply to law revisions. When the legislature enacts a revision to clean up the form of the law, rather than to improve its substance, the presumption is just the opposite of the usual rule. Then new words are read to carry forward the old meaning, even if through faulty draftsmanship they say something different.

§ 54–4. **Repeal; non-use..** The canon of construction that instructs readers to give meaning to the whole act is consistent with the presumption that repeal is not implied. If the legislature wants to eliminate a section of law, it ought to repeal that provision explicitly; until it does so, the reader should attempt to give meaning to the retained provision, even in the face of a contradictory later act. Other canons relevant to repeal are: the repeal of an act that repealed another act does not revive the original act; a statute is not impliedly repealed because there is no reason for it to be continued in the law; and a statute is not repealed automatically because it is not used.

§ 54–5. Some bits of Latin. Several canons of construction are expressed in Latin phrases, perhaps to conceal the fact that they are based on obvious logic. The Latin phrases make those who use them appear scholarly; the English translations make the user sound sensible and clear-headed. All are qualified by the basic rule that legislative intent controls.

Noscitur a sociis (known by its associates)— When a word has a variety of meanings, its meaning in a statute may be determined from the words it is associated with. *Doctor*, for example, used with one set of words means medical doctor; in another set of words it includes chiropractors, podiatrists and optometrists; in a further set of words, it includes doctors of philosophy and even possessors of juris doctor degrees.

Ejusdem generis (of the same class)—When a general word or phrase is used in a list, its general meaning is limited to things that fit with the more specific items in the list. This rule is usually applied when a list ends with a phrase like "and

other written documents." The rule adds by implication the phrase "of the same type as those in this
list."

Expressio unius est exclusio alterious (expression of one excludes others)—This is a rule of
negative implication or backspin. If the drafter of
a statute mentions one circumstance specifically,
the implication is that other circumstances that
just as logically could have been mentioned were
intentionally omitted. This rule is a particular
problem in legislation when a lobbyist refuses to be
satisfied with a general limitation and insists on a
specific exclusionary clause to "take care of my
client." If the desired clause is inserted, the general limitation may be undermined and the whole
statute thrown out of balance.

Pari materia (of the same matter)—When more
than one statute relates to a subject, the statutes
must be considered together. The reason for this
is that the whole body of law must be kept consistent with itself; one act must not be read to
undermine or distort another act. One consequence of this bonding of acts is that a word must
carry the same meaning from one statute over into
another related statute, just as a word should carry
one meaning throughout a single enactment. This
canon makes the interpretation given a statute in
one case relevant in a later case involving a different, but related, statute.

§ 54–6. **Some bits of English.** Several canons of construction have escaped translation into Latin.

(a) Words and phrases are construed according to ordinary rules of grammar and ordinary dictionary meanings.

(b) Technical and legal words and words with special meanings are construed according to the technical, legal, or special meaning appropriate to the context of the statute.

(c) Words of any gender, number, or tense may be read to include any other gender, number, or tense appropriate to the context. Generally statutes are written in the singular number, and in the present tense, and, until the 1980's, in the masculine gender.

(d) Interpretations of statutes contemporaneous with their passage are relevant guides to later interpretation.

(e) Interpretations of similar statutes in other jurisdictions are relevant guides to interpretation of statutes.

E. LEGISLATIVE HISTORY

§ 55–1. **Legislative history as extrinsic guide.** A person puzzling over the words of a statute longs for a helping hand. The reader thinks: surely there must be some document to supplement this obscure directive; surely somewhere there is a clue to what the lawmakers thought about my situation; surely there is more law than this; and surely there must be some authority to muster in support of the interpretation I desire.

Lawyers seeking legislative intent feel their job has not been done if they "discover" the meaning of a statute after simply reading its words. Lawyers are accustomed to researching the law, not just announcing it. When faced with a statute, the legal advocate feels compelled to look for extrinsic guides to supplement the naked words of the act. This compulsion is most intense when the legal researcher is a young lawyer or law clerk seeking to build a reputation for thoroughness and competence. Then the pressure to find authority—any authority—is irresistable.

For better or worse, the law does allow advocates a limited opportunity to supplement statutory language with evidence of legislative intent beyond the statutory words themselves. The seeker of legislative intent may try to document the meaning of a statute with the materials of legislative history. Today judicially recognized legislative history extends to almost everything. It includes: commentaries by those who drafted the bill; all explanations of the bill, even press reports; testimony before the committee; transcripts of committee and floor debate; official committee reports; and the record of procedural steps in the processing of the bill, including the record of amendments offered and whether each was rejected or adopted.

This list barely suggests how difficult it is to judge any item of history for its reliability as a guide to legislative intent. And it comes nowhere close to suggesting how burdensome the pursuit of legislative history has become. To use extrinsic hints of meaning seems intuitively sensible, but most commentators believe the evils that accompany use of history far exceed the dubious value claimed for it.

§ 55–2. The problems of legislative history. Legislative history presents a number of evils, among which are: its undemocratic nature, its unreliability, its uneven availability, and its expense.

Undemocratic nature.. The legislative process is designed to consider, kill, amend, and pass bills. To be accurate and honest, legislative history must come as a natural byproduct of the ordinary bill-passing process. However, clever advocates have found ways to create favorable legislative history, history that supplements their legislative victories and hedges their defeats. They plant speeches and edit committee reports. Legislatures do not take roll call votes on what is recorded as legislature history. The minority caucus, usually cut off from direct control of legislative staff, has little to say about the details of committee reports, or about which witnesses have their testimony transcribed or attached to committee minutes, or about which legislator is called on at the critical moment during committee or floor debate. Because legislative history can be tailored by participants, especially by the majority caucus, it does not always reflect the bipartisan consensus of the body.

Unreliability. Legislative history often misleads. The speeches in legislatures, as elsewhere, are full of slips and omissions. The best legislators ration their time and energy. They do not dot all I's or cross all T's in bills, and they give to the materials of legislative history even less attention. Legislators ignore off-the-wall comments, comments that then show up uncontradicted in the legislative history.

Uneven availability. The potentially relevant materials of legislative history now crush law libraries, and the problem compounds. Statutes are long-lived, but legislatures constantly tamper with them. The history of live and dead phrases of statutory law, therefore, are inextricably mixed. Because items of legislative history almost never become irrelevant to all possible future questions, law librarians cannot freely discard any of it. So the well endowed libraries, and their patrons, suffocate in the avalanche of material, while other readers of statutes cannot find even the most basic items of history anywhere within their city or state.

Expense. The search for legislative history imposes huge costs on litigants. The materials of history are voluminous, varied, and obscure. They are badly indexed, or not indexed at all. Some history is in rough form; some is as difficult to find and utilize, for example, as untranscribed tape recordings of floor and committee deliberations. A lawyer could spend a client's fortune chasing the disparate, scattered, and endless history that exists for almost every statutory provision. Once started on a search for history, a lawyer will find no clear clues as to where the quest should end, for legal rules draw no authoritative lines on relevance or materiality.

Society may pay even higher costs to support the manufacture of history. Some legislative staff justifies its existence primarily by the history it produces; in Congress the history making functionaries are a significant portion of its large bureaucracy.

§ 55–3. **What to do with legislative history.** Courts do not yet understand the problems inherent in trying to discover honest legislative history, so they still use it pretty much without restraint. The advocate facing an issue of statutory interpretation, therefore, must seek and use the materials of history to the extent justified by the client's resources and the significance of the issue. Because most jurisdictions do not have rules that draw meaningful distinctions between history that is appropriate and admissible and that which is not, the advocate should try to make use of anything that appears credible in the circumstances of the case.

Why have judges and legal scholars not drawn appropriate distinctions between good and bad materials of history? It may be that whenever an insightful examination of the question is begun, the study shows history to be so flawed that it all should be barred. If all should be barred, it is impossible to establish useful guidelines as to what history should be used and what should not.

One reason courts have not ruled against the use of history, or even shaped any meaningful restrictions on its use, is that few advocates dare ask a court to ignore it or to draw subtle distinctions between good history and bad. Each side in a case affected by an issue of interpretation plays it safe by offering its own arsenal of history, rather than attacking the legitimacy of the material offered by the other side. To attack the use of history seems to be an admission of weakness because it looks like the last refuge of a party who has found legislative history to be entirely against her position. Anyone who has in hand any credible material finds it difficult to say: "Here is my evidence of legislative history; it shows I should win; and I ask the court to ignore it." To so argue goes against the grain. In addition, the advocate who asks the judge to approve her history, but to reject that of the other side, seems too clever.

Litigators have another reason to avoid arguing against the admission of legislative history. Making that argument is a misallocation of litigation resources. Those resources are better spent establishing the merits of the substantive case, rather than pressing for a fundamental change in the judicial approach to statutory interpretation. A party in any single case should not give to such a peripheral, yet difficult, issue the resources necessary to undo the established practice on the use of history. That is certainly true when the party has no continuing interest in ending the current custom. Courts take guidance from litigants and, on history, litigants always guide toward its use.

Therefore, the rules on legislative history must be reformed through legislation. But, alas, resources will not be forthcoming to pursue reform by that route either. No interest group, except lawyers, has a significant continuing interest in the use of legislative history to help interpret statutes; and the lawyers' economic interest lies on the side of inefficiency, at least in the short run. So no interest group spends its resources lobbying for a response to the problem of legislative history. That which is nobody's business does not get done.

§ 55–4. **Drafter's commentary.** Only one kind of "history" can claim a special legitimacy. That is history in the form of a drafter's commentary presented to the legislature along with the bill. Such commentary, prepared before the bill is taken up by the legislature, is not subject to manipulation during the process by either opponents or proponents. To the extent the bill is adopted by the legislature without modification, adoption can be viewed as ratification of both the drafter's statutory words and the drafter's gloss of commentary on them. The best example of this kind of "history" are the official comments to the uniform acts prepared by the National Conference of Commissioners on Uniform State Laws. Even with this kind of history, however, there are problems of expense and availability.

CHAPTER 14

THE LAWMAKING ROLES OF COURTS AND LEGISLATURES

A. THE SEPARATENESS OF COURTS AND LEGISLATURES

§ 56–1. **Interpreting with an eye to the court.** Readers of a statute adjust its meaning to the interpretation they expect a court to give it, for courts possess the authoritative role in statutory interpretation. Law-trained readers of statutes, even when litigation is not foreseen, tend to think about how a judge would read the statute. The client's question is: Can we do this? But the lawyer's questions are: What favorable meaning can we give the act without prompting a lawsuit? What unfortunate meaning might a court impose on us if there were a lawsuit?

Furthermore, if the meaning of a statute has already been litigated, lawyers religiously examine the judicial interpretation given to the statute; lawyers, perhaps inappropriately, give more attention to the prior judicial reading than they give to the words of the statute itself. Thus, the meaning of a statute depends finally on how the appellate court will read it.

Even though a miniscule percentage of statutory reading occurs in the context of litigation, the extensive literature on statutory interpretation creates the impression that most interpretation is done by appellate judges. Academics seem rarely to think about the business of statutory interpretation without focusing on the nature of the relationship between courts and legislatures. The question of the proper function of courts dealing with legislation pervades almost everything written about statutory interpretation.

§ 56–2. **Separation of powers.** Legislatures make laws and courts adjudicate—at least that is the theory. But when a court judging a case decides what the law is—whether or not a statute applies—the court makes law for the parties to the case. And, because we have a system of binding judicial precedent, the court also makes law for the future.

When judges decide cases affected by statutes, their lawmaking function is complex. Judicial lawmaking in the world of legislative law consists of firming up the edges of statutes and filling in gaps. As to each statutory provision at issue, the judges confirm one possible meaning, while rejecting others. The meaning selected, because of the principles of *stare decisis,* thereafter has the force of law. Separation of powers assigns lawmaking to legislatures, but it leaves significant lawmaking power to the courts. This raises this question: What is the proper lawmaking role for judges when the legislature has acted?

§ 56–3. A continuum of judicial deference.
Attitudes toward judicial lawmaking fall on a continuum. At one theoretical extreme we could have
a system based on the idea that the legislative
branch should monopolize lawmaking, not just
reign over it. In that system the legislature would
make all rules; boundaries for each rule would be
defined in precise detail. Even though most cases
might fall clearly within or without the various
rules, some cases would fall on the ill-defined mar-
gins. Courts would be required to submit marginal
cases to the legislature so the lawmaking body
could spell out whether the demarcation of coverage encompassed or excluded the case at hand.
The legislature—the lawmaking body—would thus
determine the winner and the loser of actual disputes.

This method would not protect our revered separation of powers, for it would put the legislature
into the judging business. The legislative decision,
even if reported as an amendment to a statute, of
necessity would have retroactive effect. This system would not work, for the rules defining legislative power—and the rules applicable to legislative
advocacy—do not contemplate retroactivity. Responsive legislative institutions could not tolerate
having the authority to retroactively decide the
legal rights of litigants.

A reasonable attitude—closer to the middle of
the continuum of attitudes about the judicial role
in the court-legislature relationship—is that judi-

cial lawmaking is an unavoidable by-product of the judging function, even in cases involving statutory interpretation. Under this view, judges should recognize that judge-made law naturally arises out of judicial work, but that they should limit their law production as much as possible. Still another attitude, also reasonable, is that, even though the lawmaking authority rests with the legislature, that branch cannot keep up with the job. Courts, therefore, should make whatever law needs to be made—but only so long as the judicially created law does not conflict with the principles implicit in the whole body of legislative law.

And, finally, a position at the end of the continuum opposite that first described, would brand legislation as an illegitimate intrusion on the revered body of common law. This view—neither republican nor democratic—would allow judges to ignore legislation to their heart's content and with a clear conscience.

§ 56–4. Historical conflicts. The historical relationships between courts and legislatures are perceived with the same distortion that plagues legislatures in daily press reports of their activity. Conflict gets the attention. Cooperation and accommodation do not make news—or history. Journalists, historians, and legal commentators are tempted to tell interesting tales, so they convey the inaccurate impression that courts are invariably antagonistic to legislatures. This view began when the English parliament first struggled to win power for itself and to challenge the power of the crown. Kings sought to retain power and to construct what checks they could around the legislative branch. Appointed judges, allied with the crown, used every ambiguity in parliamentary acts to preserve lawmaking and governing authority for themselves and for the monarch who appointed them.

In this century, generations of law students and scholars were taught that legislature and court are instinctive rivals, if not enemies. The lesson came from the dramatic conflict that arose from judicial use of the doctrine of substantive due process to strike down state and federal regulatory legislation, and from President Roosevelt's response, the 1937 court-packing plan. This story crowded out appreciation of the hundreds of legislative policies that have been enhanced and mistakes that have been corrected by judges sympathetic with legislative goals or, more to the point, respectful of the legislative prerogatives in policy making. History has reported well those occasions when the struggle for power caused judges to frustrate the legislature, but the occasions when judicial decisions advanced legislative objectives without conflict are lost in the routine of the law.

§ 56–5. Competing constituencies. Study of judicial and legislative relations must take account of their respective constituencies. When legislative power first developed, parliament and monarch came to office through different conduits—

one by election, the other by inheritance. Conflict was normal and inevitable. Different forces in the society were allied with each branch. The more recent major conflict of court and legislature also had roots in divergent constituencies. In the early 20th century, sitting judges had received their appointments from the politicians of the pre-progressive era. Those judges came from corporate law practices. Legislatures, on the other hand, were shaped by a political tide of reform and populism. Both court and legislature were part of the democratic political system, but new attitudes came to the two branches at different times. By chance the judges holding over from the prior period in that era had a particularly perverse antagonism to the new age.

B. THE PARTNERSHIP OF COURTS AND LEGISLATURES

§ 57–1. **Merging constituencies; shared responsibility.** A reasonable expectation for the future is that judges and legislators will continue to march to much the same drummer, although discord may arise occasionally. Some conflict between court and legislature is bearable when the legal system takes advantage of the best characteristics of both branches. There is more to be gained than lost if courts free themselves from the literal words of a statute when doing so is appropriate. Common sense and justice often require a loose reading of a statute if law is to serve the best

interests of citizens who are the constituents of
both judge and legislator. The need for courts to
respect the importance of the words of a statute,
but not to exaggerate their reliability, is obvious to
those who understand that courts, by default, hold
much of the responsibility for producing the law
which regulates relations between private individuals. The legislature gives low priority to the making of private laws because of the burdens of other
legislative work.

The statutory rules on interpretation cited in
§ 51–5 suggest a legislative desire that courts provide lawmaking help as they interpret statutes.
Such a partnership makes sense, for the two lawmaking institutions have different strengths and
weaknesses. The strength of the legislature is in
its power to set the law in new directions, to
establish comprehensive programs attacking the
problems of society, and to generalize rules that
can be made accessible and understandable to most
of the community. The weakness of the legislature
is an inability to imagine the infinite variety of
circumstances in which its rules will be applied
and to draft the limitations and exceptions required to fit all circumstances.

The adjudicatory process is strong at the precise
points where the legislative institution is weak.
The judiciary deals with specific fact situations.
Courts examine the actions of the parties and with
perfect hindsight find just resolutions of disputes.

Decisions in appellate court cases produce narrow rules, but they are rules of precision and justice.

This perspective on the complementary strengths of our lawmaking institutions supports the proposal discussed in § 31–5 for giving judges increased authority to modify old statutes. It also supports the pragmatic combination of the plain-meaning approach, the golden rule exception, and the purpose approach followed by wise judges. This combination capitalizes on the power of the judiciary to establish refined and detailed precedents (legal rules) for future cases. It also capitalizes on the strength of the legislature for generalization, leaving to the courts the tasks of smoothing rough edges, mitigating harsh results, adding overlooked distinctions, and repairing imperfect drafting.

§ 57–2. **Reasoning from statutes.** Dean Roscoe Pound in 1908 urged courts to borrow from the civil law system the practice of using legislative acts as guides to just decisions in cases beyond the four corners of the act. Legal scholars continue to urge that statutes not be ignored in the development of the common law. This idea encompasses more than mere use of the purpose approach to statutory interpretation. It suggests that courts might give statutes the same intellectual respect they accord judicial precedents. If a case falls within the logic of a judicial precedent, but outside its holding, a court reasons by analogy and applies the logic of the precedent to the new fact situation.

Similarly, if a case falls within the policy of a statute, but outside the legislature's conscious intent, a court should reason from the statute by analogy to find a just, but new, common law rule for the situation. Just because the legislature did not cover the case in the statute, the court ought not presume a legislative intention to have the case decided by an old rule that does not work as well as a rule consistent with the statute.

Over the decades since Dean Pound made this suggestion few lawyers and judges have demonstrated the kind of appreciation of the intellectual content of legislative work he suggested. His advice is occasionally followed, but too often the rich vein of wisdom found in statutes goes unappreciated—unappreciated like the wonderfully complex and human institutions that enact those statutes.

*

INDEX

329

†